Ceramics: Mastering the Craft

Second Edition

Richard Zakin

Published by

 **krause publications**

700 E. State St.
Iola, WI 54990-0001
Telephone 715-445-2214
www.krause.com

Please call or write for our free catalog. Our toll-free number to
place an order or obtain a free catalog is 800-258-0929 or please
use our regular business telephone 715-445-2214 for editorial
comment and further information.

Library of Congress Catalog Number: 00-107846

ISBN: 0-87341-867-0

Printed in the United States of America

Front cover photo: Bruce Taylor, "Ball and Wedge"

Acknowledgments

I am very grateful to the many ceramists who were willing to send me slides of their work. These inform the book with their creative skill and energy. I particularly want to thank those who helped me with the work series photographs: Linda Huey, David MacDonald, Angelo diPetta, Michael Sheba, Dale Zheutlin, Nina Hole, and Barbara Frey. A particular note of thanks goes to my photographer T. C. Eckersley. Tom has worked with me for many years and knows my needs very well.

Special thanks go to Peter Pinnell who helped me with the analysis section. There was a great deal of information in this section, information that required both a knowledge of the science and a knowledge of the proper nomenclature. Peter was a truly generous resource for me in this area and I am very grateful to him.

I am very grateful to Val Cushing for his very generous Foreword. He has contributed so much to our field and I am proud that he was able to write as he did about this book.

I want to thank my editor Barbara Case for her help with this project. For me the hardest part of writing a book comes at the end when the whole project must be tied together. Her help with this task was invaluable.

Finally I want to acknowledge the many contributions of my wife in our effort to lead a meaningful and work-centered life.

Contents

Foreword

Val Cushing

Back in 1964 when we accepted Richard Zakin into the MFA program of the New York State College of Ceramics at Alfred University, I remember having some questions. I wondered if this student, who was trained in painting and who was devoted to music and the intellectual life, would be able to embrace the significance of pushing his hands around in clay. Would he understand the importance of mastering the skills and techniques of the potter's craft? And, most important, would he be able to accept the relevance of these sorts of things in forming a personal ceramic art aesthetic? Although many painters do make the switch to clay, it must be hard to leave the world of ideas in two-dimensional space and instant color for three-dimensional space and the transformation process inherent in making ceramic forms. Everything changes in the fire! The final look and feel of the work is not determined by the artist. The conceptual basis for ceramic art involves seeing the crucial relationships between ideas, understanding a bewildering number of processes and methods, and having intimate knowledge of the earthy and sensual materials. Richard quickly put my doubts to rest. His ceramic expression was filled with insight and understanding. He was able to grasp the whole of the craft. He understood the importance of knowing materials and processes and of having the skills and technology for ceramic art. He has become one of the authorities in the field.

With the publication of this book, Richard shows us just how comprehensive his knowledge is and how clearly he can structure and explain this sort of material to others.

Over the years of our friendship, I have watched him grow from an energetic young student, sitting in my lectures hearing about the technology of the ceramic medium for more or less the first time, to becoming a definitive voice in our field. His first book, *Electric Kiln Ceramics* (Chilton; A&C Black; 1981), opened up an important aspect of the craft to people everywhere at all levels of experience and interests. That book filled an important gap in the literature of standard reference books for ceramic art. It also became obvious then that a new author had come along who would help inform and educate ceramists who needed help and encouragement.

This book has a much wider scope. It encompasses all aspects of the potter's craft and will become another essential book in the standard reference list. It was written by a person who is an artist and educator, as well as an author.

Contemporary American ceramics has developed and matured to a position of world leadership since the mid 1940s. There are many reasons for this rise to the top, and for the development of an American style in ceramic art. I use the word "style" here after a definition of the word once given by George Bernard Shaw: "Style is force of assertion." This style was created by talented American ceramic artists, writers, and teachers. Some of our best have been all of the above, including Richard Zakin. Something fresh and different and exciting has happened here in less than fifty years. Bernard Leach once said it would take America one hundred years to learn to make good pottery and to have some sort of ceramic tradition. He was wrong about that, but his landmark *Potter's Book* (1946) was a major influence on the post-World War II surge of interest, information, and inspiration that got us all going.

The teachers and students at Alfred University were another reason. I was affected and very much inspired by the "Alfred tradition" and the remarkable teachers here. Richard also carries on some of that tradition. Charles Binns was the first director (1900) and founder of the New York State College of Ceramics, which is a college of Alfred University. From the very beginning he taught that art and science were crucial studies for the ceramist. That idea has continued to this day. Binns also believed that books were needed and that authorities in the field should write them. Binns was the first Alfred teacher to write books. He was followed by Dan Rhodes and Larry Lawrence, who have written books for artists, and several others here who have written books for ceramic science and engineering as the field has become more specialized. Alumni authors of distinction have included Donald Frith, John Kenny, Susan Peterson, Hal Reiger, and, of course, Richard Zakin.

In this book Richard takes us on a very comprehensive journey through the information and ideas of the potter's craft. He includes photographs of pieces made by leading artists as well as comments by them concerning various aspects of their work. This book is unique in its scope and the depth of its information and photographic documentation. It will become a standard reference in the field and will help bring us into the 21st century, maintaining a world-class reputation in ceramic art. Writing this book was indeed a monumental task. There are many fine books that give us various pieces of the puzzle of ceramic technology. This book attempts to be the one book we need to cover most of the ground. Few people could do a book like this and even fewer would ever dream of trying. But America's leadership role in ceramic art has depended on people with the energy, talent, knowledge, and motivation to do the hard work that makes quality and produces leaders. Richard Zakin continues the tradition.

Further Thoughts

The new edition of *Ceramics: Mastering the Craft* by Richard Zakin does, in exemplary fashion, what it should do. A very good book has become an even better book. Most chapters are expanded, with new information and new insights. It is filled with new color photographs that are a pleasure to see. They help bring contemporary American ceramics up to date by showing new work by many of this country's established ceramic artists, as well as introducing some emerging talent.

Richard continues to demonstrate his comprehensive knowledge about ceramics and his ability and interest to keep learning and growing. Someone once said, "An educated person is one who knows everything about something and something about everything." Ceramic art is a powerful force in American culture and through his books, Richard Zakin is one of our important voices.

Val Cushing
Alfred, New York

Introduction

I feel lucky to be in this complex field, with all of its many facets and its odd, special, almost secret places, its great, continuing traditions, and its strange dead ends. In writing this book I have had the chance to deal with some of the aspects of ceramics that fascinate me most. I have also had to deal with aspects of ceramics that seemed unfamiliar and strange. So I have tried to be open and to have the courage to deal with ways of thinking that at first glance seemed pointless and unpromising. In time I got to know them and often to enjoy them, learn from them, and respect them.

Yet I want to have a point of view. I suppose that I would characterize that point of view as a commitment to growth, vitality, movement, and change in all the aspects of ceramics. I see no areas of our field that have to be relegated to the status of traditional and resistant to change. In every area there is room for growth. On the other hand, I have studied our tradition a great deal, and honor it. The traditions of ceramics have power and vitality, it is the vitality that is most worth emulating.

This complex landscape needs to be explored and those explorations reported upon. I feel very much like an explorer, impelled by curiosity and waiting to encounter the next surprising development in the field. It is obvious that these explorations and the writing that results from them take time that I could spend working on my own pieces. Nobody is making me set out on these explorations, however. I find them novel and fascinating and I am doing what I most want to do. I feel lucky to have this job.

I want to describe the organization of this book. I have tried to make it as straightforward and logical as possible. I start with our materials, move on to the forming process, from there to creation of the surface, and then to firing. Where possible I give specific descriptions and directions. At this point I shift to more theoretical matters; analysis, studio practice, recipes for bodies, slips, engobes, and glazes, and finally a small glossary of ceramic terms.

I hope that you enjoy this book and find it useful.

- Richard Zakin

1

Understanding Ceramic Materials

A collection of dry materials used for the creation of clays, washes, slips, engobes, and glazes.

The basic physical makeup and character of our materials strongly affect the way our pieces look when they come from the kiln. To understand ceramic materials as a group it is important that we understand a bit about their basic architecture. The materials we ceramists use to make up our clay bodies and glazes - those rather anonymous looking powders - are compounds made up of atoms and elements. These compounds are affected by the kinds of elements that make them up and the way in which the elements are structured. The elements in a glaze compound affect such things as its fluxing (melting) and glassmaking character. Their atomic and molecular structures too are important. For example, the molecular and particle architecture of a clay has a great deal to do with its character and helps make a material which is workable and can withstand the rigors of the fire.

The Basic Building Blocks

The architecture of our material universe can be understood as a step-by-step progression of the basic building blocks of matter - from atoms, to elements, to compounds.

➤ All matter is composed of atoms; they are the fundamental units of all material things.

➤ An element is a grouping of identical atoms. While we ceramists do not deal with pure elements, we must understand the concept, for it is essential in comprehending the structure of the material world.

➤ Molecules are structural units composed of atoms. They may be composed all of one kind of atom or of several kinds.

➤ Compounds are substances formed by two or more elements or molecules in defined proportions. All ceramic materials are compounds; some are fairly simple, while others are quite complex, containing many different elements.

➤ Before firing, some ceramic materials are compounded with oxygen and others with carbon. Those compounded with oxygen are called oxides and those compounded with carbon, carbonates. Oxides are compounds of metallic elements and oxygen. Since firing is an oxidizing process, oxides are little changed in the fire. Carbonates used by ceramists are compounds of metallic atoms and carbon. In the fire they are converted to oxides and the carbon is released as the gases carbon monoxide and carbon dioxide.

➤ Crystals are compounds whose structure is three-dimensional and composed of repeated identical units. Each crystal type has its own unique structure and properties that help define the structure and properties of the materials they make up. Crystal development occurs in all ceramic materials and strongly influences their appearance and character.

➤ Particles are composed of crystals. They are significant to ceramists because a number of materials, including clay, are made up of particles. Particle size as well as particle size variations strongly influence the character of the clay. It is at the particle stage that our senses of perception come into play. Here we arrive at things we can see and feel. This is the world of materials and their physical characteristics - the characteristics that we deal with day by day while dealing with our medium.

Elements Found in Ceramic Materials

Elements are composed of identical atoms. They affect the character of the compounds they are part of and it can be very useful to understand their behavior. If we know the element composition of a recipe we will understand a great deal about its fired character. The following is a list of the elements commonly found in clays and glazes.

Silicon (called silicon until it is compounded with oxygen to become silica). If ceramists have one indispensable element it would have to be silica: it is found in almost every ceramic recipe. It is a glassmaker and so is central to the character of glazes. It also is found in clays and renders them stone-like. Silica is a common component in many compounds found in the earth's crust.

Aluminum (called aluminum until it is compounded with oxygen to become alumina). Aluminum, along with silicon, is the main building block of clay. It is also found in slips, engobes, and glazes where it controls glaze flow and durability and encourages mat surfaces.

The other elements on this list are found in compounds used by ceramists to "dope" or modify silicon and aluminum in order to make them more useful - often by encouraging melting - in clays, slips, engobes, and glazes.

Elements That Encourage Melting:
Potassium
Sodium
Barium (toxic, not used)
Boron
Calcium
Lead (toxic, not used)
Lithium
Magnesium
Titanium
Zinc

Elements That Modify Color:
Cobalt
Copper
Iron
Manganese
Nickel (toxic, not used here except in stains)
Vanadium (toxic, not used here except in stains)

Elements Added to Glazes to Make Them Opaque:
Tin
Zirconium

Elements That Take Part in Chemical Reactions:
Carbon (found in carbonates such as calcium carbonate, whiting)
Oxygen (found in oxides, such as iron oxide, Fe_2O_3)

Compounds Used in Ceramics

Compounds are combinations of two or more elements. For example, two important compounds used in ceramics are whiting and soda feldspar. Whiting is composed of calcium and carbon. Soda feldspar, somewhat more complex than whiting, is composed of silica, alumina,

High-, Medium-, and Low-Clay Percentages in Clay Bodies

Clay Bodies with High Clay Content
stoneware, terra-cotta

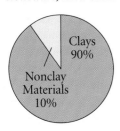

Clays 90%

Nonclay Materials 10%

Clay Bodies with Medium Clay Content
porcelaneous bodies

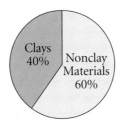

Clays 40%

Nonclay Materials 60%

Clay Bodies with Low Clay Content
porcelains talc bodies

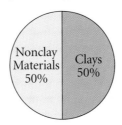

Nonclay Materials 50%

Clays 50%

Slips, Engobes, and Glazes - Clay to Nonclay Ratio

Slips

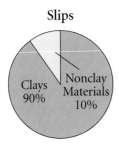

Clays 90%

Nonclay Materials 10%

Engobes

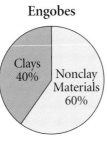

Clays 40%

Nonclay Materials 60%

Glazes

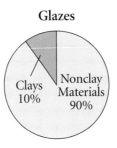

Clays 10%

Nonclay Materials 90%

Materials Used in Glazes

Clays

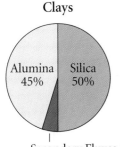

Alumina 45%

Silica 50%

Secondary Fluxes 5%

Silica

Silica 100%

Silicates

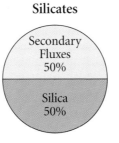

Secondary Fluxes 50%

Silica 50%

Feldspars

Secondary Fluxes 10%

Alumina 20%

Silica 70%

Modifying Compounds

Secondary Fluxes 100%

The Ceramist's Materials Cupboard

1. Feldspars and Feldspar-like Materials
Soda feldspar
Potash feldspar
Nepheline syenite
Spodumene - a lithium feldspar
Optional:
Pumice
Volcanic ash

2. Silica, Ground Silica (Flint)

3. Clays
Ball clay
Kaolin
Stoneware clay (buff-colored clays of mixed particle size)
Fire clay
Red burning clay
Dark burning clay

4. Silicates
Talc
Wollastonite

5. Modifying Compounds
Bone ash
Dolomite
Gerstley borate
Titanium dioxide
Whiting
Optional:
Magnesium carbonate
Tin oxide

6. Frits
High-soda frit (over 10% soda)
Boron-containing frit (between 8% and 20% boron)
Optional:
High-boron frit (over 20% boron)
Barium frit

TOXIC MATERIALS
Barium carbonate
Lithium carbonate (substitute spodumene)
Finely ground manganese dioxide
Compounds that contain cadmium, lead, fluroine, vanadium

Clays

Clays are natural earthy materials. They consist of fine grains of silica and alumina. The grains are plate shaped and slide along each other's surface. Clays also contain a level of impurities. The impurities contribute to plasticity, melt, and color. The ceramist makes clays workable by adding enough water to make them moist; at this point clays can be given form. Aside from use in clay bodies, ceramists use clays in slips, engobes, and glazes to contribute silica and alumina and encourage suspension.

We use six main types of clays:
   Kaolin (silica and alumina)
   Ball clay (silica, alumina, titanium, and iron)
   Stoneware clay (silica, alumina, titanium, and iron)
   Fire clay (silica, alumina, titanium, and iron)
   Red burning clay (silica, alumina, iron, potassium, magnesium, and titanium)
   Dark-burning clay (silica, iron, alumina, potassium, and magnesium)

Feldspars

Feldspars are found in nature. They are composed of silica, alumina, and melting materials. They are economical and extremely useful in ceramics. Feldspars contain a good deal of silica as well as some alumina and some elements that encourage melting, especially sodium or potassium. They can be very useful in clay bodies and supply most of the elements necessary for slips and glazes to produce good results in the kiln. They are used as the primary material in many clay body, slip, and glaze recipes. Ceramists use several types of feldspars: feldspars rich in potassium (potassium feldspars), feldspars rich in sodium (sodium feldspars), and feldspars with a significant lithium content (lithium feldspars).

   Soda spar (silica, alumina, potassium, and sodium)
   Potash feldspar (silica, alumina, sodium, and potassium)
   Nepheline syenite (silica, alumina, potassium, and sodium)
   Spodumene (silica, alumina, and lithium)

Frits

It is useful to think of a frit as a kind of manufactured feldspar, one tailored for a particular job. Frits are manufactured in a process that begins with a recipe, proceeds to the melting of the materials in a crucible to make a glass, and finally to cooling and grinding. Although somewhat expensive, this process has its advantages. Most frits, like feldspars, contain silica, alumina, and melters. Frits, however, contain elements not found in natural feldspars and can be formulated to contain melters in greater amounts than those in natural feldspars. The result is a powerful melting compound precisely tailored for a specific job. There

Dry clays. The two darker clays contain iron and other impurities while the light-colored one contains few impurities.

sodium, potassium, and oxygen. Clays too are compounds. They are made up of silica, alumina, and varying percentages of other elements that encourage melting or color the clay.

We use various compounds in our work. We use them because they can survive the rigors of the ceramic fire and because they produce interesting results. The ceramist's list of useful chemicals is fairly small because most materials burn away in the very high temperatures of the ceramic kiln. All organic materials burn away at these temperatures, as do many minerals. Among the compounds used in ceramics are:

The Materials Cupboard - A List of Useful Ceramic Materials
   Clays
   Feldspars
   Frits
   Silicates
   Ground silica (flint - silica dioxide)
   Fluxes and anti-fluxes (materials that modify the character or the look of the recipe)

are very many frit types. The two most popular among studio ceramists are frits based on sodium and those based on boron.

   Soda frits (silica, sodium, calcium, and alumina)
   Boron frits (silica, calcium, boron alumina, and sodium)

Ground Silica (Flint)

Ground silica is sometimes called flint. It is derived from ground quartz and is used in ceramic recipes when additions of pure silica are desirable.

Silica/Melter Materials

Ceramists use two of these compounds - talc and wollastonite. They are used most often in clay bodies.

   Talc (silica, calcium, and magnesium)
   Wollastonite (silica and calcium)

Modifying Materials (Fluxes and Anti-Fluxes)

These materials contain no silica or alumina and are composed only of elements that modify the melting properties of silica. Ceramists use a number of different modifying materials:

Melting Materials:
   Bone ash (calcium, phosphorus, and fluorine)
   Dolomite (calcium and magnesium)
   Magnesium carbonate (magnesium)
   Titanium dioxide (titanium)
   Whiting (calcium)
   Zinc (zinc)

Note: Gerstley borate contains boron, calcium, and sodium. For many years this has been a popular melter for use in slips, engobes, and glazes, especially in the United States and Canada. It appears that this useful material will soon be unavailable. Therefore, boron content in a recipe will be limited to boron frits. These are fine materials, they are reliable and they should remain readily available. Their high silica (and usually alumina) content, however, makes it impossible to substitute boron frits for Gerstley borate on a one-for-one basis. The old recipe must be analyzed and its chemical makeup reproduced as closely as possible with the new material.

Opacifiers:
   Tin oxide (tin)
   Zirconium opacifiers (zirconium and silica)

Colorants (used to color ceramic materials):
   Chrome
   Copper
   Cobalt
   Iron
   Manganese
   Rutile (a compound of iron and titanium)
   Vanadium

Glaze and Body Stains

Glaze and body stains are compounds of clay, colorants, and materials that modify the color response of the colorants. Stains are more stable than the original colorant and may be less toxic.

Toxic Materials

The following materials, though useful, are toxic. For more information see the section on toxic and dangerous materials and Appendix B.

   Barium
   Lithium carbonate (spodumene, another source of
      lithium is much safer)
   Finely ground manganese dioxide
   Cadmium
   Lead
   Fluorides
   Vanadium

Eutectics

Eutectics encourage strong melting. It would seem natural that a combination of two materials would have a melting point dictated in a straightforward way by the melting point of each material. If this were so, material "A" melting at 1800°F and material "B" melting at 2000° would, if mixed half and half, create a compound with a melting point of 1900°F. This makes excellent sense but it is not how nature works. Because of the way compounds react to heat at the atomic level, the melting point of a compound is usually lower than that of its individual components. Furthermore, different oxide proportions will produce different melting temperatures. The classic example of this is a combination of whiting (calcium carbonate) and feldspar fired to cone 8. By itself, whiting is a dry powder when fired to this temperature and feldspar a stiff mass. The 75 feldspar, 25 whiting mixture will, in fact, be very strongly melting and will be a glass. In these proportions calcium and feldspar form a eutectic and melt strongly.

What this means is that some combinations of oxides in a glassy slip or glaze recipe will cause more fluxing than expected. This phenomenon is especially important for the ceramist who works in the low fire.

Purchasing Ceramic Materials

The market for ceramic materials obviously is a specialized one. Most of our materials are specially prepared for ceramic use and must be purchased from a ceramic supply house. Ceramic supply houses are located in or near most large cities. Look for advertisements from suppliers in craft magazines. A good supplier will be reliable, offer reasonable prices, have a good stock, and be familiar with that stock. Suppliers will often know a fair amount about the craft (or have someone on staff who does) and be willing to give you advice on technical matters. It is also important that the supplier have reasonable procedures for ordering and delivery of materials. Look for a supplier you can trust who will deal with you on the basis of resonable trust.

Ceramic Recipes

In ceramics, more than in many other arts, technological matters strongly influence the look of the finished piece. One place where this is strongly in evidence is in the phenomenon of the ceramic recipe. Ceramic recipes are composed of materials which are sources of silica, alumina, and various other elements that influence the character of the melt. Ceramic recipes are written in a format that allows them to be compared one to another and can be used easily by contemporary ceramists. For example, they are generally formulated for a total of 100% to allow easy comparison with other recipes. Colorants are often written as percentages over and above the 100%. This is because other colorants can be used in their place with few substantive changes in the character of the fired product other than color. Furthermore, ceramic recipes draw from a limited palette of materials - those that have been proven in use and are readily available from ceramic suppliers. While we have a limited choice of materials, their proportions vary a great deal. These different proportions are what give each recipe its unique flavor.

2

Ceramic Color

One of the things we notice first about a ceramic piece is its color. Ceramic color is very complex. Our ceramic materials have specific color characteristics, many of which are revealed only when they are fired in the kiln. These reactions can be (and often are) modified by other materials in the glaze and by the atmosphere and firing temperature of the kiln. Those unfamiliar with ceramics will compare ceramic color to paint. While there are some similarities, the differences between the two are most significant. Unlike paint, ceramic color must pass through the rigors of the kiln fire: in this process it is transformed in ways which are not fully predictable (and at times are wildly unpredictable). While this is often a problem, ceramic color has a great advantage as well - once the piece is fired the color will be durable and unchanging.

Few coloring materials can withstand the heat of the fire. For millennia ceramists had to rely solely upon a limited group of naturally occurring minerals. These coloring minerals were of natural origin and only needed to be refined. In the 18th century ceramists discovered new, naturally occurring coloring minerals, which extended the color possibilities open to ceramists. They also learned how to create a new group of compounds in which oxides were added to colorants: this altered their color and produced a whole new color palette for the ceramist (these compounds are referred to as ceramic stains). Each type has advantages: the natural minerals are relatively inexpensive and are very powerful. Ceramic stains are less economical and less powerful but offer a wide choice of unusual colors. Between the two different sources contemporary ceramists now have ready access to a very wide palette of color.

The Physics of Ceramic Color

Ceramic color is created by the presence of minerals which react in a characteristic way to light energy. When thinking about ceramic color, it is best to think of light as individual units of energy or quanta. These units vibrate at differing frequencies. Ceramic color is generally produced because the clay, slip, or glaze absorbs most of these vibrations and reflects only a narrow band of light energy back to the viewer. We perceive the vibrations that are reflected back to us as colors.

Colorants Found in Nature

Chrome oxide. A strong grass green. In stains it is also used for chrome tin pinks. *Note:* All chrome-containing compounds are potentially toxic and should be used in stain form.

Clays. High-impurity clays will encourage cream, gray, burnt orange, rust, and brown.

Cobalt. Blue.

Copper. Green in the oxidation fire, often blood red in the reduction fire.

Red iron oxide. Earth yellow in the presence of calcium, bright red in a pure oxidation atmosphere, brown, rust, brick red, soft green celadon in a reduction atmosphere, or black if used in a saturated iron glaze (up to 12% iron, reduction fired).

Black iron oxide. Encourages gray and brown colors.

Manganese. Soft browns and pinks. Manganese-containing compounds are toxic unless in stain form.

Rutile. Tans and browns.

Vanadium. Bright yellows. *Note:* Vanadium-containing compounds are potentially toxic and are therefore used in the form of a stain.

Ceramic Stains

At one time ceramists used a small number of naturally occurring colorants. During the course of normal work, they

Sue Abbrescia, "Vessel," height 10½", 1999, low-fire earthenware clay body and low-fire glazes. Coil formed using an earthenware body. Abbrescia created a contrast between the textured outer surface of the piece with its muted color and the brilliant orange color derived from ceramic stains on the inside of the piece. Photo by Karen Weyer.

A group of brilliantly colored stains.

began to notice that sometimes the glaze color would be modified by other materials in the recipe. When ceramists began to understand the mechanisms underlying these changes, they realized they could combine the naturally occurring coloring minerals and their modifiers to create new ceramic colors. In the next logical step, experimenters combined colorants with modifying chemicals to create "artificial" colorants. These colors were dubbed stains because they are used to stain glazes, slips and engobes, and clay bodies. Because they are already fired, their color before firing is the same as after. Most stains can be mixed to create an intermediate color. Today there are many suppliers of

Kathryn Sharbaugh, "Night Jump," teapot, 10" x 9" x 2", porcelain clay body, stiff slab construction. Sharbaugh created the surface by painting imagery with underglaze stains and then over this sprayed a transparent glaze. She fired the piece to cone 10 in a reduction atmosphere. The result is a complex graphic imagery. Photo by Chuck Sharbaugh.

these specialized coloring compounds; typically each manufacturer will produce a list of 20 to 50 colors.

Ceramic stains are compounds made by calcining mixtures of kaolin and ceramic colorants. The colorants are often modified by the addition of materials that affect their color. As a result, ceramic stains come in a wide variety of colors. Furthermore, due to the calcining process toxic materials in the resulting compounds are rendered harmless and stains will not harm the ceramist in normal use. Stains are added to the glaze in varying amounts, usually 3% to 8%.

While relatively expensive, they have certain advantages over naturally occurring colorants: their color range is wide and their action is generally predictable and reliable. There is one important exception to this, however. Ceramic stains are very sensitive to the other materials in the recipe. Many materials in a normal recipe will significantly modify them, so they must be tested before use. For example, tin will cause a chrome green to turn a brilliant pink or crimson. Cobalt creates purples and royal blues in the presence of magnesium. Other combinations are less pleasing. Materials in the recipe may bleach stains and rob them of color. For example, magnesium in any form (magnesium carbonate, talc, or dolomite) will completely bleach away the rich colors of chrome tin pink and some violet stains.

Earth Colors	Yellow	Orange	Red	Blue
tan	warm yellow	burnt orange	scarlet	French blue
ocher	strong canary	pumpkin	deep crimson	medium blue
barn red	yellow	bright orange	soft pink red	blue green
brown	orange yellow		maroon	aqua
	corn yellow		purple	
			deep rose	

Green	Gray	Black		
yellow green	light gray	charcoal		
blue green	dark gray	umber		
	gray blue	blue black		
		true black		

Nan Smith, "Oneness," 1999, detail, airbrushed, glazed earthenware. Photo by Allen Cheuvront.

Colors Found in Stains

Most stains follow principals of manufacture that have been used for 100 years or more. Their palette extended from yellow to amber, ocher, burnt orange, pink, violet, green, blue, gray, and black colors. Some of these stains were soft in color while others were quite brilliant. Red and orange colors were available but only for the very low fire.

In recent years ceramic artists have had access to stains that represent a significant widening of our color palette. We now have orange and red colors that can withstand the heat of the mid and high fire in both oxidation and reduction firings. These stains are much more powerful and reliable than the orange and red stains available to ceramists in the past. These stains are expensive but their color effects are so striking that many ceramists value them greatly and many ceramic supply houses now carry them.

The color palette of stains is very wide. It includes light and dark colors, dull and bright, earthy and brilliant.

Using Stains in Ceramic Recipes

As mentioned above, stains can be very sensitive to their environment. If you know the makeup of a stain you can choose recipes to use with it that will not bleach the stain. Most manufacturers will tell you the ingredients in their stains. Certain broad stain types are fairly common. The information below is a listing of a number of popular stain types and the way they react to other materials in the recipe.

Chromium based - green. Use: high percentages of calcium. Do not use: tin. Use: zinc and high percentages of calcium. Be wary of the potentially dangerous gases from chrome during the firing.

Chrome/tin based - burgundy, pinks, and crimsons. Use: calcium, alumina, silica, tin. Use little: alkalies, boron. Do not use: zinc, phosphorus, titanium, or magnesium. Use chrome/tin stains only in the oxidation fire.

Chrome/alumina based - usually pink or crimson. Use: zinc. Use little: calcium and boron. Do not use: lithium.

Louis Marak, "Smoke Rings Teapot," 14½" x 19½" x 4½", 1999, low-fire ceramic stains. Marak used engobes colored with stains to paint a tromp l'oeil combination of two- and three-dimensional imagery.

Chrome/iron based - usually brown or amber. Use: zinc. Use a great deal of: clay. Use little: calcium. Do not use: tin.

Manganese/alumina based - usually pink. Use: alumina in high percentages. Do not use: zinc.

Cobalt based - may be blue, purple, violet, or black. Do not use: titanium or zinc in amounts over 2%.

Praseodymium - yellow. Use: zirconium and perhaps zinc.

Titanium based - usually yellow. Use little: calcium. Do not use: tin.

Vanadium - yellow/**Vanadium-zirconium** - usually greens and blue greens. Be wary during the firing of vanadium stains. The gases from vanadium stains are potentially dangerous during the firing.

A Note on Toxicity

Oxides that are potentially toxic (chrome, manganese, nickel, vanadium) are much safer if compounded with other materials to form a stain. Even in this form, however, there is danger during firing - make sure the kiln area is well ventilated so that dangerous gases cannot concentrate in the kiln area during the firing.

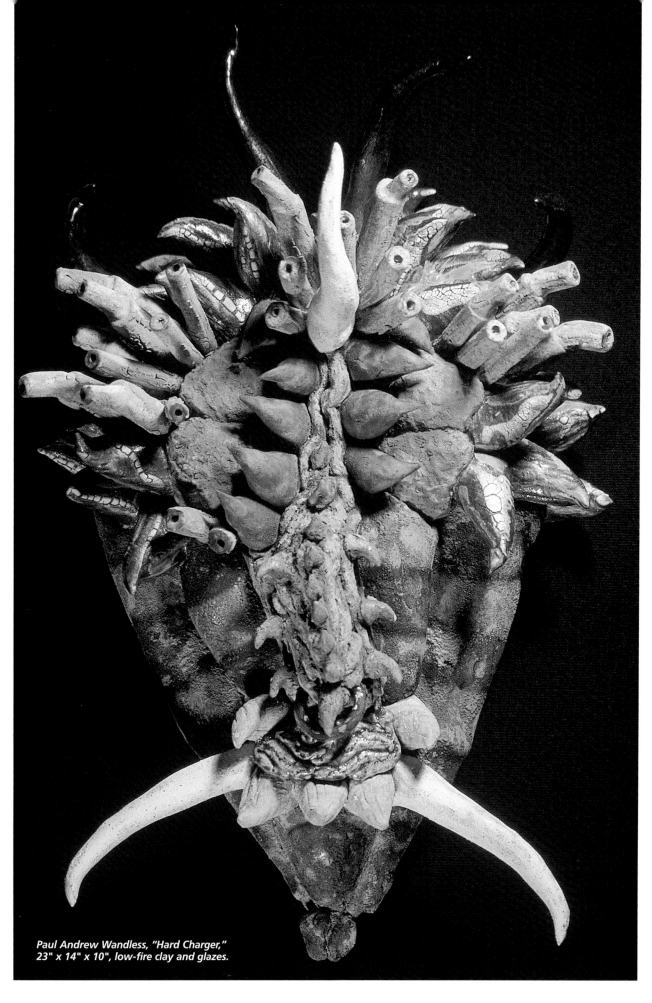

Paul Andrew Wandless, "Hard Charger,"
23" x 14" x 10", low-fire clay and glazes.

3

Clay Bodies:
Making and Buying

Why do we who work with clay find it so fascinating? The answer to this question is no further away than the nearest container of clay. Clay is a very special material and we who work with it know this very well. The character of clays is defined by many possibilities: first and foremost they are plastic, that is, they can be worked. Clays are shapeless. This is a distinct advantage - because they have no shape the ceramist has great freedom in giving them shapes. The process of giving clay a shape can be very pleasing. Clay is easily and naturally worked and responds to the touch. Many sorts of shaping processes do not even require tools. Clays can be worked directly with the hands. As they dry, clays hold their new shape. Once dry they may be fired in a kiln; the shape is now given great permanence. Clay is pleasing to manipulate and many work in clay solely out of love for the material and the process.

Contemporary ceramists use "clay bodies" to create their pieces. They use this term to define a composition made up of two or more clays, or of a combination of clay and nonclay materials. While it is possible to take a clay out of the earth, clean it a bit and use it to form ceramic pieces, this is not often done. Clay bodies can be "tuned" to offer the ceramist a particular working character and behavior in the fire. They can be customized for use at particular firing temperatures, or for use with particular forms, or with particular forming or finishing techniques. Ceramists have been making clay bodies for a very long time; even the earliest potters tinkered with their clay by adding ashes, sand, other clays, and minerals to the mixture to modify it to their liking.

Important Attributes of Clay Bodies

There are many attributes ceramists use to judge clay bodies. These include plasticity, durability, color, maturity and absorption, texture, resistance to warping, and intended use.

Plasticity

This is a very important consideration in choosing a clay body. Plasticity is the ability to be formed, shaped, and bent. No other material can match clay's plasticity. Plasticity is enhanced by the presence of fine particle clays (such as ball clay) and by the presence of a great deal of clay in the recipe (bodies low in clay, such as porcelains, are low in plasticity).

Working Strength

Working strength is the ability to withstand the stress of forming without collapsing. A number of factors influence working strength. These include thixotropy, particle size differentiation, and clay body chemistry.

Thixotropy is a chemical term used to describe the property exhibited by the moist clay body of becoming limp, relaxed, and much wetter during the forming process. Highly thixotropic bodies appear to be firm until they are worked and then they seem to lose all their strength. Such bodies are not easily formed. Generally, ceramists want to limit or completely eliminate thixotropy. They do this by avoiding strongly alkaline fluxes in the body (soda- and boron-containing materials for example). These can partially break the bonds that hold the clay particles together. It is especially difficult to maintain low alkalinity in clay bodies meant for the low fire because they require strong fluxes, which are usually highly alkaline.

Strength is also enhanced and thixotropy diminished when there is a mixture of clays of varying particle sizes in the body (this is known as "good particle size differentiation"). A well thought out clay body will contain, for example, a fine particle clay (a ball clay), a clay with a good amount of midsize particles (a stoneware clay), and a clay that is coarse in particle size (a fire clay). Also useful are fillers such as grog or chopped nylon; these have particle sizes much larger than those of most clays and thus further diversify particle size.

Clay Body Color

Ceramists can create clay bodies in a wide variety of colors just using the natural colors of clays. These colors range from the pure white of porcelain to oyster white to tan, gray, and brown. Most clay bodies have some color, contributed by impurities in the clay. These vary from buff to gray or brown. It is also possible to create colored bodies whose color is not found in nature. These bodies may be, for example, yellow, blue, green, or black. They are special and challenging but are expensive and can be difficult to use.

Maturity

Ceramists use the term "maturity" to describe the density of the fired clay body. A mature body will be dense and hard. An immature body will be less dense and less strong. While the terms may seem to place a higher value on a mature body, a body of this sort is not always necessary or even desirable. Immature bodies are less prone to cracking, shrinking, and warping.

Clay Body Absorption

Absorption refers to the amount of water a fired clay body can absorb. Low-fire bodies will usually absorb a fair amount of water (10% to 12% is common). Stoneware bodies should have a lower absorption (2% to 3%). Those bodies that have a very low absorption (0% to 1%) are special and challenging. Porcelain bodies are both white (an unusual color) and low in absorption (ideally 0%). They are very special, very challenging, and greatly admired.

Clay Body Texture

Clay body texture is also something ceramists think about. Especially interesting are those bodies with very little texture, such as porcelains, or those "loaded" bodies with very coarse, gritty, textures.

Resistance to Warping

Very few ceramists are fond of warping. They avoid it by working with immature clay bodies or by varying the particle sizes in the body or by adding coarse clays or aggregates such as grog to the recipe. They also use strong, stable forms that resist warping.

Intended Use

Finally we come to intended use. Ceramists make many of their clay body decisions based on this factor. The ceramic sculptor looks for a highly durable, warp and crack resistant clay body; body color is not a big issue and plasticity is not that high on the list either. Working strength, on the other hand, is very important. Most utilitarian potters place great emphasis on great plasticity and good working strength. For these reasons many utilitarian potters choose a good strong stoneware body with excellent workability. Other utilitarian potters choose to work in porcelain. Working strength and plasticity are not as good as that found in stoneware bodies but the bond between body and glaze is very strong and fired porcelain has excellent durability.

Materials Used in Clay Bodies

Clays

Ball clay - low impurity clay, light cream in color. Neither highly refractory nor strongly melting, it is used at all firing temperatures. Ball clay is a very fine particle clay and shrinks a great deal. It encourages that kind of workability called plasticity - the ability to take a form easily and naturally.

Stoneware clay - medium impurity clays, tan gray. They have moderate melting powers. Their particle size is mixed and they contribute excellent workability. Mid- and high-fire buff and even moderately dark clay bodies are based on these clays.

Kaolin - very low impurity clays, white. They are valued for their white color. Porcelain bodies are based on kaolin clays. Their particle size is quite uniform and they do not contribute to good workability. They are quite refractory (nonmelting).

Dark-colored clays - these are very high-impurity clays with a high iron content. Their color is an intense earth red. They have strong fluxing powers. Their particle size is varied, which contributes to good workability but this is often offset by the alkaline character of the impurities because alkaline materials do not encourage good workability. In the low fire they may serve as the basis for the clay body. In the high fire they are used to modify the color and the melt of the clay body.

Fire clays - medium impurity clays, tan gray in color and their particle size is quite coarse. They are added to clay bodies to improve workability and durability. They vary in their melting powers from moderately melting to quite refractory.

Nonclay Materials

Silica
ground silica (flint)

The only source of pure silica for clay bodies is ground silica. If silica is added to the clay body, along with a flux such as feldspar, the two partially fuse, binding the clay particles together. This significantly hardens the clay body.

Silicates
talc (ingredients silica, magnesium, and calcium) and wollastonite (ingredients silica and calcium)

The composition of talc and wollastonite is approximately half silica and half melter. This silica/melter combination causes a partial fusing during the firing, which strengthens the body.

Talc is a powerful and economical clay body flux and is used a great deal in clay bodies, especially those intended for the low fire. In the low fire, talc bodies encourage the formation of cristobalite (a form of silica) in clay bodies and discourage glaze crazing. In the high fire, talc bodies encourage resistance to heat shock. Wollastonite is a strong flux, similar in action to talc. It is highly valued in clay bodies, especially tile bodies, because its particles take a fibrous form: this stabilizes the body and helps it resist warping.

Feldspars

nepheline syenite (ingredients silica, alumina, soda, and potash)

This is one of our most powerful clay body fluxes. It has a high soda content and is most useful in the low and mid fire.

Soda feldspar (ingredients silica, alumina, soda, and potash). This is a powerful melting compound, high in soda and especially useful in the mid and low fire. It is alkaline and can discourage workability.

Potash feldspar (ingredients silica, alumina, potash, and soda). This is a strong flux (though not as strong as feldspars, which have more soda). It does not volatilize in the high fire and therefore is especially suited to that range.

Spodumene (ingredients silica, alumina, soda, potash, and lithium). This is a lithium feldspar It is a very strong melter. It is mainly used in clay bodies because of its resistance to heat shock. *Note:* Gases released by this material during the firing may be dangerous - the kiln room should always be well ventilated.

Frits

Frits are useful for fluxing clay bodies, especially those meant for the low fire. The most useful frits in clay bodies are the soda frits. These contain significant amounts of soda plus silica, alumina, and small amounts of other elements that modify the melt. They are very powerful melters. Over time they may leach alkalies and may exert a negative effect on the workability of the clay body. Frits must be used with great care in clay bodies, especially low-fire clay bodies. Low-fire bodies containing strongly fluxing frits will have a very narrow maturation range and are very easily overfired.

Fluxing Materials

(no silica content) - bone ash (ingredients calcium and phosphorus)

This material encourages very strong melts. It is used in mid-fire porcelain bodies where it imparts translucency and a warm tone. It is highly alkaline and deflocculates the body. Because of this it is most often used in slipcast bodies rather than bodies meant for hand forming (deflocculated bodies do not lend themselves to hand forming). Because it is so highly alkaline, gloves must be worn when working with clay bodies that contain this material. Furthermore, a good dust mask should be worn when working with the dry powder and dust from the clay body should not be allowed to accumulate.

Dolomite (contains calcium and magnesium). Additions of 5% to 10% may be used in mid-fire porcelainous bodies to encourage workability, a good melt, and translucency.

Fillers

Materials called fillers are also often added to the clay body. These are coarse substances which help to "open up" the clay body so it can dry evenly and thoroughly; they also reduce shrinkage and warping, enabling the ceramist to dry the body and fire safely. The most commonly used fillers are grog, sand, organic particles, and chopped nylon.

Grog - Grog is made from ground fired clay. Though it may be made in any of a wide variety of colors, it is usually made from a buff-colored clay and looks like sand. Grog reduces clay shrinkage and warping, cracks, and heat shock. Grog additions strengthen the clay body and make complex construction less risky. Furthermore, grog additions open up the clay body; such bodies do not retain moisture as readily as bodies without grog. Therefore, grogged bodies are not as likely to crack or blow up in the fire. Grog is generally added during the clay mixing process but it also can be added directly to wet clay that has already been mixed. As a starting point, add a half cup of grog for every ten pounds of clay. If added to already mixed clay, the grog should be moistened so it doesn't dry out the body.

Sand - Sand is similar to grog in its action, though its edges may be less sharp than grog's. Common sand has a high percentage of impurities, including iron. These impurities may express themselves as spots and encourage running. Their presence is obvious. White sand has few of these impurities and will act more like grog in the fire.

Organic Materials - Materials such as sawdust and coffee grounds can be added to the clay body. These organic particles strengthen the clay body while it is in the wet state. When they are fired, they burn out. If the clay body is fired to a mature and dense state, the resulting openings will shrink and the body will shrink a great deal as well; if the body is fired to a point short of maturity, then the holes will remain and the body will be quite open. While a mature, dense body is desirable for its low absorption of water, an open body is desirable if the body is under a great deal of stress. Sculpture bodies (where this is often the case) are often in this open category and as a result may be more useful than a mature body to the sculptor.

Chopped Nylon - Chopped nylon is made of short lengths of very fine nylon filaments. During the mixing process they are dispersed throughout the clay body. Introducing chopped nylon into the body produces particle size and shape variation, which reduces warping and cracking. It also opens up the body, which encourages workability and reduces the possibility of explosions: chopped nylon burns away during the fire (the effect of this on the elements of the electric kiln is negligible). Chopped nylon can easily be added while the clay body is being mixed or with more difficulty after mixing. As a starting point, try adding a teaspoon of chopped nylon for each 100 pounds of clay. If you wish to add chopped nylon to already mixed clay it should be moistened so it can be distributed in a uniform manner.

Foam Pellets - Tiny plastic foam pellets can be introduced in the clay body. Like sawdust and coffee grounds, these contribute strength and workability to the unfired clay and then burn out in the fire. They do not, however, make much smoke in the firing and so are useful in bodies fired in the electric kiln.

Types of Silica and Their Effect on Clay Bodies

The physical characteristics of clay bodies affect their behavior. For example, silica exists in a number of forms and these play a big part in influencing the character of the clay body. All of the silica in our clay bodies is chemically the same but we have many materials that contribute silica and these materials differ in their effect on the body. Much of the silica in a clay body is bonded chemically with alumina and flux (clays and feldspars are examples of this). Other silica appears in the form of very fine sand or silica flour. The type of silica that is bonded chemically with alumina or flux is known as "chemically bound," that which is not bound up with alumina or flux is known as "free" silica.

Free silica is useful because it forms a glassy binding which welds the clay particles together and strengthens the clay body. We are used to thinking of silica as refractory but some forms of silica encourage more melting than others because they are very fine grained (below 600 mesh).

In dealing with chemically bound silica we find a number of types: two with a very definite structure - quartz and cristobalite - and one that is amorphous (that is, it has no structure) - glass. In the structured arrangements, silica atoms are grouped together with atoms of oxygen. These atoms form a triangular pyramid which we refer to as the "silica tetrahedron." These tetrahedrons in their turn are organized along orderly structural lines; quartz has one such arrangement, cristobalite another. This dictates the way they react during the cooling cycle of the firing. At 573°C/1063°F quartz suddenly undergoes 1% shrinkage (this is called quartz inversion). Most glazes are still quite fluid at this point and are little affected by quartz inversion. At 226°C/439°F cristobalite rapidly contracts by 3%. At this point the glaze is solid; this puts the glaze in a squeeze - the body contracts but the glaze (which has already cooled) cannot do so. This compression of the glaze can help to prevent crazing.

Therefore, cristobalite can be a powerful tool to help cure crazing problems in low-fire work where crazing is an especially difficult problem. We can encourage the formation of cristobalite in clay bodies by using magnesium in the body (talc is a good source of magnesium and is the traditional source of magnesium in clay bodies). We can also prolong the firing (especially at or near its height - this also encourages cristobalite production). Finally, ground cristobalite can be added to the body.

When is cristobalite a problem? High-fire bodies can be rendered brittle by cristobalite. Refired bodies often crack from the presence of cristobalite. Ovenware should not be too rich in cristobalite as cooking temperatures may occasionally be high enough to crack the piece.

The silica alumina bond also has its own structure - mullite. Mullite ($3Al_2O_3 . 2SiO_2$) is an alumina silicate created in the clay body during firing. Mullite crystals are long needles which interlace and strengthen the body. The presence of mullite in the body is guaranteed at temperatures above cone 1 (1150°C/2102°F). Therefore, if a durable clay body is a priority it is a good idea to fire above cone 1.

Materials in Clay Body Recipes

Clays

Most clay body recipes contain two or three different clays of varying particle size and character. Usually there will be a fairly large amount of one clay in the recipe and smaller amounts of a few others whose purpose is to modify such characteristics as body color, workability, and durability. If moderate amounts of either very fine particle or very coarse clays are added to the body they encourage particle size variation and improved workability; often a little of each is found in the recipe. White or light-colored clays are added to raise the firing temperature and lighten body color. Darker clays are added to lower the maturation temperature of the body and darken its color

Nonclay Materials

Aside from clays, most clay body recipes contain important nonclay materials. The clay, of course, is the backbone of the recipe but the nonclay materials are quite significant and strongly influence the character of the body as well.

Nonclay materials are added to a clay body to modify its silica or melter content or to change its color or workability. Ground silica (flint) is added to raise the silica content of the body; silica is a significant ingredient in porcelain and dense clay bodies. Feldspars, frits, and silicates, such as talc, contain silica and flux; they also encourage dense nonporous bodies. Furthermore, their melter content lowers the maturation temperature of the body. Those melters that contain no alumina or silica may also be added to the body to lower its maturation temperature, though they are not as useful in this regard as those materials that also contain silica.

Clay Body Types

It is useful to place individual clay body recipes in groups

Walter Keeler, "Teapot," height 5½", 1999, thrown, press molded, extruded, and modeled, cone 04. This piece strongly communicates its identity as low fire. It does this in its loosely thrown, emphatic form with exaggerated details, its bright color, and satin shiny transparent glaze.

or categories. When we talk of a stoneware body or a porcelain body, we are using such categories. While each clay body recipe has unique characteristics, it also shares many characteristics with other bodies in its category.

It is not unusual for ceramists to prefer to work with recipes that belong to a favorite category. The reasons for these preferences vary but the most often mentioned are: workability, durability, color, economy, suitability of firing temperature, suitability for a firing atmosphere, visual texture, and availability of materials.

Clay body types move in and out of fashion due to shifts in the way ceramists look at their field. An interest in functional ceramics for everyday use made durable stoneware bodies the norm during the 1950s. In recent years a great many ceramists have taken up work which is low fired, highly colored, and nonfunctional; this encourages the popularity of high talc bodies which are useful with the brilliantly colored glazes of the low fire.

There is also some interest in clay bodies whose category

can be called unconventional. As ceramists seek to establish their own identity and create their own unique imagery they may become interested in recipes and strategies that can be used to explore the frontiers of the medium. Many types of unusual clay bodies are of this sort: some of these are discussed on pages 34 and 100.

Clay Body Types in Common Use

Earthenware Bodies

These are low-fire clay bodies; they are fired at temperatures between 920° to 1100°C (1700° to 2000°F). They contain ingredients which encourage as much durability as possible from the comparatively low temperatures of this part of the firing spectrum.

Earthenware bodies are divided into two types: the white

Gail Kendall, "Cake Stand," 7" x 12", 1999, earthenware, terra cotta. Here we see a form made in an absorbent clay body that speaks strongly of earthenware. This form, with its striking flat top, would have been very difficult to form with a less absorbent, high-fire clay body. Photo by Larry Gawell.

Bill Stewart, "Red Head," 30" x 13" x 7". Stewart hand formed this piece using a low-fire terra cotta clay body. We see the influence of the body in those areas left free of glaze and in the thin, elongated forms he uses here. Photo by Bruce Miller.

and buff firing bodies and those whose color is dark. The white and buff firing bodies are composed of half clay and half melter (usually talc); talc bodies are fairly workable and appropriate for use with transparent and translucent glazes as well as those which are opaque. Low-fire, light-colored bodies have little visual appeal: terra sigillata can be applied to any areas that will remain unglazed. These dry surfaces will greatly benefit from a thin wash of the smooth terra sigillata surface. Though their surface and color are not very appealing, these bodies tend to be workable and reliable. Furthermore, glazes look well when applied over their light color. At present they are the most commonly used low-fire bodies.

The dark-colored low-fire bodies have a high clay content; they derive their color from the high iron bearing clays that make up a good part of these recipes. These bodies have appealing color and good workability. They are often marked, however, with a white haze that covers the surface of the piece where it is unglazed. This haze is the result of the efflorescence of calcium on the surface of the piece. The classic remedy for this is the inclusion of 2% barium carbonate in the clay recipe. Once barium has been added to

Richard Hirsch, "Primal Bowl with Bone Artifact #5," 14" x 13" x 13", 1997. Low fired, slips and glazes, and sandblasted surfaces. This piece has a very strong earthenware identity in its complex form and in Hirsch's freedom in combining a great variety of shapes including rounded and flat-topped shapes. The flat shapes are especially difficult to use in high-fire work.

the body, it unites with the calcium in the body in such a way as to encourage the calcium to melt. For those ceramists who would rather not keep barium in their studios (it is toxic), a useful alternate strategy is to apply a red terra sigillata to those areas of the piece that will remain unglazed. Furthermore, the very smooth terra sigillata is not as likely to scratch any surfaces upon which it is resting.

Low-fire bodies cannot be as durable or sanitary as those for the high fire. Furthermore, water seeps through these permeable bodies. While an earthenware body theoretically could be designed to be mature and watertight, in actual practice this is difficult and impractical. Highly fluxed earthenware bodies do not have a tolerance for marginal overfiring (a normal occurrence in most kilns). Therefore, low-fire bodies must be fired to a point short of maturity. These bodies also lack durability because the mullite crystals that grow in bodies fired above cone 2 are not present in low-fire bodies.

On the other hand, very dense bodies shrink, warp, and sag. Low-fire bodies suffer from none of these problems. As

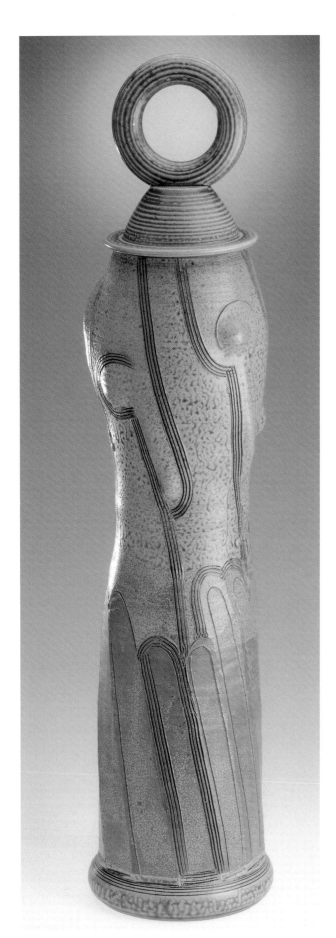

a result the ceramist who works in the low fire does not need to worry as much about structural questions as other ceramists. You may notice that low-fire pieces feature flat tops, unsupported sections, and sharp changes of direction which would be very likely to deform if the clay bodies were fired to maturity.

Stoneware Bodies

These mid- and high-fire bodies are very workable, strong, dense, and reliable. They are fired at temperatures between 1150° and 1300°C (2100° and 2400°F). They are especially appropriate for functional ware because they stand up well to constant use and cleaning. They generally contain about 90% clay; the rest is evenly divided between ground silica and a potassium or sodium feldspar. Fairly refractory clays make up the bulk of the material in these bodies, some coarse, some mixed, and some fine in particle size. This mix encourages good workability and durability.

Most ceramists who work in the mid and high fire use these bodies; they are easily worked and very reliable. They range in color from a very light ivory to tan, red, and brown. They tend to be somewhat rugged in character, which in good part accounts for their natural appeal.

In reduction their character is especially pleasing. Color is rich and warm; their visual texture is quite active so that upon inspection a tan body will be seen to contain particles ranging from a light tan to a medium brown, occasionally punctuated with black speckles (a result of the transformation of red iron oxide to black in the reduction fire). Many reduction-fired stoneware bodies are dark and rich in color.

In oxidation many of the stoneware bodies (especially those light buff in color) lack much of this appeal. At one point a number of suppliers added materials such as manganese or ilmenite particles to oxidation-fired stoneware bodies to improve their appearance: unfortunately these tended to look like poor copies of reduction-fired bodies. Generally the oxidation firing ceramist has to be content with clay bodies that lack richness when compared to bodies fired in reduction. On the other hand, few body types offer as much usefulness and reliability as oxidation-fired stoneware bodies.

High-Fire Sculpture Bodies

These are special variants of normal stoneware bodies. They have a high content of coarse clays and aggregates. These very coarse bodies can be rich and varied in color and texture. They are durable, resist shrinkage and warping, and are useful for large sculpture and vessel forms.

Val Cushing, "Covered Jar - Column Series," height 38", 1990, stoneware body, wheel formed, combed clay imagery, glazed, fired to cone 9 in a reduction atmosphere. This piece has a strong stoneware identity in its strong but controlled curves. These are complemented by its rich but sober colors. Photo by Brian Oglesbee.

Sandra Byers, "Bulb," height 3⅛", 1984. Byers fires in porcelain, in an oxidation atmosphere, which is very effective when used to fire porcelain. Glaze color and visual texture are emphasized by this fire. True porcelain must be fired to cone 9 and the elements in oxidation-firing electric kilns may have a diminished life at this temperature but with care the elements will last a long time. Photo by the artist.

Ruska Valkova, "Decorative Forms: Cobweb." 1200°C. The influence of the European porcelain tradition can often be seen in contemporary porcelain work from Europe. This is the case here. Valkova's porcelain pieces are precise, carefully thought out, and make it clear that they are made with a clay body that has its own character, one of spareness and austerity and remote beauty. Photo by Valentin Kirov.

Nan McKinnell, "Porcelain Vase," 8" high, thrown and fluted with a clear glaze over iron in the decoration. To finish the piece McKinnell applied a mother of pearl luster on the lip and on the raised areas of the piece. She fired the piece to cone 9/10 in a reduction atmosphere. The elegant, shell-like character of this piece speaks strongly of the character of porcelain. Photo by Jim McKinnell.

Porcelain Bodies

Porcelain has such special associations that we must remind ourselves that essentially it is merely a clay body. True porcelain is pure white (sometimes ethereally white), very hard and very dense: where thin it is translucent. Its composition is very narrowly defined: it must be evenly divided between clay and nonclay materials. Its clays must be either all or almost all kaolin; its nonclay content must be composed only of silica and feldspars. Finally, true porcelain must be fired at high temperatures - 1280° to 1300°C (2300 to 2400°F) - in either an oxidation or reduction atmosphere. Porcelain bodies look very rich when fired in any atmosphere, in oxidation they have a creamy cast, while in reduction a grayed cast.

Workability is limited in porcelains, in part because of their low clay content and in part because the clays they do contain have limited plasticity. Form choices also are limited because the material, being so close to the glassy state, will

Tom Folino, "The Waiting Room," 12" x 12" x 12", 1997, porcelain and aluminum, oxidation fired to cone 9/10 in an electric kiln. Oxidation-fired porcelain has a very white body color, which encourages a clear and bright sense of color. Folino created an aluminum environment for this ceramic grouping.

often warp or sag in the fire; forms which would be quite appropriate in a less dense body may be disastrously altered if made in porcelain. Ceramists who wish to use these bodies learn to work around the problems, making size and form compromises that enable them to work with the material. They must do this or abandon its use.

According to Nigel Wood (see page see the Bibliography), the Sung Dynasty Chinese potters used locally available clays whose significant mica content helped them to create a body which was quite plastic. Contemporary ceramists do not have access to such clays but those in North America do have access to a low impurity micaceous feldspar called Plastic Vitrox. Its platelet-like particles encourage good workability (and unfortunately some extra shrinkage as well).

Porcelain is known for its richness. The unadorned white body is called porcelain bisque: its character is at once spare and yet rich in its smooth, pure, white surface. Covered with a clear glaze, porcelains are celebrated for their simplicity and elegance. Covered with colored glaze we witness a change in glaze character which transforms a run of the mill glaze surface into one that is subtle and lively.

Porcelainous Bodies

Porcelainous means "like porcelain." This term is used to designate a clay body which contains a high proportion of nonclay materials (generally around 30%): the rest is clay. Their firing temperature lies between 1160° and 1300°C (2130° and 2400°F). They tend to be halfway between a stoneware and a porcelain in character. Most are white or buff-colored but there are darker porcelainous bodies with color varying from tan to umber. White porcelainous bodies are made solely from ball clay and kaolin, buff-colored porcelainous bodies are made from clays that are less pure, such as stoneware, and dark-colored porcelainous bodies are made from darker clays. Color is often influenced by the body's significant nonclay content, which moderates and "grays" the color.

While not as workable as true stoneware bodies, the workability of porcelainous bodies is quite good and the ceramist who uses these clay bodies is far less constricted in form choice than is the ceramist who works in porcelain. While not translucent, their texture and surface tend to have

Vincent Suez, "Birds," height 14", porcelainous clay body. Suez throws these forms and alters them by working the clay from the inside and by stamping the outer surface of the piece. He applies the glazes by dipping and spraying. Fired to cone 6 in a reduction atmosphere. Suez is very interested in controlling the reduction by varying the intensity and length of the reduction period. He also experiments with activating the reduction at different points in the firing to create different effects.

much of the refined character characteristic of porcelains. Porcelainous bodies are especially useful in the oxidation fire for their grayed color is quite pleasing.

Unconventional Clay Bodies

Most clay bodies are quite conventional, and in most cases that is the way we want it. We do not want our clay bodies to surprise us because most surprises have a negative effect on the work. In this time of emphasis on the new and the experimental, there are those who strive to find ways to work with clay bodies that are anything but conventional. These experiments have a way of taking over the work. They encourage the ceramist to try all sorts of new forms and images. The ceramist has many choices in this part of ceramics. These include highly-melted or reactive bodies, self-glazing bodies, colored bodies, and bodies with little clay or even no clay content at all.

Self-Glazing Clay Bodies

The concept of a clay body that also contains a glaze is extremely appealing: how much better it would be to use a clay that would be naturally glazed during the firing! Such clay bodies do exist: in fact, the earliest glazed pieces, made from Egyptian paste, fall in this category and recipes of this sort continue to attract attention. Self-glazing bodies contain water-soluble fluxes which migrate to the surface of the piece as it dries: these fluxes are deposited as a film over the surface of the piece. When the piece is fired, these deposits combine with the silica and alumina in the body to create a thin layer of glaze on the surface of the ware. Unfortunately, these melters are quite alkaline and greatly diminish the workability of the body. Therefore, forming strategies such as press mold forming are generally used by ceramists who work with bodies of this type.

Low-Clay Content Bodies

Low-clay content bodies can be seen as a type of porcelain, perhaps as a kind of porcelain carried to the extreme. Porcelain is traditionally composed of half clay and half nonclay materials: however, these bodies have an even lower clay content. They show that many of the characteristics we associate with porcelain are enhanced by lowering its clay content even further.

Working with clay bodies that contain very little clay is quite an experience for the ceramist who is used to normal clay bodies. They are usually very difficult to manipulate. However, one can become quite accustomed to their difficult character and can come to enjoy their unique qualities. Though these unique qualities vary from recipe to recipe, the following characteristics are often found in low-clay bodies: translucency, striking color, low shrinkage, durability, and rich, glassy surfaces.

Many low-clay bodies are translucent: since clay discourages translucency, it is much easier to achieve translucency in bodies low in clay. Many low-clay bodies feature striking, saturated color: clay bleaches color, a low clay content encourages strong color. These bodies tend to shrink very little; clay shrinks, nonclay materials do not. Being low in clay, these bodies resist shrinkage. This also helps them resist warping and cracking. They can be extremely dense and rock hard after firing. Some very highly fluxed bodies become completely smooth and glassy, thus blurring the line between a clay and a glaze. They will often look quite finished and need no glaze.

Colored Clay Bodies

All clay bodies have a color: some of these colors (such as the brick of a red earthenware body or the strikingly white of some porcelains) are very beautiful. In fact, these can serve as the final finish for the piece. The idea of using clay bodies whose color or surface is so rich that you do not need

Robin Hopper, "Shell Form," thrown and altered, blue and white agate bodies, once fired in an electric kiln at cone 08. The form, combined with and the blue and white clay body and striped pattern, creates a shell-like imagery. Photo by the artist.

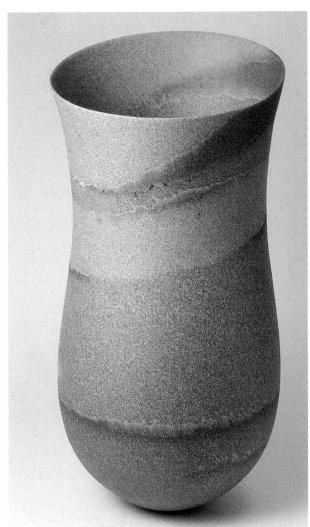

Jennifer Lee, "Dark Smoky Pot, Haloed Bands," 36.3 x 18.7 cm, 1998. Lee hand forms her pieces with colored stoneware, fired to cone 8 or 9 in an oxidation atmosphere (generally in an electric kiln). As the kiln approaches cone 8 she fires very slowly, soaking the kiln for one to two hours to allow the colored clay to mature and the kiln to reach maturity. After firing she smooths the surface with emery paper and glass grinding materials to refine and polish the surfaces. She works with bands and streaks of color in a colored clay work strategy. She uses simple forms and limited color and plays extremely careful attention to the character of the surface of her pieces. Photo by the artist.

substances. Therefore, most of the colorants including cobalt, chrome, and manganese cannot be recommended for use in colored clays (see page 233). Stains are much less toxic than colorants and with care can be used in a safe manner for colored clay techniques.

You should add stain color to a clay body by adding the coloring material to a clay slurry; then blend this thoroughly (use a propeller mixer for amounts of more than 1,000 grams). You can then dry the mixture on an absorbent surface. In this way you can guarantee that the color will completely mix with the other ingredients of the body.

You may use a monochrome (one color) or a polychrome (multicolored) colored clay technique. Monochrome colored clay techniques require the use of a clay body whose color is unusually rich. Colors often seen in such bodies are blues, greens, reds, blacks, and whites. In a polychrome technique, clays of various colors are used together to create rich surfaces and vivid imagery.

Low-Clay Content Colored Clay Bodies

When normal clay bodies are colored by adding colorants or stains to the recipe, the ceramist runs into many problems. Most clay bodies are much harder to color than glazes and require much larger additions of colorant or stain if their color is to be effective. Clay bodies that are highly charged with colorant tend to be very unworkable and when fired very brittle. Furthermore, if you use differently colored clay inlays you may run into problems where one area of inlaid clay meets another. The inlays tend to shrink away from each other, leaving a fine crack between each inlaid section, thereby creating a very obvious fault. One of the best ways to deal with this problem is to use low-clay content clay bodies, which shrink very little. These bodies are quite dense and glassy and serve well as the base for a colored clay technique. They contain little clay (50% of the total or less) and accept color much more readily than a clay body with a normal clay content. This is because clay bleaches colorant additions - less clay means less bleaching of color.

Low clay content does limit workability. While workability is limited, however, a body of this sort can have a very rich surface, often reminding one of a polished rock.

Low-clay content bodies may be colored with stains or with high-impurity clays. This latter strategy can be very interesting; color is warm, but not at all heavy. Such recipes are very similar to those employed in the 18th century by Bottger and von Tschirnhausen for their red porcelain (see page 206).

Highly Active Fluxes in Clay Bodies

A very interesting type of clay body contains highly active fluxes such as boron (borax is the usual source) and lithium (here the usual source is spodumene). These bodies are very

to apply glazes is very appealing. While you will encounter many problems when working with colored clay bodies, the results can be very much worth the trouble.

Colored clay techniques may be as simple as the use of a very rich red or white body which derives its colors from the natural color of its clay constituents. Often, however, these techniques require additions of oxides or stains. You are urged to use stains rather than colorants in colored clay bodies; they are much safer than oxides for this use because you must touch and manipulate the clay, and this may expose you to dangerous materials. This is far more threatening than a slip or glaze colored with the same

Thomas Hoadley, "Nerikomi Vase," 10⅛" x 8" x 7½", 1999. Hoadley has made a real specialty of colored clay work. His imagery is quite inventive and unexpected. Rich pattern plays a strong part in his work.

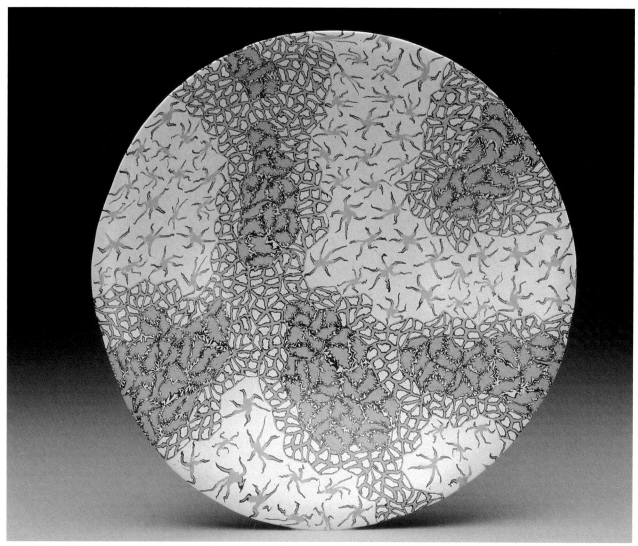

Lou Miller, "Platter," cone 3 porcelain, colored clay. Miller has said about his work methods: "After using stains and metallic compounds to color a cone 5 porcelain clay, I produce up to 2,000 sticks (approximately 2" long) with a variety of cross-sections and colors. I combine these into a loaf as high as the sticks and the overall dimensions of the piece. I slice off thin slabs (up to seven per loaf) and use a plaster mold to form them into the desired shape. I sand, bisque, wet sand, high fire (cone 3/4 to allow for a final sanding and wax penetration), wet sand, and apply six coats of two kinds of wax." Photo by Hap Sakawa.

obviously different from other clay bodies - they are light and frothy and marked by a pattern of fine bubbles. Many ceramists first encounter these bodies as kiln accidents: their effects can be quite spectacular for they have a tendency to boil and bubble and to weld neighboring pieces together during the firing.

Colored Grog in Clay Bodies

The addition of colored grog to a clay body serves not only to improve workability but also to modify the look of the body and enhance its visual appeal. The addition of multicolored grogs in large amounts can create a highly colored and textured surface. Such grogs can be made in the normal manner by crushing sheets of colored clay to a desired particle size and firing this to bisque temperature.

Theoretically, it is also possible to make an unfired grog: it would only need a binding material to hold it together. An

appropriate binder would be glue, wax, or resin. If this kind of grog were added to a clay body, its surface when cut or sanded would reveal upon firing a smooth, visually textured surface similar to terrazzo.

Making, Purchasing, and Testing Clay Bodies

Clay bodies are important to us because they can profoundly influence the way we make our work as well as the way it looks. Contemporary ceramists can rely on a complex infrastructure created to supply either dry ingredients for our clay bodies or bodies that have been already prepared. Therefore, contemporary ceramists must decide whether to make or buy their clay bodies.

If the clay body is purchased, who will supply it? If it is made in the studio, what kind of mixing machine must be purchased? Many ceramists avoid the drawbacks of clay

Richard Zakin, "Vase," height 8¼", 1996, low clay content, low absorption, colored clay bodies, formed over a bisque-fired clay slump mold, fired in oxidation to cone 3. I formed the piece using small "patches" and coils of clay, one hammered into the other to build up a clay wall .5 cm. thick. In my initial work with pieces in this group I used no glaze but in time decided that their surface and color were richer when I rubbed a black glaze into the cracks and crevices of the surface.

mixing by letting somebody else do the work. There are, however, ceramists who insist that a studio-made clay body is best and buy dry materials and mix the clay body in their own studios. There is no doubt that the ceramist must be more highly committed to the quality of the clay body than any other person. Both approaches require judgment and knowledge and both have their advantages. Clearly an argument can be made for either approach.

Purchasing Clay Bodies

Commercial clay body suppliers must purchase the materials and machines and hire the workers necessary to prepare, mix, and bag these clay bodies. Many ceramists buy their clay bodies from these suppliers. They do this mostly for convenience and safety. Commercial suppliers usually mix a wide range of clay bodies, from very low-fire on up to high-fire stoneware and porcelain. In recent years the best

suppliers have become quite sophisticated when dealing with the problems of mixing clay bodies. The winners in the marketplace have been those who are willing to take the trouble to do a good job. Of course, the market has become more sophisticated as well and complaints persist.

If you use commercially produced bodies, you must deal with a number of problems. The clay body mixing process requires great attention to detail. The mixing machinery must be cleaned between loads of different kinds. If your supplier has not made sure the machine is carefully cleaned, the leavings of one body can contaminate the next one in the mixer. Cleaning the machine is physically demanding, tedious, dirty work: good suppliers make sure that it is done well. Weighing of materials must be at least fairly accurate; here again the supplier must make sure that no corners are cut. Expense is also a factor but the expense of the clay body is never large compared to the ceramist's investment of time and effort in forming and glazing the piece. Quality is a

Making a Teapot in Colored Clay

Photos by Barbara Frey

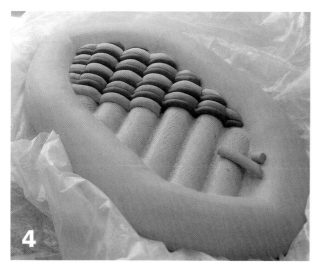

For the last few years Barbara Frey has been making a group of boat/teapots. She wanted this piece to continue in this vein but to be more color oriented than her work has been in the recent past. She began the teapot by preparing a cone 6 porcelain clay body which she made into porcelain slabs. She made hollow tubes and half tubes from the slabs and used these to create the hull section of the boat/teapot. She attached separate pieces by scoring and slipping the joins. She also constructed air holes to aid in drying and firing.

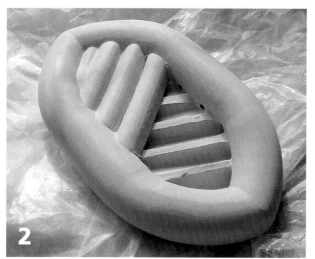

Here we see the completed upper surface of the piece. All the half-tubes are in place.

Frey prepared seven stained versions of the porcelain clay body. She extruded these to form coils and rounded strips and readied these for attachment to the surface of the piece. She placed these under a plastic sheet to keep them moist.

Frey attached the colored clay coils to the surface and sides of the piece.

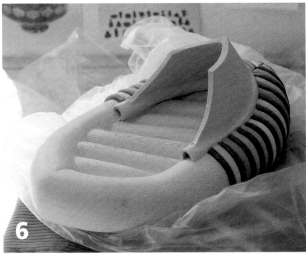

She now constructed the boat cabin from white porcelain slabs.

Here we see the piece with many of its colored clay elements in place.

Frey completed the teapot by adding a handle, spout, and lid. She made these forms in the same way she made the hull and

cabin, by starting with white porcelain slab forms then covering them with colored porcelain.

Some of the group of "rocks" were made from white porcelain with colored clay fragments paddled into the surface. Others were made by mixing two colors to create a marbled look. Frey attached the "rocks" together in the leather-hard stage to form a rock pile.

Finally, she prepared to attach the teapot to the rock pile base after firing.

more important consideration than price. Sometimes the supplier will substitute one material for another. The supplier may wish to make a substitution due to the economical availability of a substitute material or because an older material may be getting scarce. The supplier should inform you if a substitution seems necessary.

It is important that you check a new clay body shipment and that you quickly make and fire test tiles and a piece or two from the body. You should perform an absorption test (see page 44) on a small tile. It is important that you understand your needs and know how to test for them. If you are making ceramic sculptures it is likely that you will not be satisfied with a dense body with a low absorption rate, whereas if you are a utilitarian potter you may require a dense clay body that does not absorb water. You must know before you use a clay body that it is appropriate for your intended use. An absorption test will tell you this in an objective manner.

Making Clay Bodies

Many contemporary ceramists persist in making clay bodies in their own studios. They buy clay in 50 pound bags filled with powdered, dry clay and nonclay materials. These materials have been mined, ground, and refined. The ceramist mixes them with water to turn them into a clay body.

None of the ways we have for mixing clay are without significant drawbacks. These drawbacks occur because of one underlying truth: clay bodies are heavy and unyielding when moist. They are difficult to mix and the machinery can be dangerous. Most require the ceramist or clay body supplier to spend a good deal of money on complex machines that need maintenance. Most methods for mixing clay require powerful mixing machines.

The most common types of clay mixing machines are tub mixers and pug mills. Tub mixers rely on a large motor and blade to cut through the moist clay. This is a kind of brute force method but it is effective and widely used. Pug mills run the clay through a screw mechanism. They work on only a small portion of clay body at a time. They can mix clay more effectively than tub mixers and can be built with a de-airing chamber to produce a smooth mixture in which little wedging is needed. Since they only mix a small portion of the clay body at any one time, the process is slow and the overall mixture may not be uniform. Both types have their advantages - blade mixers may be superior when used to mix clay bodies from dry bagged materials while pug mills are best if used to rework scrap and discarded work.

The problems faced by the ceramist who wishes to make clay in the studio, however, are very formidable. The mixing process requires a machine dedicated to the process. Unfortunately, the purchase of such a clay body mixer requires a substantial outlay of money and these machines require good maintenance and can be dangerous. It is likely that you will create a great deal of clay dust during the mixing process. This is more than an inconvenience, it is dangerous and can lead to silicosis. It is extremely important

that you employ an effective method of ventilation and wear a good dust mask. Furthermore, clay mixers can be misused and then are quite dangerous. They contain powerfully driven mixing blades that can injure, break, or, in some designs, even sever limbs, and should be used with extreme care. At some point during the mixing process, the machine may falter and the ceramist may be tempted to insert a hand or arm into the clay mixer. To the person who has never used a clay mixer this doesn't seem to be a likely prospect, but anyone who has ever had to use one of these machines knows that when the mixing process is going poorly it can be a tempting impulse. The ceramist must resist this impulse.

Clay bodies may also be mixed by hand. It is useful to know how to make clay bodies by hand even if you normally mix your clay in a clay mixer or buy most of your clay bodies already prepared from a ceramic supply house. There may come a time when you wish to make small lots of a special clay body, such as a low-clay porcelain body or a colored body. In very small test lots (1,000 grams or less), you may mix a clay body in a plastic bucket with a rubber spatula. If the resulting mixture is too wet, you may dry it on a plaster bat or layers of newspapers. This process is called de-watering. Wedge the clay after the de-watering process is finished. The same methods may be used on a slightly larger scale (up to 10,000 grams or 20 lbs.). When mixing amounts of this sort, fill a bucket with wet clay slurry and mix with a propeller mixer attached to a small electric drill. Dry the clay on bats or layers of newspaper. This is a slow process but not terribly demanding and it produces highly workable clay bodies.

Material Substitutions in Clay Bodies

Those ceramists who make their clay bodies from dry materials must always be ready to substitute materials if necessary. This may be because a particular material is in short supply or is no longer available. Or it's just as likely that a material has been introduced to the market and is now readily available. Substitutions are also necessary if a recipe developed in one place is used in another where different materials are available. Clays in particular are subject to variations in availability but appropriate substitutes are generally available for most clays. The new recipe may have somewhat different characteristics, however; be sure to test before using it.

Clays fall very naturally into one of four or five categories; groupings which are distinguished by impurity content, particle size, and shrinkage. The difference between any clay in a given category is less significant than the similarities. Therefore, it is common to substitute one clay for another in the same category.

Clay Categories:	_Example:_
High-impurity clays	Barnard clay
Stoneware clays	Goldart clay or Foundry Hill Cream
Ball clays	OM4 clay or Tennessee ball clay
Kaolins	EPK or grolleg
Fire clays	Hawthorne clay

In high-impurity clays, iron is always present; their color is generally red or brown. Clays in this category will differ from one another due to differences in the type and the amount of impurities they contain but it is usually possible to substitute one high-impurity clay for another in a body recipe. The other clay types are perhaps even more uniform and it is usually quite easy to substitute one stoneware clay, ball clay, kaolin, or fire clay for another in the same category.

Nonclay materials used in clay bodies fall into the following categories: soda feldspars, potash feldspars, lithium feldspars, frits, and silicates. If you need to make a substitute, use another material from the same category. It is, however, very important that you test the results because the new recipe may have a somewhat different character from the original.

Testing Clay Bodies

If you want to understand the characteristics of a clay body, you must be able to test for the following: working strength, plasticity, shrinkage, warping, and absorption.

Testing for Working Strength

Start with a sample of the clay recipe with a water content typical of your normal clay bodies. Make a slab ⅜" thick and 10" high. Let it sit under plastic for four or five hours. Bend the slab into a cylinder and place it on the work table. If the cylinder remains upright and does not sag, it has a good working strength.

Testing for Plasticity

Start with a sample of the clay recipe with a water content typical of your normal clay bodies. Roll out a ½" coil and bend it into the shape of a hand written e. If it does not crack or break where it is bent, the clay has a reasonable plasticity.

Testing for Shrinkage

All clay bodies shrink. It is common for a piece 20" tall when you first form it to shrink to 17" or 18" after the final firing. Shrinkage is dependent on the amount and type of clay in the recipe. Nonclay materials do not shrink and do not contribute to clay body shrinkage. Therefore, high-clay recipes will shrink more than bodies low in clay. The type of clay is also important - a very fine particle clay such as ball clay will shrink more than one with coarse particles such as fire clay. A very plastic and workable clay body will shrink more than a clay body mostly made up of coarse clays (such as a sculpture body). A body that is very dense will shrink

A simple test for plasticity.

more than an open and absorbent clay body.

Start with a sample of the clay recipe with a water content typical of your normal clay bodies. Make up a test tile 13 x 4 x .7 cm. Carefully draw a 10 cm mark on the tile. Let the tile dry and fire it to the desired temperature. Measure the new length of the drawn line and subtract this length from 10 cm (the length of the line when it was originally drawn). Move the decimal point one place to the right (in effect dividing this figure by 10). The result is the percentage of shrinkage.

For example, if you inscribe a 10 cm line into a moist tile, fire it, and measure the line again, the measurement might be 8.7 cm. When you subtract 8.7 from 10, the result is 1.3. Moving the decimal point one place to the right gives the amount of shrinkage - 13%.

Testing for Warping

Uneven shrinkage is the primary cause of warping. Shrinkage never takes place in a perfectly linear manner: it is always uneven. It is this uneven shrinkage that causes warping. Warping, therefore, is a fact of ceramic life. To discourage shrinkage and warping, avoid clay bodies with a high percentage of ball clay and look for clay bodies that contain a reasonable percentage of coarse particles and fillers such as grog or chopped nylon.

Body fluxes can also encourage warping: especially those which melt in an abrupt manner. Some fluxes move very quickly from the inert state to highly melting. If such fluxes (among them boron) are present, they can cause warping in reaction to normal kiln temperature variations.

Another cause of warping is glassification. If a clay body becomes glassy in the fire, it is liable to warp. Glassy clay bodies, however, are dense and rich in surface. Sometimes the ceramist will be willing to forego surface richness for good structural integrity. On the other hand, the ceramist may be willing to deal with warping in order to use a very dense and rich clay body.

Making up the clay body test.

Adding water.

Immersing the fired test tile.

Weighing the tile after immersion to find the percent of absorption.

Testing Clay Body Absorption

One of the most important characteristics of a clay body is its absorption rate; that is the amount of moisture it is capable of absorbing. A body that can absorb a great deal of moisture (perhaps equal to 12% of its fired weight) is said to be open, while a clay body that can absorb very little moisture (perhaps 2% of its fired weight) is said to be tight or dense. Absorption is significant to the ceramic sculptor because most sculptors prefer a clay body that is very open. Such bodies resist warping and cracking and work well for large scale work. Most utilitarian potters prefer to work with clay bodies that are dense and have a low rate of absorption because such bodies are watertight and very durable.

The absorption rate of a clay body is controlled by a number of factors: the firing temperature, the amount of the clays and fluxes in the recipe, and their fluxing power. Use larger amounts of strongly fluxing clays and fluxes or raise the firing temperature, and the body will become progressively more dense. Use larger amounts of refractory clays and fluxes or lower the firing temperature, and you will raise the absorption rate.

There is no one ideal absorption rate, the chart that follows shows absorption rates which are customary and normal. They work well most of the time for most needs.

Normal Absorption

Low-fire bodies	= 8% to 12%
Stoneware bodies for food containment	= 4% to 5%
Utilitarian stoneware	= 3% to 5%
Decorative stoneware	= 5% to 8%
Porcelain and porcelain-like bodies	= 1% to 3%
Sculpture bodies	= 10% to 20%
Glassy bodies	= 2% to 0%

The process of testing for clay body absorption is not difficult though it takes a bit of time and patience. It is an accurate test of the absorbency of a clay body.

Fire a test tile, weigh it on a gram scale, then soak it in water for 24 hours. Re-weigh the test tile and subtract the soaked weight from the original weight. The resulting figure is the weight of absorbed water. Divide this figure by the weight of the tile before immersion. Move the decimal point two places to the right to find the percent of absorption.

For example, if the weight of the fired test tile is 22.3 grams and the weight of the test tile after immersion is 26.7 grams, subtract 26.7 from 22.3 for a total of 4.4 grams. This is the weight of the absorbed water. When you divide 4.4 by 22.3 (the original weight of the tile), you arrive at the figure .1973. Moving the decimal point two places to the right gives you the absorption rate of 19.73%.

Ceramic Forms:
Vessels, Sculpture, and Wall Pieces

From the very beginning of ceramics, ceramists have worked with three work categories: vessels, sculptures, and wall pieces. Each of these formats presents the ceramist with a wide range of challenges and possibilities, each with its own special character and its own demands.

Vessel Forms

Vessel forms are ubiquitous, useful, and satisfying forms with a very long history. They are universally recognizable and highly admired. This has led ceramists to use the format in many different ways. Vessels have been made for more than 9,000 years and ceramists show no signs of exhausting the form. With their long history, clay vessels can speak of timeless values. Nor is the format limited to expression in clay. Vessels are made from basketry materials, iron or bronze, stone, ivory or lacquer, glass, and more recently, plastics. Until fairly recently, however, most containers were made from clay. This is understandable because the character of the vessel form is complementary to clay. During the forming process clay is soft and flexible and works well with the encircled and enclosed vessel form.

Vessels vary in such important aspects as material, intent, character, and imagery. Vessel pieces may be made as a personal expression or may be the impersonal product of an efficiently organized process. They may be unornamented or ornamented with the abstract patterns glazes can take on in the kiln, or they may be covered with complex pictorial imagery. Ceramists use the vessel form not only to make utilitarian objects but also nonutilitarian pieces that are ceremonial or decorative in intent.

Utilitarian Vessels

Utilitarian pottery is an integral part of the ceramic tradition and has played a very important part in the history of our material. Clay lends itself to many functional uses and is still the best material for many objects we really need.

Malcolm Davis, "Covered Jar," porcelain clay body, Shino type glazes fired to cone 9/10 in a reduction fire. Davis is very interested in the challenges of utilitarian pottery. "My desire is to bring to life pots that are friendly and intimate, growing ever more personal with daily use." The artist is very interested in the technical as well as the historic aspects of reduction firing. The two studies overlap to create the history of ceramic technology. This study is more than an arcane corner of ceramics because it can lead us to real understanding of many of the characteristics of our medium. This piece, in fact, is a direct result of Davis' studies. Furthermore, it proves that studies of this sort, when blended with an emotional approach to the work, can produce pieces of great power.

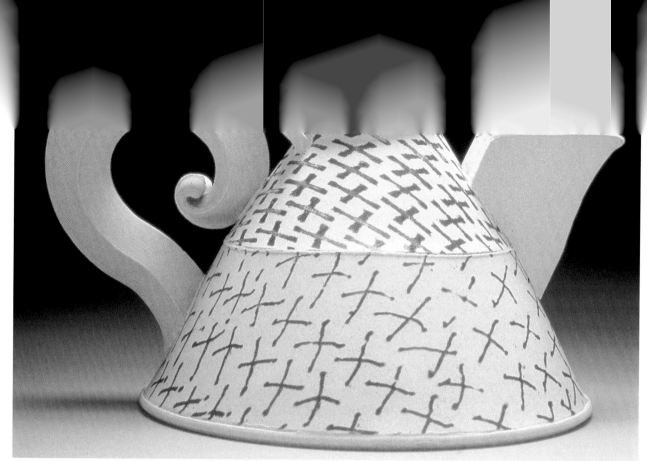

D. Hayne Bayless, "Teapot with Hinged Lid," 7" x 11" x 8", 1999, white stoneware, stretched slab, extrusions, black slips. The decorative character of Bayless' pieces in no way interferes with their utility. In this piece Bayless visually dramatizes the hinge that holds the lid to the body of the teapot. The hinged lid, however, also makes the teapot far easier to use. Photo by the artist.

Val Cushing, "Casserole," 6¾" x 10", 1997, stoneware body, wheel formed, fired to cone 9 in a reduction atmosphere. Though this piece looks very relaxed and natural, a great deal of thought and planning has gone into it. Cushing is very concerned with the way his utilitarian ware will be used and strongly wishes to combine beauty and real usefulness. Bases are broad and stable, lids are well balanced. Handles are placed carefully and designed for ease of use and safety.

Elmer Taylor, "Stoneware Casserole," diameter 12", stoneware body, wheel formed, fired to cone 9 in a reduction atmosphere. This piece has much in common with Val Cushing's casserole. A great deal of thought and planning has gone into it. Taylor is very concerned with the way this casserole will be used. The base is broad and stable, the lid is well balanced. The piece is designed to look well but beyond that, for ease of use and safety.

Alec Karros, "Coffee Pot Set," height 11" with cup and saucer 4½" x 5", porcelain, fired to cone 6 in an oxidation atmosphere. Karros wants to combine utility with a strongly contemporary character.

Steven Hill, "Three Mugs," 4" x 5", slip-trailed imagery. Hill's work is very much in the tradition of utilitarian stoneware. The throwing is relaxed, the forms are elegant but strong, and the color and visual texture are quite dramatic.

Suze Lindsay, "Darted Teapot," 9" x 7" x 3", 1998, cone 10 salt-fired stoneware. We see in this piece Lindsay's use of the salt firing to create energetic and vivacious pieces. Lindsay has integrated all aspects of her image creation strategies to create a unity of form and imagery. Photo by Tom Mills.

Greg Pitts, "Bulb Forcing Pot," diameter 8", 1999, terra cotta clay body, lead glaze, sgraffito.

Consumers no longer, however, need to use clay-formed, hand-crafted, utilitarian pieces. They can use vessels manufactured from materials other than clay. If made from clay, they can use the products of the ceramics industry. Yet many consumers prefer to use hand-crafted products, for they see these objects as expressions of an individual sensibility.

The potter who creates utilitarian objects has the opportunity to make pieces which are at once objects of beauty and truly useful. In a time when so much around us can seem frivolous and ephemeral, this is potentially a source of great vigor. Particular utilitarian pieces that come

Julia Galloway, "Salt and Pepper Pot," 3" x 3" x 5", 1999. Wheel formed with slab additions. Cone 6 porcelainous clay body, soda fired. Galloway's work is strongly oriented to utility. Her pieces are well thought out for use and have pleasing and interesting imagery. This is yet another example of a rethinking of the way utilitarian pots should look. Galloway mentions as one of her sources Persian miniature paintings. This work is celebrated for its rich patterning and attention to detail. The discovery of new imagery sources for utilitarian pottery is an important task. The utilitarian aspect of ceramics has traditionally been a wellspring for invention and a significant source of energy in the ceramics. Photo by the artist.

Linda Sikora, "Ewer," height 6", 1999, porcelain, cone 9. Sikora created the unusual imagery on the surface of this piece using a latex resist process. She fired the piece in a salt kiln to cone 9. Sikora is part of a new generation of utilitarian potters who are trying to renew this approach to ceramics. She has done this in part by finding new sources of form design, mainly in the ceramics of ancient Iran and in developing new kinds of surface imagery. Photo by Peter Lee.

to mind include the austere cups used in the Japanese tea ceremony, the simple elegant Ting Ware bowls from Sung Dynasty China, Yixing teapots (still being made in China), Nigerian village pottery, and the richly glazed pieces of Bernard Leach and Shoji Hamada.

Nonutilitarian Vessels

A very different view of the vessel form is popular among contemporary ceramists who see it as a pure form with no links to utility. They are interested in the vessel because it is a resonant and universally recognized form. The surface of a vessel - the vessel wall - is a strong and dramatic form. It affords the artist great possibilities for creating a very wide variety of rich and dramatic imagery.

In many cultures of the past the best work was nonutilitarian. It is a very common phenomenon to see pottery unearthed from very ancient grave sites whose sole purpose was the religious veneration of the dead and was never intended for everyday use. Quite often these pieces were ornamented with complex imagery. In many cases it is this complex imagery that separates the pieces from others intended for utilitarian use. Much of this work has for its subject imagery of humans or animals or natural forms usually pictured in stylized, shorthand imagery and often carried out with verve and acute observation. Other imagery is abstract and often colorful and rhythmic.

Noteworthy examples of work in the nonutilitarian vessel format include the richly painted, feather light, coil pieces

Arthur Sennett, "Jar," height 13", wheel thrown, stoneware body finished with a temmoku glaze sprayed with Gerstley borate, fired to cone 9 in a reduction atmosphere. Sennett gives us a personal version of the classic cookie jar, well thought out and sensitively handled. Photo by Carol Barclay.

Erroll Willett, "Summus quid Summus," height 42", 1994. Earthenware, low fire from cone 02 to 2. To make these pieces the artist works with a large cylinder. He has thrown some of these forms and used others made in a sewer pipe plant. Willett starts by making a simple drawing on the surface of the cylinder. In this drawing he divides the surface into forms and shapes. He uses the lines as cues for where he pushes into the cylinder wall. Then placing his hand on the inside of the cylinder he looks for places that are not sunken. At these points he begins to push out. He often adds another cylinder (or a number of cylinders over a period of time) in order to gain height. As he moves on up the piece he continues to work the surface and create form by pushing into the form inside and out. He says that it takes him about a month to make a group of two or three of these pieces. He glazes the completed piece using a spray gun and fires multiple times, adding more glaze layers to rework the surface after each firing. He fires in a gas kiln. His glaze firings range in temperature from cone 02 to cone 2. While not particularly looking for reduction, it often occurs spontaneously. Parts of the piece show color changes where it has occurred. Willett wants the vessel walls to seem alive; to swell and compress and to breathe in and out. Photo by the artist.

George Kokis, "Sounding Tube," 1998, hand formed, finished with a high manganese glaze, salt-fired to cone 10. This piece has the look of a vessel but though related to the vessel form it is not one. Kokis says of it: "The piece has no bottom, the intention is to set it down on the ground as a sounding tube to hear the earth. Kind of a reverse megaphone." The repetition of the small form elements gives it the look of a manifestation of the order we find so often in the world of nature.

from the Yang Shao potters of the second millennium B.C. China, the rich, complex imagery of the Nazca and Moche potters of pre-Columbian Peru and the intense and elegant carved porcelain vases made by Adelaide Alsop Robineau in the early part of the 20th century in the United States.

Sculpture

The term sculpture is very hard to define. Traditionally, the subject of sculpture was defined as limited to human or animal figures. This changed as contemporary abstract art achieved a level of acceptance in the 1920s. In the 1930s there was an attempt to import an abstract piece made by the Rumanian sculptor Constantine Brancusi into the United States. Customs officials, using the traditional definition, concluded that Brancusi's piece was not an art object because it was not figurative. They were left with no better category to place the piece under than that of "scrap metal." In a suit, the definition was rejected and the customs officials were compelled to redefine the definition of sculpture. At present there seems to be broad agreement that the term sculpture can be applied to any art object which is three dimensional and is neither a vessel nor an architectural structure.

Though more often associated with marble or bronze, clay is a primary medium for the creation of sculpture. In many ways clay lends itself very well to sculpture. Unlike most sculptural media, clay offers a kind of freedom and immediacy that is very valuable. A piece that might take months to carve in marble or might require the resources of a large foundry if it were to be cast in bronze can be built very inexpensively in a few days, in clay.

On the other hand, sculptors often wish to work on large scale pieces, and clay has definite size limitations; furthermore, sculptors often wish to use attenuated, drawn out forms and clay does not lend itself to forms of this sort. These problems can be dealt with. The ceramic sculptor can tackle scale problems by pushing the forming and firing process to its limits or by segmenting the piece and firing it

Donna Nicholas, "Admonitions," 20" x 37" x 13", 2000, mixed media. At one time Nicholas' work was completely abstract in its subject matter. Furthermore, the clay medium, as a medium, was very important to her. Now her work centers on a message. She wants to deal with the place of women in her ceramic sculpture. This message gives meaning and a sense of force and urgency to her forms.

Ted Vogel, "Fish Cage," 23" x 22", 1997, earthenware, terra sigillatas, gold leaf. Vogel makes it a practice to use imagery from the human and animal world in his sculpture. Photo by Bill Bachhuber.

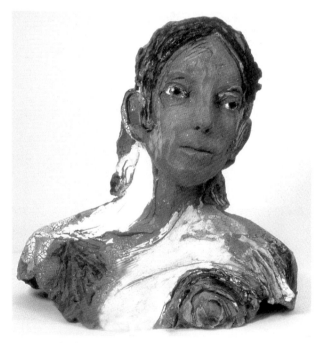

Marcia Polenberg, "Lydia," 17" x 16", slips, terra sigillatas, vitreous engobes, glazes fired at cone 04 and at cone 06. Not all ceramists have the inclination and the interest to make portrait sculpture. The history of ceramics gives us many fine examples of the genre and this piece shows us that it is possible to do fine ceramic portraiture and make it look very current.

Hiroaki T. Morino, "Work #99-2," 1145 x 95 x 440 cm, 1999. This piece is rich in color and the color is exciting and unexpected. The contour is very strongly stated. The space is limited but enhanced by the rectangular openings that allow us to see inside and beyond the bounds of the piece. Morino combines slab and coil construction to make these pieces. He fires them first to a high temperature for durability and then applies a low-fire glaze and fires them to a low temperature. Morino deals with the challenges of complex form creation and large size. The size of these pieces is a very important aspect of their character and contributes to their power. Photo by Takashai Hatakeyama.

Russell Wrankle, "Dog With Mask," earthenware clay body. Wrankle says of the building process: "I add the clay to the form as needed, so the form can get rather thick in areas, especially the legs and hips. Once it is leather-hard I cut the form in half or thirds and hollow it out. After I put it back together I continue to shape it by paddling from the inside out. For this piece I made a mask from coils and used a stiff brush to give the clay the appearance of leather." Wrankle went on to paint the piece with a red terra sigillata and fired it in a low-fire kiln.

in sections, assembling them after firing. These assembled pieces can be held together with wire, bolts, or other fasteners or cemented with mortar, mastic, or glue. This technique allows the ceramist to build a large piece from small, easily handled forms. It also allows the use of materials such as wood, plastic, or metal along with clay. In this way the positive characteristics of clay as a material for sculpture are maximized and its limitations are minimized.

Because of the constraints of the medium, some sculptural forms work better than others in clay. Clay is at its best when used to create compact, blocky forms. It is most weak when used to create attenuated, elongated forms. Most sculptors who work in clay know this and choose forms appropriate to the medium. This gives ceramic sculpture its own characteristic look. Formal limitations and scale limitations can also be dealt with by combining clay with other media.

Important examples of ceramic sculpture are the intense and elegant figural pieces of the Haniwa period from Japan, the complex, threatening, figural sculpture of pre-Columbian Mexico, the elegant dancing figures of Leonard Agathon made at the turn of the century in France, the inventive ceramic collages of Joan Miro and Lorens Artigas, and the brilliantly painted figural work of the contemporary ceramic artist Robert Arneson.

Imagery

The sculptural ceramist will need to use all sorts of technology and may indeed be very adept at using it. Ceramic sculpture, however, is not about the technology - it is about space, form, and subject. The imagery of ceramic sculpture is extremely varied in its subject matter. In fact, that is often seen as one of its great strengths. In the group of sculptural pieces on the following pages we see work dealing with images of the human figure, of animals, natural forms,

Angelica Pozo, "Blossom Series: Honey-Combed Striata," 11" x 14½" x 11", 1998, hand-formed terra cotta. The artist began forming this piece with a press mold for the rounded base. She then laid the form in a chuck and continued forming the piece using coils. It is made from a terra cotta clay body fired to cone 04. It was glaze fired by propping it up on its rim with stilts. In this way she can create a radiating glaze drip effect, simulating floral growth patterns. Plant imagery has become a major form subject for ceramic sculptures. We see that Pozo is aware of the way plant forms are never straight lined but rather marked by waves and undulations. In this piece this is expressed in the striations on the rim of the form.

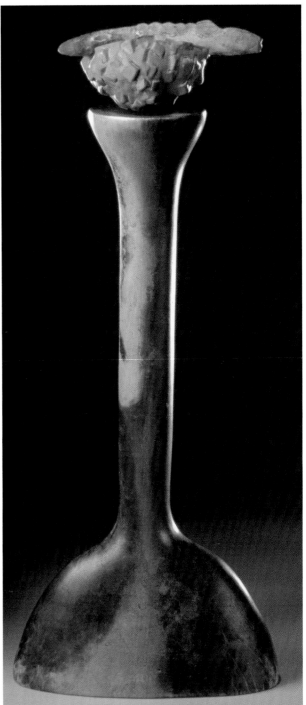

Richard Hirsch, "Pedestal Bowl With Weapon Artifact #15," 53½" x 12" x 10", 1997. Hirsch used a complex group of finishes including terra sigillatas, raku glazes, underglaze slips, and a clear low-fire glaze to finish this piece. This piece has the character of a ritual object, perhaps even a very threatening object. The onlooker is reminded of an ancient altar and of the violence one might see there.

Left: Roy Cartwright, "Perforated Landscape," 32" x 22" x 16", 1996, cone 2 oxidation, finished with paint. Cartwright uses forms and colors that evoke the lush natural world of marshes and lake shores. His use of paint gives him the control over the imagery that he needs.

Sally Michener, "Herstory/History," 51 x 38 x 10 cm, 1997, cup forms and ceramic tiles. Michener has always told stories in her work. Here she has invested familiar objects with a sense of personal history. She has written that in this piece we see a wooden breakfast tray clad in ceramic mosaic, a mixture of ceramic tiles and mirror/glass made by her and her friends, and commercial and found shards, surrounded by colored grout. In the center we see a game board of black and white tiles with computer-generated ceramic decals (fired to cone 020) spelling out the following messages: feeling frisky, mad as hell, sorry, maybe later, your turn, yes! We also see Ikea coffee cups labeled with computer generated decals (fired to cone 020) such as 2 history or 2 herstory to allow people of various gender assortments to be the "players." She worked out this concept in collaboration with Alf Bogusky, director of the Vancouver Art Gallery, as part of a project for the Canadian Craft Museum Collaborations. Materials collected and crafted by the artist. Photo by the artist.

Victor Spinski, "Carving a Teapot," 16" x 14" x 12". Spinski made this piece using cast and hand-forming methods. He used low-fire stains and glazes to create the surface finishes. Here we see Spinski using the low fire as a way to generate complex form and brilliant color to mirror the form and color of familiar objects. As a result, only after study can we begin to "see" his forms and colors as sculptural attributes because we are so taken with their hyper-realistic portrayal of familiar objects. Photo by Tom Stiltz.

Opposite: Jamie Walker, "Natura Morta," 1998, porcelain clay body, wheel formed with hand-formed flowers. Glaze applied with a sprayer, fired to cone 6. Walker's sculpture is quite unorthodox in surface, color, and form. The surface is smooth and almost enamel-like, the color is bright and saturated, and the forms are not ones often associated with sculpture.

Ellen Day, "Cradle Journey II," 16" x 14" x 19", 1999, stoneware clay body. Day's piece is a structure made of many parts knit together. The imagery has a boat-like character. Photo by D. James Dee.

Sana Musasama, "Maple Tree Series, Untitled," height 58", 1994, low fire. Musasama has said of this work: "These sculptures were inspired by the Maple Tree abolitionist movement in the late 18th century in New York and Holland. Dutch colonists, Native Americans, and freed African servants joined together in protest against slave labor on sugar plantations in the West Indies. They took as their symbol the maple tree - a source of sugar that did not entail the exploitation of slave labor. At once trees and aspects of the human body, these sculptures explore links between trees and human sexuality, between trees and human agency."

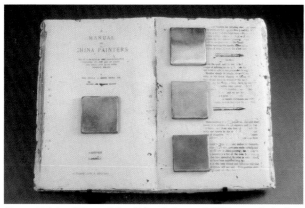

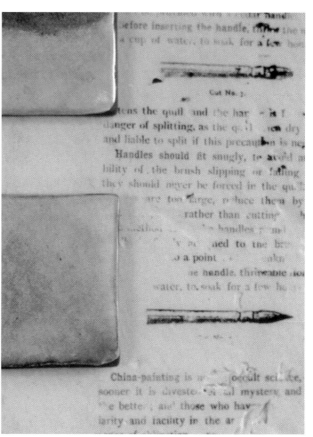

Nancy Selvin, "Manual for China Painters," 1999, cast-in built terra cotta, underglaze and screened underglaze images and text, china paint samples on terra cotta. When the old definition of sculpture as an image of a human or animal was abandoned it became clear after a time that any subject could be used as a subject for sculpture. This piece is an example of that. The piece is very successful both as a sculpture and as a beautiful and interesting object.

Nancy Selvin, detail of "Manual for China Painters."

Anne Currier, "Eleusis," 19" x 18" x 11", 1999, hand formed, low fired. Currier uses a white stoneware clay body. All pieces are hollow and slab constructed. She uses the basic procedures of scoring and reinforcing seams. She uses cardboard tubes of various diameters to form clay cylinders. She makes cone shapes from a flat disk. (Imagine a pie-shaped disk, then remove ⅓ of the pie, bring the edges together and join them with slip. The resulting form will be a cone.) She bisque fires her pieces to cone 03. The first glaze, usually black, is sponged on and fired (again to cone 03). The fired surface of the first glaze is a soft, satin finish. She spray applies a second glaze and while it's still wet, she scrapes the edges of the piece to expose the first glaze. She then refires the piece to cone 08. The fired surface of the second glaze has a gritty texture, comparable to 220-grit sandpaper. The edges of the piece reveal the soft, satin finish of the first glaze, while away from the edges the surface has a fine grit texture. The resulting surface suggests a subtle, understated complexity. Courtesy of the Helen Drutt Gallery, Philadelphia. Photo by Brian Oglesbee.

Elyse Saperstein, "Golden Orb," 28" x 13" x 7", 1999, earthenware, glaze, slip wash, slab constructed, cone 05/06. Saperstein uses human imagery in almost all of her work. These subjects look at times like characters from a fable, or a myth, or perhaps like characters from a story by Italo Calvino.

familiar objects, and abstract forms. We also see sculpture made for architectural environments, large scale sculpture and installation pieces.

The human form is a classic subject of ceramic sculpture and one of the favorites of contemporary ceramic sculptors. The nature of clay (with its characteristically compact forms) lends itself to a stylized imagery. Funk potters of the 1960s put human imagery at the core of their work. Their imagery was ironic, highly stylized, and very funny. Human imagery remains the favorite subject of many ceramic sculptors. Contemporary ceramists use this imagery as a springboard for ideas and comments about contemporary life.

Animal forms are also classic subjects and have often been used by ceramic sculptors. This strategy has a long and honorable history. The multiple figures that make up the "Monkey Orchestra" made in Meissen, Germany, in the early 18th century come quickly to mind. The sculptor Johann Joachim Kändler used animals as stand-ins for humans to create a piece with an ironical message. In the1960s in the United States this was a favorite strategy of the Funk potters. In contemporary work the nature of clay lends itself to a stylized imagery.

Forms found in nature are rich in themselves and symbolize life. Ceramists have worked with this subject for a very long time. It especially finds favor among contemporary ceramists as the springboard for highly stylized imagery. Natural forms are a rich source for the ceramist because they have the breath of life and form character that can be challenging and useful.

At the present time there is a good deal of interest in the depiction of everyday objects in contemporary ceramics. Some of this work is startlingly real looking (tromp l'oeil) while other examples are highly simplified and stylized.

There is great interest in portraying such objects because the subject matter is new and the forms can be quite interesting. These objects carry symbolic weight.

There is a tendency among artists who use abstract imagery in their ceramic sculpture to concentrate on space or form. The ceramic medium is well suited to these subjects because the medium can be manipulated very freely. This encourages exploration and experiment. It has often been noted that potters and sculptors have very different ways of dealing with space and form. Potters start with the container form, the wall that encloses space. Sculptors deal with forms that weave in and out and that often seem to come from a solid core. Sculpture is less predictable; it includes container forms but we see also forms that more fully emphasize the three-dimensional nature of space. So too forms will often seem to come from a solid core rather than from the empty space at the center of a vessel.

The ceramic medium would seem to be ill suited to large scale work. Fired clay is a heavy, awkward material in the large scale and large scale pieces are prone to cracking and explosion. On the other hand, clay lends itself to modular construction. Ceramic sculptors who work with large scale ceramic pieces almost always employ modular construction strategies. This is especially useful for architectural sculpture because architecture is modular and so the two - the modular sculpture and the building - go together in a sympathetic way.

Sculptures in the installation format are constructed environments, perhaps in the form of a slice of real life, perhaps in the form of a collection of objects combining various art media to create a large scale art object. In recent years many artists who do not work in clay have come to be very interested in the installation format. Ceramists, especially ceramists who pay attention to what is going on in other

Virginia Scotchie, "Bronze Green Knobs," 12" x 21" x 21", 2000. Scotchie employs striking and surprising forms in her work. She finishes her pieces with brilliantly colored slips and glazes and makes great use of contrasting textures as well. She goes to great lengths to make all aspects of her pieces work together.

Mary Jo Bole, "The Moody Pete Bathroom Show: Acme Bathroom," 7' x 3' x 8', 1990-1998, clay, mosaic, wood. This photo shows how appropriate clay is as a medium for installation work in its spatial character and in the way it lends itself to the fluent creation of a wide variety of forms.

Nancy Jurs, "Triad," 16' x 15' x 15", 1992, low-fire clay and ceramic surfaces. Jurs first made the maquette and then the final piece for a large public space at the airport in Rochester, New York. In scale and in its heroic mood this piece elevates an otherwise uninteresting space. It makes the experience of flight, which has come to seem very normal and everyday, into an experience that is quite special.

Nancy Jurs, "Maquette for Triad," 1992.

Katherine Ross, "Prophylaxis/Hygiene," installation view, 1999, porcelain. Ross has been working with mixed media installations for a number of years. She uses clay in a great variety of ways here and it plays a big part in these pieces. Photo by the artist.

Tori Arpad, "Grove: Accumulated Urges" (installation detail), 1995, clay, stains, glazes, and sand. The clay medium lends itself to modular forming. Here we see modular forms repeated a great many times to create a powerful image from numerous small elements.

Elizabeth MacDonald, "Inner Landscape," 16" x 16". In this piece MacDonald emphasizes the spaces between the tiles. They play a strong part in defining the imagery and let us know that the artist wants us not to see a landscape but rather a mosaic of a landscape. Photo by Joseph Kugielsky.

artistic media, have taken up the format. In their installations the imagery is usually modular and they often mix ceramic and other media.

Ceramic Wall Pieces

Ceramic wall pieces are clay constructions meant for wall placement. Tiles may be made from simple, flat sheets of clay or from complex, highly modeled forms. Wall pieces may be made from a single tile or from groups of tiles. Scale will vary from a 6 x 6 cm tile which hangs on the wall to large groups of tiles covering a wall the size of a city block.

The ceramist who works in the wall piece format has great freedom and can employ complex and rich image-centered strategies. Wall pieces can free the ceramist from certain kinds of formal restraints as well: the wall or the backing supports the form, creating the opportunity to use form elements which would not otherwise work in clay. In the past most wall pieces were intended for public use. They were meant to be seen by large numbers of people and to be strongly communicative. This strategy is as viable as ever;

George Mason, "This Coin," 14⅝" x 12⅝" (each piece), 1996, terra cotta, low fired. This is a diptych tile work. For many years Mason has worked exclusively in the tile medium. His mastery of the format is evident. Photo by Dennis Griggs.

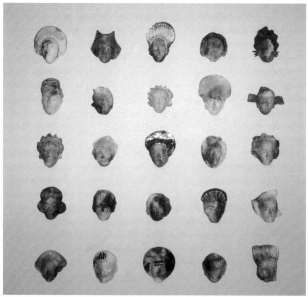

Roberta Griffith, "Five x Five: Twenty-Five Transposed," 10' x 10', 1999, life-size masks. In recent years a number of ceramists have worked with wall pieces made up of a number of repeated elements placed near each other. The grouping can be very powerful.

Nancy McCroskey, "Red Leaf Field," 4" x 6" x 3", 1999, low-fire terra cotta. McCroskey used repetition as an important aspect of the imagery to create this piece.

Kenneth Vavrek, "Windfall," 29½" x 63" x 12½", 1997-98, glazed stoneware. Vavrek calls his pieces "wall sculpture" and the name is very appropriate. The pieces move very far out from the wall and have a real sculptural identity. We are used to sculpture that rests on the floor or the table, it is a pleasing surprise to see highly sculptural pieces intended for wall mounting.

Roy Strassberg, "Holocaust Bone House #5," low fire, wall hanging piece. In recent years Strassberg's work has been transformed by his studies of the Holocaust. The imagery he uses now is not that dissimilar to that he has used in the past. This piece is an image of a house; he has made such images for many years. Now, however, the imagery has deepened and grown much more somber and has a much stronger impact.

some of the best contemporary work in the wall piece format is done in this way. These tile pieces, decorative in character, serve as a kind of background for the business of the day. On the other hand, wall pieces can be private and personal in orientation. These pieces are assertive, highly personal statements. In character they differ little from contemporary art objects made in any media.

Wall piece imagery may be created from a single element or from many elements. A tile piece can be composed of one tile or many tiles. In a piece composed of multiple elements each particular segment may carry a complete image or it may have no individual identity and only when they are assembled will an image be created. Pieces made from a single element (panel compositions) have their advantages: they are uncomplicated, easy to place in a home or gallery, and are intimate in character. Furthermore, the artist need not worry about the demarcations that separate one tile element from another. In some cases ceramic wall panels are very reminiscent of paintings; in others the dimensional characteristics of clay are exploited.

Wall pieces made from multiple elements also have advantages, the main one being that since they are assembled from many elements, they may reach any size. This is an important characteristic. Normally the ceramic medium has size limitations: generally no single piece can be more than 25" or 30" in its largest dimension. Using multiple elements, whole walls, buildings, and even complexes of buildings have

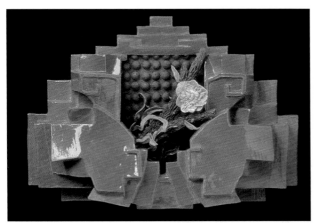

Frank Ozereko, "Pre-Columbian Chinoiserie," 26" x 18" x 9", 1998-99, hand-formed wall piece. Ozereko finishes his pieces with commercially produced slips and glazes. He applies his glazes by brushing, spraying, or even by sprinkling a bit of stain on a surface to get the results he wants. He then fires, sometimes only once but often more than once, to arrive at the finished piece. At one point Ozereko drew a great deal. He liked these drawings but they did not have much to do with his ceramic work. He felt a sense of conflict because he wanted to bring these different kinds of work together. His work has evolved over the years. When it began to evolve in the direction of wall pieces he began to feel that he was bringing the two faces of his work together and was grateful for the opportunity.

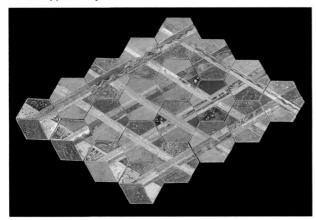

Susan Tunick, "Blue Notes," 56" x 37", 1999, ceramic medallions inset with clay bands, reglazed antique tiles, and gold glass mosaics. In this piece Tunick has fashioned an abstract composition for an architectural setting. She has made great use of many of the artistic tools available to the tile worker. The artist has carefully studied the history and historic technology of the tile maker. Photo by Peter Mauss/Esto.

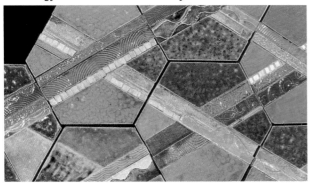

Susan Tunick, detail "Blue Notes," 1999. Photo by Peter M. Mauss/Esto.

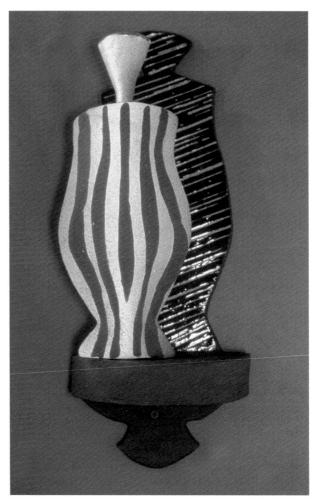

Anna Calluori Holcombe, "Vasaio III," 16" x 7" x 4", 1999, earthenware clay, low-fire slips and glazes. In our culture the vessel form is a very rich symbol. A number of ceramic artists have chosen to work with the vessel form as a sculptural subject.

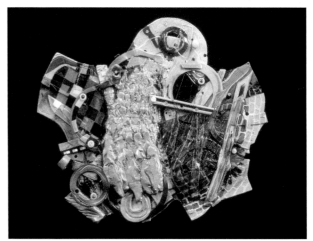

Thomas Seawell, "Vienna Ring VI: Inner Ring," 15" x 17" x 2", 1996, ceramic with mixed media. Seawell has worked with ceramics with mixed media for a long time. His art training was in the area of printmaking but he never was content to limit himself to one medium. In recent years he has concentrated on pieces in which he mixes ceramic and other media to create complex, thought-provoking imagery. Photo by T.C. Eckersley.

Nino Caruso, "Wall Sculpture," installation in the Rocca Paolina, Perugia, Italy, 1991. Caruso uses a mixture of ancient (press molding) and contemporary work strategies (hot wire cut Styrofoam as forms for the creation of plaster molds) to create his large sculptures and wall pieces. Their imagery too is a blend of classic Mediterranean imagery with that of contemporary abstraction.

been ornamented with tiles. Tiles of this sort do not have an individual identity; it is only when they are assembled that an image is created. When a number of tiles are placed together, the interstices between each tile may be obtrusive. Is the artist to ignore these demarcations, to try to minimize them and ask us to pretend that they do not exist? Or should the artist work with the demarcations and integrate them with the imagery of the piece? As a practical matter, in those pieces that are meant for large (often public) spaces, which are to be seen from a distance, the demarcations are often ignored. From a distance the imagery seems to blend together and each individual segment becomes part of the whole. In pieces meant for smaller spaces, to be viewed up close, the demarcations cannot be ignored so easily; they are often acknowledged and designed into the imagery.

Scale will vary from a 6 by 6 cm tile which hangs on the wall to large groups of tiles covering a wall the size of a city block. Tiles can be freely movable (like a painting) or can be permanently attached to the wall. While less attention is paid to this format than to vessels or sculpture, it is a marvelous format for the ceramist.

If we wish to look for precedents for wall piece work we can look to many wonderful examples. These include the monumental glazed brick relief imagery of the Ishtar Gate from ancient Babylon (7th century B.C.), the relief tile Mihrabs (prayer niches) and tiled mosques of Iran, the relief

tile facades designed by the architect Louis Henri Sullivan, and the relief tile panels made by the Grueby studio at the turn of the century for the Lexington Avenue Subway in New York City. In recent years there has been a heightened interest in the tile format, encouraged by a general enthusiasm for exploratory work. Many contemporary ceramists have made important and expressive work in this format.

Wall pieces are often imagery-centered. In those illustrated here we see work dealing with images of humans, animals, nature, familiar objects, and abstract images. We also see wall pieces whose character is defined by their use in architecture or their scale (often a very large scale).

Just as in sculpture the human form is a favorite of contemporary ceramists working in the wall piece format. Animal forms are also classic subjects. The nature of clay lends itself to stylized images of these subjects.

Natural forms are another favorite subject of ceramic artists. Natural forms are rich in themselves and symbolize life. While some artists use imagery that is quite literal, other artists use natural forms as a springboard for highly abstracted imagery. Particularly interesting are highly patterned pieces where forms are repeated to establish a rich and rhythmic imagery. These forms are full of life and have great appeal.

Many contemporary ceramists have a strong interest in depicting objects of symbolic significance. A particular type

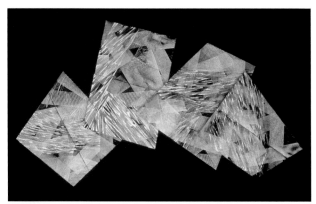

Dale Zheutlin, "Wall Piece," 4' x 6', ceramic slab construction, porcelainous clay body. Zheutlin's pieces are designed for placement in public spaces. They are custom-made pieces meant for a particular space, intended to enrich their environment and give them a personal note.

Lana Wilson, "Ritual Pause," wall piece with ceramic mosaic elements, concrete grout, and green beach glass. The artist starts by making and glazing the ceramic elements. She works first with cone 6 glazes and then refires at cone 04 to get the bright color we see on the larger tile-like elements. She then assembles the other materials she needs to complete the piece including backing materials, grout, and beach glass. Wilson combines a wide variety of materials in her work. The results are highly personal and easily recognized as her own.

Aurore Chabot, "Cellular Synchronicity," 15' x 15', ceramic tile, site: the Marley Building, University of Arizona. Here we see an abstract composition intended for an architectural setting.

that has become popular has the ceramist employing the vessel form on wall pieces. As the artist transfers the image to the wall, it loses its identity as a functioning vessel. Instead the form becomes a powerful symbol and is usually simplified and highly stylized.

Artists who work with abstract imagery in wall pieces tend to deal with color, pattern, and the problems of transforming imagery from three dimensions to relief imagery. At their best these are not paintings transferred to another medium but images authentically belonging to ceramics, in which the artist deals with the particular problems of relief imagery. These problems are especially interesting because the particular problems of relief imagery

are not often taught in the schools of art where ceramic artists are trained.

Ceramic wall pieces work extremely well in the environment of architectural form. They are particularly suited for use in public spaces. They can be used to create large compositions of modular units. They can make spaces elegant and inviting. They can improve the mood of otherwise dark and uninviting environments. These wall pieces are durable and easily maintained. For example, the large ceramic wall piece constructions in the New York City subway system have successfully withstood the pressures of the city for almost 100 years. These include grime, graffiti, occasional flooding, and misdirected "improvements."

Ceramic Slab Construction

"Fractals," created by Dale Zheutlin, commissioned wall piece for the Citibank Tower, Phoenix, Arizona. 34' x 8'. Photos by Craig Wells.

The original space. Site of the wall without the ceramic construction.

The maquette for the wall piece in its environment.

The design process in which Zheutlin plans shapes and sizes for the forms on a computer. In the studio she generates precise computer simulations to show the client what the piece will actually look like and to make sure each plate, fitting, and screw will line up exactly.

Painting clay presents special problems. What you see in the wet stage is not what you get in the fired state. Zheutlin places slabs face up on the table to paint them.

The work table.

Painting the clay elements.

Drying the clay elements. Zheutlin air-dries the slabs in vertical storage racks in preparation for firing.

Installation - scaffolding and a paper template help locate the exact position of each section.

The completed project. Detail and full view.

Robert Harrison

Robert Harrison, "Gibson Gateway," 1993.

Robert Harrison is an architectural sculptor. He travels to do his work and is free to spend a good deal of time on the site where the piece will be located, wherever that may be. Harrison has not had a full-time teaching position for many years. He values the freedom that this gives him. He can pick up and go to a site when he wishes. Recently, for example, he has worked in Staffordshire in England. He was immediately attracted to the area because of its long and distinguished history as a center of clay work in England.

Much of Harrison's work is hand formed. He works with thick slabs (often ¾"). He also uses extruded elements. He researches the site neighborhood to find industrial clay manufacturers where he purchases extruded parts and alters their shape and form. He then returns the piece or pieces to the factory for firing and incorporates them in his final

piece. He likes this both because it helps him create interesting pieces and because he admires the consistency and reliability attained by industrial ceramics firms. He uses these forms with others that he has made in order to create modular pieces.

Many of Harrison's pieces are intended for use outdoors. Glazes that are applied to pieces sited outdoors are subject to a very challenging environment. They are attacked by

Robert Harrison, "Chimney Stack Pair," 2000, Arapaho Community College, Littleton, Colorado.

pollution and weather conditions. Harrison tries to use clay surfaces as much as possible because they are much more stable than glazes. His color is then derived from clay bodies rather than from an applied layer that may part company from the clay body over time. He looks for the most stable types of glazes - often also industrial products. He is especially interested in industrially produced tile glazes and characterizes them as "problem free." While their visual character is usually quite simple, they are very stable and durable. Harrison has used them often enough to know how to get rich results with them. These glazes are intended for spray applications and he uses this application method more than any other. He likes the consistency and uniformity of spray applied glazes. Harrison likes to use materials with an historic background from the local area. He also likes to use

recycled materials and nonclay materials. He generally fires in the mid-fire range - cones 3 to 6.

The site is very important to Harrison. "The work must have an affinity for the site," he states. When he takes up a new project, he visits the site and begins research on the area. He makes it a practice to thoroughly document the site. He is especially interested in researching the weather conditions in the area. He then tries, as much as possible, to work in a place at the site or nearby. As a result he does a lot of his work away from his studio. He is interested in the products, resources, and character of the area and lets this interest enrich his work. Harrison has developed his own unique approach to work in clay. As a result he travels a great deal and works in interesting places. Furthermore, he has learned how to make the most of his opportunities.

5

Creating Form in Clay

Dong Hee Suh, "Rhythm 24," 16½" x 5", fired to cone 06. Suh uses her wire cutter as a forming tool. In her hands it is a tool for the creation of expressive work. This is important to her because Suh uses her work "as a means of artistic expression which ranges from abstract forms to explicit interpretation of my beliefs." In recent years especially, Suh has used her work to reflect these deeply held beliefs and the work reflects this in its subject matter and its sense of commitment.

We ceramists can choose among many methods when we create our forms. We can make our forms from slabs or coils, throw our forms on the potter's wheel, or use mold-forming methods. The descriptions and illustrations of these methods that appear in this section are by necessity limited, general, and very basic. They are a starting point, a foundation. This foundation must be built upon over a period of time and requires experimentation, identification with the medium, and very hard work.

Preparing the Clay for Work

First you must prepare the clay for the forming work. To prepare the clay you season, wedge, and cut it.

Seasoning the Clay Body

In the seasoning process you store the clay after you have mixed it. Even a short aging period is useful because it will encourage an acidic bacterial growth in the watery areas between the particles. This helps the particles slide past each other. The result is a clay body which is greatly improved in workability. Both those who throw on the wheel and those who hand form will find that they can work with much more assurance and control after the clay has been seasoned.

If you are throwing on the wheel or are coil forming, prepare lumps of clay of the appropriate size and store them for a time in a covered plastic container.

If you are using slabs to form your pieces, form the clay into slabs and store them under plastic for a day or two.

Wedging

In the wedging or kneading process you force one part of a lump of clay into another; you roll and knead the clay into

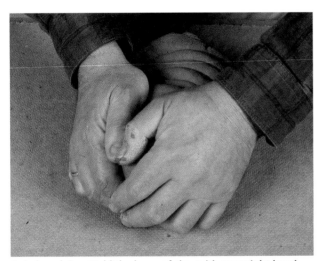

"Dog's head" wedging. Hold the lump of clay in such a way as to simultaneously place pressure on both its top and shoulder. Press down and in at the same time. Use a gentle pressure to press the clay into itself.

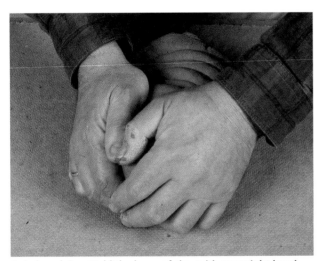

Spiral wedging. Hold the lump of clay with your right hand higher up on the lump than your left hand. Press a bit harder with your right hand than your left and wedge a section of the clay lump. As you wedge keep on shifting from one section of the lump to the next until the whole lump is wedged.

itself. During this process you force much of the air out of the clay and encourage a uniform moisture content. You will find the wedging process easier if you lean into the clay and let your body weight do most of the work rather than trying to use the strength of your arms. You may perform the wedging procedure either on the whole lump of clay or on one section at a time. The first method is called dog's head wedging: here you wedge the whole lump at once. Ceramists have given this method its memorable name because of the shape the lump takes during the process.

The second method, spiral wedging, is given its name because you turn the clay lump in a spiral pattern in order to wedge one section after another. This allows you to wedge large lumps of clay one section at a time.

Cutting

In the cutting process you cut the clay into slices; you then throw the clay slices on a wedging table with some force. The slicing action breaks down lumps and the throwing action drives the air out of the clay body. Generally ceramists wedge the clay, cut it, and wedge it again.

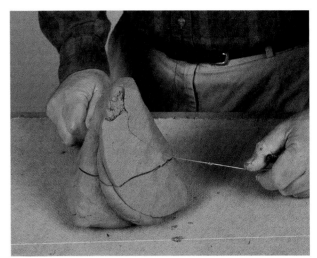

Cutting the clay. Cut the lump of clay into slices to break down lumps and air bubbles.

Slicing the clay. Throw the slices onto the wedging table and wedge them together.

Ceramic Forming Methods

Pinch Forming

The pinch forming method is simple and easy to learn. It is therefore, often used as a way to introduce students to clay. There are ceramists who stay with the method, however, because it lets them emphasize the earthy character of the medium.

Bruce Taylor, "Ball & Wedge," height 39" x 26" x 33", 1993, clay, lead, and wood.

Though most pinch formed pieces are quite small, an accomplished ceramist can use the method to build large pieces as well. Extra wads or coils of clay can be added to the top of the piece. These can then be pinched to extend the height and modify the shape of the piece. Furthermore, you can employ other forming methods along with pinch forming. For example, you can use slabs or coils to modify the form and create pieces unmarked by the limitations of the basic pinch forming technique. Most small pinch formed pieces take the form of cups, bowls, or elongated cup forms.

Building a Small Pinch Form

- ➤Wedge a lump of clay into a spheroid form.
- ➤Place your thumbs together on the surface of the spheroid.
- ➤Press into the spheroid with both thumbs.
- ➤Turn the sphere in your hands.
- ➤Again press your thumbs into the spheroid.
- ➤Continue this process of pressing and turning until the piece begins to take on a hollow bowl-like form.
- ➤Pinch the clay so that you raise the form and widen it at the top.
- ➤Continue this process of creating and defining the form.
- ➤Finish the lip with a sponge.
- ➤You may wish to use a rib and a paddle to define the form as well.
- ➤Allow the piece to become firm.
- ➤Create a base by adding a coil of clay to the bottom of the piece and weld this into the form.
- ➤Smooth and finish the form.

Robert Wood, "Dual," height 109", 1996, earthenware clay, slab construction, finished with slips, stains, and frits. Wood once-fired the piece to cone 3 in a medium reduction atmosphere in a gas kiln. This is an example of the use of large flat slabs. The complex silhouette becomes a focal point in this approach to dealing with slab forms.

Building a Large Pinch Form

- ➤Start with a small pinch formed piece and add pinched clay wall segments to the lip of the piece.
- ➤Weld the elements together using pinch methods.
- ➤Raise the wall as high as you wish.
- ➤Smooth and finish the form.

Solid Forming

In the solid forming process you form the piece from a solid lump of clay. You must open up or hollow out any parts of the form that are more than 2" or 3" thick. The method is mostly used for sculpture and for thick-walled vessels. Solid formed pieces are liable to cracks and explosions during firing, but a piece with a hollowed or pierced center is much less prone to these problems.

Joe Molinaro, "Teapot," 16" x 10" x 6", porcelain, hand formed with thrown and extruded elements, fired to cone 8 in an oxidation atmosphere. Molinaro alters the shapes of his slabs before assembling them. The result is an elliptical form with a tightly controlled curve that serves as the body of this piece. He contrasts these with thrown and extruded handles and spout.

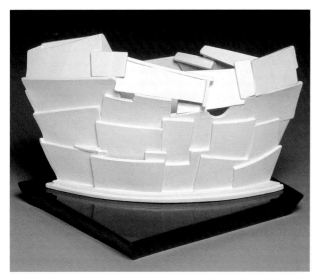

Judith Salomon, "White Vase on Black Base," 19" x 12" x 10", 1998, terra cotta clay body, slab construction, fired to cone 04. Salomon here creates a slab wall using many small slabs luted together. The result has the look of an architectural construction. Photo by Dan Milner.

Piercing a Solid Form

One way to open up a solid block of clay is by using rods. In this method you open channels into the interior of the piece to encourage even drying and allow moisture and steam to escape during the firing process. The resulting pieces are heavy because they have not been hollowed out. You can make a great variety of shapes using this method because it is not necessary to create complex hollow forms. For this method you will need a long metal rod with a sharpened point.

➤ Wedge a lump of clay and create the form.
➤ Finish the surface with a sponge and allow the piece to become firm.
➤ On the worktable, position a large slab of sponge rubber or a thickly folded blanket and place the piece on its side resting on this cushion.
➤ Pierce the base of the piece a number of times with a metal rod.
➤ Smooth the surface of the piece, taking special care to fill in any openings where the rod has broken through to the surface of the clay.
➤ Dry the piece carefully, examining it periodically out for cracking.

Hollowing a Solid Block of Clay

In this method you hollow out the interior of the piece. This lightens it and ensures that there will be a place for moisture and steam to escape during firing. You will need a cushion and a loop tool to carry out this procedure.

➤ Allow the piece to become firm.
➤ Place a cushion on the worktable and rest the piece on this cushion.
➤ Hollow out the inner cavity with a loop tool; attempt to follow the outer contour as closely as possible. (Save the discarded clay for rewetting and reuse.)

➤ Dry the piece carefully, examining it periodically inside and out for cracking.

Slab Forming

A clay slab is a sheet-like building form. Slabs are fairly easy to make in clay and can be used as the basic building block for many kinds of forms. Slab forming techniques are a good introduction to clay forming. Beginning projects can be simple and easily learned, yet slab forming can present the experienced ceramist with challenges as demanding as any in ceramics.

There are many methods for forming clay slabs. The method that follows is quick, makes no great physical demands, and requires no expensive machinery. All you need is a lump of wedged clay and a work board. (The thick cardboard material called Homosote makes a fine work board.)

➤ Flatten the top of the lump of clay a bit.
➤ Pick up the lump at one corner with both hands and stretch out your arms as far as possible.
➤ Snap the lump of clay onto the board at a point close to your torso and let the clay hit the board in a kind of skidding motion.
➤ Repeat this process until you have a slab ½" thick. It will take you a few minutes to learn how to do this.
➤ Transfer the slab from the board to a piece of fabric.
➤ Smooth the slab with a wooden roller or with a rib tool and a sponge. This method helps you to force air out of the slab and break up air pockets.

The working character of your slabs is important. This is dictated in part by the moisture content. A slab that is very wet will be flabby and you will not be able to build with it. A slab that is very stiff will be difficult to work with and difficult to join to other slabs. Crisp, geometric work requires flat,

Throwing a slab.

Trimming the slab.

Pressing down on the edge.

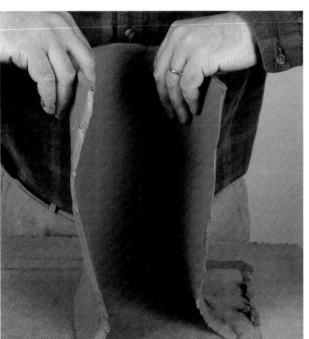

Starting the cylinder.

Working on the cylinder.

somewhat stiff slabs. More organic imagery suggests slabs which are softer and can be shaped and curved. Over time many ceramists come to prefer working with curved and billowing slabs that reflect the plastic nature of clay.

Making a Ceramic Cylindrical Form

➤ Trim the slab so that it is rectangular in shape.

➤ Pinch the ends on the right and left sides of the slab so they end in a sharp edge: leave the top and bottom edges straight.

➤ Stand the slab on its bottom edge and bend it so it makes a "U" shape that will support itself.

➤ Wet the two ends of the slab (which were pinched), join them, and smooth the join.

➤ Here we see the completed cylindrical form, the basic shape for many pottery and sculptural forms.

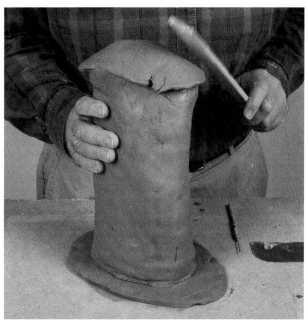

Working on the rounded top.

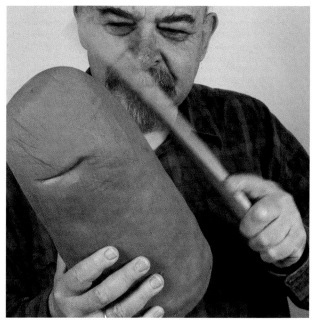

Paddling the form.

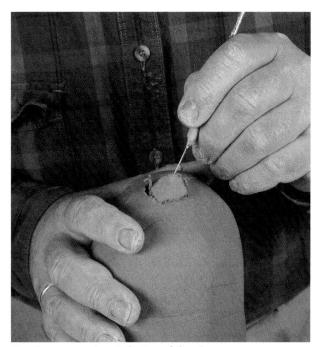

Creating an opening at the top of the piece.

Joins

There will be many occasions during the slab forming process when you will need to join pieces of clay together securely. It is good practice to join pieces together with slip - a soupy, sticky mixture of clay and water. After you have applied the slip, you may wish to fill in the join with a coil made from soft clay (called a fillet). It strengthens the join and gives it a more finished appearance.

➤ Score both surfaces where they will come together and paint them with slip.

➤ Join the two surfaces, tug and adjust them a bit so there is very good contact.
➤ Once the piece has become firm, roll out a coil of soft clay same length as the height of your piece.
➤ Paint the inside corner created by two slabs with water or slip and place the coil over the join.
➤ Smooth the coil (a long-handled brush is a good tool for this).

Working With the Cylinder

Cylinders are one of the basic forms of the ceramist. They are useful to both the potter and the sculptor and can be used in a great number of ways.

Turning the Cylinder Into a Vessel Form
➤ Place a slab on one end of a cylinder. This will be the base of the cylinder.
➤ Trim and clean the base. You may wish to trim the edge of the base so it is flush with the walls of the cylinder.
➤ Paddle the base, making it curve inward to create a stable base.
➤ Integrate the base with the rest of the form.

Turning the Cylinder Into a Closed Form
➤ Place a slab on each end of a cylinder and assemble the form.
➤ Trim this so the edge of each slab is flush with the walls of the cylinder.
➤ Paddle the ends of the capped cylinder until they take on rounded forms.
➤ If the cylinder is longer than it is wide, the form will be tubular with rounded ends. If the cylinder is

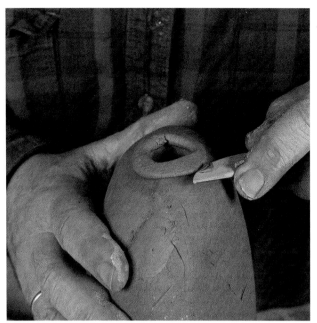

Working on the opening.

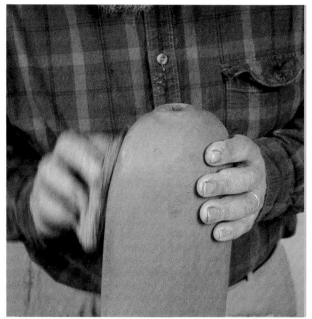

Completing the form.

only as long as it is wide, the form will be spherical.

➤Place an opening somewhere on the form (it can be a small opening if you wish) to allow gases to escape during the firing; otherwise these trapped gases may cause the piece to explode.

➤You may wish to add a base so the piece sits securely.

Making a Three-Sided Form

➤Make three slabs.

➤Pinch the corners of each slab to form a 45° angle.

➤Let the slabs partially dry until they are somewhat firm (cheese-hard).

➤Paint slip on the corners of the slabs, then assemble them. This will create a three-sided form.

➤Join and smooth the corners.

➤Place thin coils of clay at the corners where the slabs are joined to strengthen the form.

➤To make the base, place the form on a slab of clay. Join, trim, and smooth the edges.

➤Paddle the base, making it curve inward to create a stable base and integrate it with the form.

➤Experiment with irregular and asymmetric hand-built forms. There is no reason why the walls of a hand-built piece must be uniform in size and shape. In fact, hand-forming methods do not lend themselves to mechanically perfect, symmetrical forms. Furthermore, the use of irregular shapes and sizes is one way to insure that your forms are not overly predictable.

Preparing the slabs.

Putting the slabs together.

Smoothing the join on the inside of the form.

Smoothing the outer edge of the join.

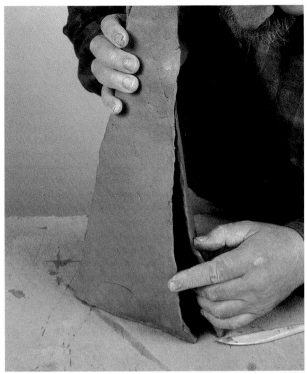
Trimming and pinching.

Ann Mortimer, "Velvet Invitation," 4½" x 2¼", 1999, low-fire clays and glazes, coil formed over a Styrofoam form. Mortimer has used coil forms to create not a piece formed coil fashion in an upward moving spiral, but rather has placed them side by side and luted them together. Finished with underglaze colors and then a coating of a satin glaze to intensify the colors, the result suggests underwater life-forms and conveys a mood of fantasy. Photo by Mark Eveson.

Coil Building

Most of us know what a coil of clay is, but the term is hard to define. A coil is what we get when we roll a lump of clay on the table for a while - a clay form about ½" thick and 8" long. Coils look like snakes, and children invariably call them by that name (we probably should call them that too, but it doesn't sound very dignified).

The coil-forming method is a bit slow compared to other methods. It has great advantages, however, because it can be used to create very complex and/or unusually large forms. Therefore, there are potters who specialize in this forming method.

Coil Forming

➤ Start a coil-built piece with a slab-built cylinder or bowl form. If coils are used to form the base of a piece, it is likely to crack.
➤ Place a coil on top of this base.
➤ Build up the form by adding coils in a tightly woven spiral. Be careful that each successive layer is joined firmly to the last.
➤ Use a sponge and a smoothing tool to smooth the coils together on one or both sides of the wall. Though this erases the coil pattern, it is necessary because it insures that the coils will not crack or open.
➤ After a time the wall of the form begins to attain some height and the soft coils have a tendency to sag. At this point you must interrupt your work for a time until the walls have a chance to set up; you may then continue the building process. Because this waiting period is necessary, coil builders often work on more than one piece at a time: while one piece is setting up, you can continue work on the other.

Throwing on the Potter's Wheel

For many people, ceramics and the potter's wheel are synonymous; the image of the potter at the wheel is one that

Forming the base.

Adding coils.

Paddling the form.

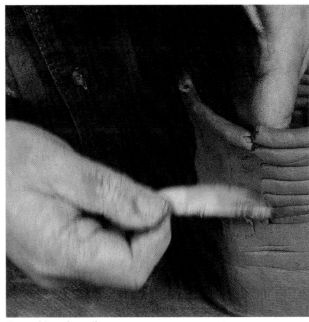

Smoothing the coils.

springs quickly to mind. This is a wonderful clay forming method. It is quick and fluid. It produces strong and visually satisfying results. Its symmetric forms can be very pleasing to the eye: they speak at once of movement and of that center point where everything is still.

The wheel is really a tool for creating a group of basic shapes. Though this is a small group of basic forms, they can be used in a very wide variety of ways and within these limits the ceramist has great opportunities for formal invention. The products of the potter's wheel are surprisingly diverse. It takes time to learn how to throw on the potter's wheel with skill and ease, often a number of years, but for many ceramists the effort is worthwhile. A

well-thrown pot speaks of the adaptability of clay and the skill of the potter.

The Process

It is a real challenge to describe what happens on the potter's wheel: words are not really adequate. The wheel is simple in principal - it is a whirling turntable upon which you have placed a lump of clay. You first "center" the clay by allowing it to pass under your hands. You hold your hands and arms still in order to "persuade" the lump to take on a symmetric form. Once the clay is centered, you must pierce it with your fingers to "open it." Once you have opened the clay lump you thin and raise the wall to create a symmetric clay form.

JoAnn Schnabel, "Tea for Who?" 15" x 18" x 10", 1999, terra cotta and glaze, cone 3. This piece is made from coils that do not spiral upward but rather are strips placed one on top of the other. Technically they are not coils at all, but this building method is obviously closer in mood to true coiling than any other. This piece is also very interesting for its source of ideas in the Middle East. We are beginning to see a real interest among contemporary ceramists in using pottery from the ancient Middle East as a source for ideas. At one time ceramists resolutely kept their attention upon forms and surfaces with roots in China and Japan. It seems very healthy to acknowledge sources from a wide variety of traditions.

Chris Gustin, "Vessel," 35" x 34" x 29", 1999, stoneware clay body. Here the artist has combined thrown with coil elements to create an imagery that speaks in a very elegant way of form rather than either throwing or coiling. He says of this piece: "I work with stoneware clay, combining both coil-building and wheel-throwing techniques to build my large forms. I start my pots by throwing simple bowl-like forms, maybe 4" to 5" tall by 16" in diameter. I then alter these by cutting, pushing, and pulling the walls of the pot out of the geometry of the circle. This creates lines that move between a hard and a soft geometry, imposing harder angles and softer, slower curves. I then continue building up the wall of the pot by adding coils of clay and basically hand building the form. This strategy takes the pots out of their symmetrical format and allows me to explore the 'architecture' of the vessel. The foot of the pot is no longer round, therefore I am able to challenge the symmetry of the wheel-formed vessel. I often throw numerous shapes on the wheel as well, using them as 'parts' that I may cut up and hand build onto the larger forms I am building. I bisque fire the pots and apply one to three glazes on the surface. I spray all of my glazes in layers and have found that by building up the glazes I am able to get a surface with a depth of color and richness that invites a sense of touch. I fire the pots to cone 10. The density of the clay and the structure of the glaze melt at this temperature allow for surfaces that I cannot attain at lower temperatures."

Throwing on the Wheel

David MacDonald

Opening up the centered lump of clay.

The first pull.

Forming the lip.

Beginning to fill out the form.

Working on the shoulder of the filled out form.

Cleaning the lip.

Refining the lip.

Examining the finished piece.

Robin Hopper, "Skyphos - Classical Series," porcelain with a bronze colored slip glaze. Hopper fired the glaze in an electric kiln to cone 08. In this piece he has used the potter's wheel to refer to the ancient Mediterranean world and to metallic vessels from that culture. The narrow pedestal foot and the dramatic handles enhance the presence of the piece. Photo by the artist.

Centering

➤ Sitting in front of the wheel, fix a lump of clay on the wheelhead.

➤ Wet the clay to assist the centering process.

➤ Brace your body, arms, and hands and let the lump pass under your hands.

➤ Periodically moisten the form with a water-filled sponge.

➤ Hold your hands and arms steady and rest them on the lump of clay.

➤ Exert subtle pressure to shift the lump on its axis until it is perfectly symmetric.

➤ By using a controlled pressure, work the clay to take on its symmetric, cone-like form.

Opening Up the Form

➤ At this stage the lump of clay is solid. Now you are ready to open it.

➤ Pierce its center with your fingers to create a symmetric opening.

➤ Enlarge the opening while keeping it symmetric.

Pulling

➤ To pull the form into a pot you place the fingers of your left hand at the inner bottom of the cylinder and the fingers of your right hand on the outside surface of the cylinder at its base.

➤ Push outward to create a ring of clay and pull that ring toward the top of the form.

➤ Moisten the form with water. This will help you to shape the clay.

➤ Repeat these actions three or four times to create a cylindrical form whose walls are reasonably uniform and controlled in thickness (¼" to ½").

➤ Shape and finish the piece to give it identity as a finished form.

Thrown and Altered Forms

One way for the potter who throws on the wheel to assure variety is to alter the form after the throwing process is complete. Thrown forms can be altered by subtracting parts of the form, by adding to the form, or by changing the shape of the piece. The additions of elements such as spouts and

Judi Dyelle, "Doubled Walled Vessel, Kamloops Series," 30.5 x 12.5 cm, wheel formed. This piece speaks of the potter's wheel as a tool to fashion forms of restraint, intelligence, and elegance. It is double walled and its sense of space is very pleasing. Photo by the artist.

handles needed to make a teapot are one kind of alteration. In another kind of manipulation, the vessel wall is altered by squeezing, molding, or pushing out from within. These modifications may be subtle or quite radical; their underlying principal is that a clay form may be shaped with energy and spontaneity on the wheel and then modified to create an image with characteristics of both throwing and hand building.

"Ovalizing" a Thrown Cylinder

➤Place a bat (a removable disk) on the wheelhead.

➤Throw a form without a base.

➤Remove the thrown form (including the bat) from the wheelhead and set it aside until it's somewhat firm though still flexible.

➤Use a wooden knife to free the form from the bat and place it on a work board.

➤Press the form inward on two sides to form an oval.

➤Make a clay slab a bit bigger than the base of the piece.

➤Place the form on the clay slab to create the base.

➤You will probably want to trim the base flush with the sides of the oval form.

➤Finish the piece using hand-forming methods.

Jim Srubek, "Covered Jar." Srubeck makes porcelain pieces using traditional Arita methods for handling the material. He studied these methods with the Japanese Arita master, Inoue Manji Sensei. Srubek uses a clay body containing grolleg kaolin, kona F-4 feldspar, silica 325 and 200, and 1.5% macaloid. These pieces are striking in their clarity and single-minded pursuit of perfection of proportion. Photo by the artist.

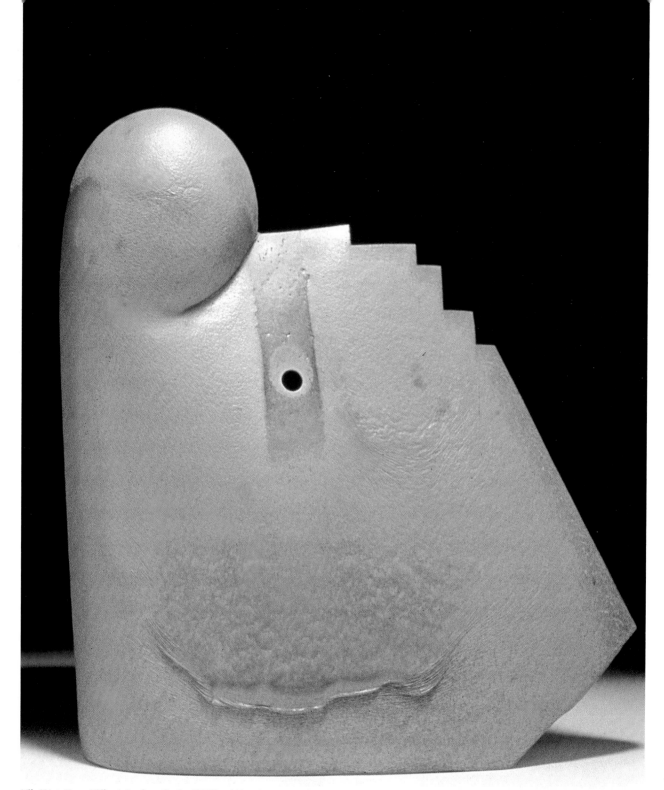

Yih-Wen Kuo, "Silent Asylum Series," 21" x 21" x 8", 1999. The artist created the form using a press mold. It is glazed and fired in gas reduction kiln. The press mold process has allowed Kuo to create a form that would be very difficult to form in clay in any other way. With its aid he has been able to establish a very high level of control of form and surface. Photo by Barry Stark.

Matrix Forming

A matrix is a tool that can be used to create a form. Matrix forms can be made from a wide variety of materials including plaster, clay, fabric, wood, plastic, or paper. They can be used to create form by draping or pressing workable clay or casting with clay in its slip state.

Drape Forming

The drape forming method is halfway between hand forming and mold forming. Here the ceramist drapes a clay slab over or into a form made from wood, bisque-fired clay, or plaster. These forms are so simple that they cannot really be called molds. The term "forming aid" seems more appropriate. The method is simple, direct, quick, and very useful.

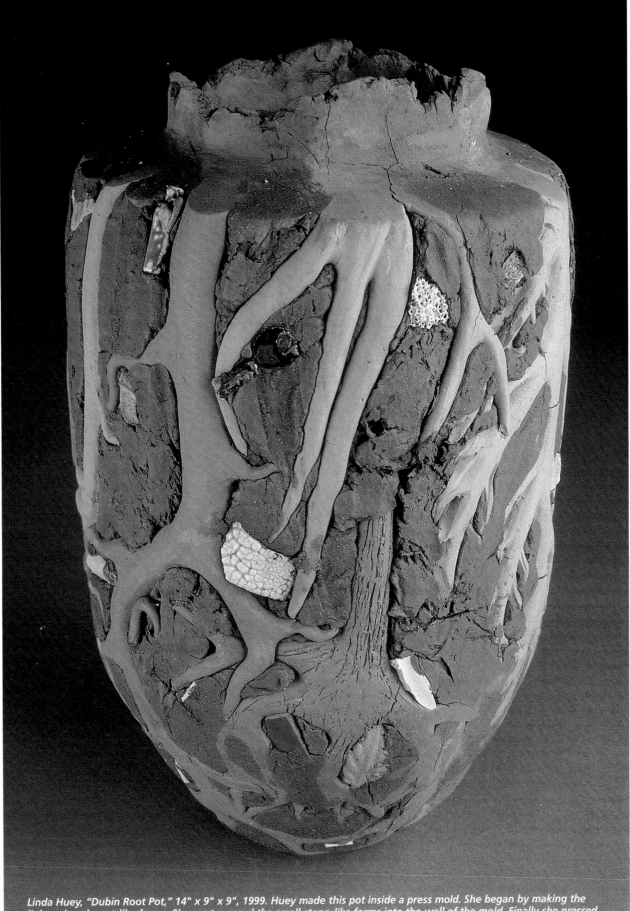

Linda Huey, "Dubin Root Pot," 14" x 9" x 9", 1999. Huey made this pot inside a press mold. She began by making the light-colored, root-like forms. She next pressed the small stone-like forms into the wall of the mold. Finally she pressed in the dark-colored clay body that serves as the matrix holding the other elements in place. Thus the piece is not only satisfying visually, it is also a fascinating record of the forming process. Photo by the artist.

Hand Forming in a Press Mold

By Linda Huey

Linda Huey prepares to make the piece. Here she works with plaster molds that she will use to make some of the imagery on the wall of the piece. She will make other imagery by hand forming it.

Creating hand-formed elements. Huey rolls out coils and places them on a slab.

Working the coils into the slab.

Huey will build the piece inside a bisque form. She begins lining the inside of the bisque form with a newsprint liner (to avoid sticking).

Beginning to place some of the wall elements.

Adding more wall elements with imagery and lining the inner wall with soft clay to strengthen the piece.

Removing the newsprint liner from the piece after it's been removed from the form.

Spraying the piece to keep it moist.

Refining the imagery.

Adding a new leaf.

Continuing the finishing process.

More work on finishing the piece.

The completed piece in its unfired state.

The fired piece.

Creating a Mold-Formed Vessel

By Angelo diPetta
Series photos by Catriona Sinclair

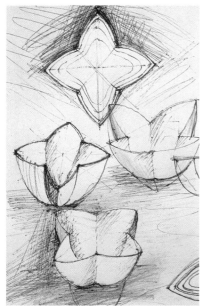

Preliminary sketches - a page from diPetta's sketchbook.

Forming the mold upside down. diPetta builds up the solid form starting from the lip and moving up to the base.

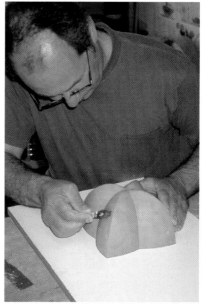

Finishing the model.

Making a plaster mix. When it begins to thicken diPetta carefully pours it over the model, being careful not to trap air pockets and making sure he fills all the detail work with plaster.

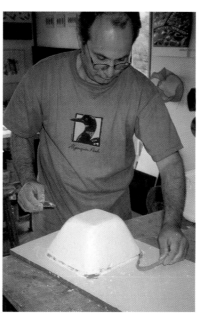

When the plaster sets to a "cream cheese-like" state he scrapes it clean and removes the coil where it joins the table.

Turning it over and inspecting the mold.

He allows the mold to dry for a number of days then pours casting slip into the mold (stopping at a point an inch or so from the top of the mold). He leaves the clay in the mold for 30 to 40 minutes (40 minutes will make a thicker piece than 30 minutes).

When the clay wall is as thick as he wishes, he pours out the slip (leaving the clay that clings to the mold to form the new cast piece).

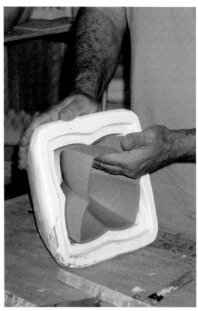

After 20 minutes or so the cast piece hardens and shrinks away from the mold, at which point diPetta can remove it from the mold.

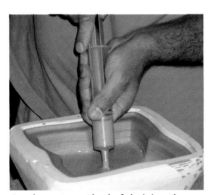

An alternate method of draining the clay from the mold - drawing off the slip a little at a time using a syringe or baster. diPetta likes to wait about ten minutes between each draw. This strategy creates ridges in relief on the inside of the cast piece.

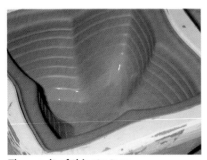

The result of this strategy.

The finished piece.

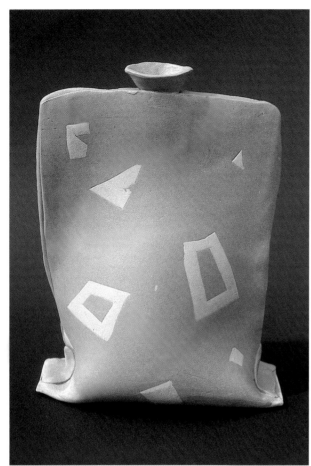

Richard Zakin, a U shaped Pot. Note the soft slumped look that can be achieved using this forming method. I am especially fond of this method using low clay content clay bodies that are a bit flabby and rubbery. Their contours take on a billowing character.

Using a Plywood Drape Form to Create a Plate

➤Make a forming aid using a piece of plywood.

➤Prepare a slab of clay. It should be somewhat larger than the forming aid.

➤Drape the slab over the forming aid.

➤Create a foot on the base of the form.

➤Allow the piece to dry for an hour on the form, then turn it over and remove the forming aid.

➤Allow the piece to dry for a few hours and trim it.

Forming a U-Shaped Pot

Here is a method for creating useful and unusual drape formed vessels. These pieces are called "u-shaped pots." The basic idea behind this method is that you slump a slab over dowels to create the walls of the piece. You then finish the form by joining its sides and letting the form hang upside down until it becomes firm. Now remove it from the dowels and finish the piece. By doing this you will be able to make a complex folded form from a single slab. The process is easy and natural and takes very little time. It results in a form with an interesting slumped look.

Sun Yong Chung, "Six Inch Bowls," 1999, colored porcelain with clear glaze. Chung created these pieces in a ram press. Though this device helps her work quickly, speed is not the most important aspect of its character. More importantly, it allows her to create an imagery that has a strongly graphic character. Color and imagery is highly defined. Photo by Bardajay.

This method is especially useful for creating tall pieces. If you are making a tall piece, roll out the slabs and cover them overnight to season and ready them for the forming process.

➤Make a slab that is narrow and long.

➤Place three reinforcing struts in the middle of the slab.

➤Place newspaper down the center of the slab.

➤Place two supports (such as tall buckets) about 15" apart.

➤Place two or three wooden rollers on the two supports.

➤Place the clay slab over the rollers. The ends of the slab will naturally fall toward the table.

➤Wet the side edges of the slab and pinch them together but stop about 1" away from the bottom of the piece.

➤Push the edges together to make a full form.

➤After a time the form becomes fairly firm.

➤Take the form, with the rods still in it, off the supports.

➤Turn it over, place it on the table, and remove the wooden rollers.

➤Rest the piece on its base. The base will slump a bit to conform to the table.

➤Cap the open areas (where the supporting rods were) on each side.

➤Pick up the form and push the base upwards to give it a stable, concave foot.

➤If desired, finish the form with a thrown spout or a carved lip.

Extruder Forming

A clay extruder is a machine that allows the ceramist to shape clay by forcing it through a form or die. The simplest extruded forms are solid. More complex extruded forms are hollow. It is also possible to create forms which curve as they

Tam Irving, "Earth Still - Series 1," 66" x 19" x 9½", 1998, clay and painted wood shelves. In these pieces Irving combines slipcast pieces and pieces thrown on the potter's wheel. In describing these pieces he talks of "the celebration of objects through a still-life format." He feels that one of the strengths of this format is that it allows him to explore forms in relation to each other. By combining slipcast and thrown elements he can vary the character of his forms to make a stronger and more interesting piece.

leave the extruder. Extrusions can be of any length but are limited to the width of the die that the machine will accommodate. Simple clay extruders are given their thrust by a hand-operated lever. More complex versions are powered by mechanical means. Extruders find their greatest use as supplemental to other forming methods. The most common of these is the use of an extruded form, such as a handle, joined to a thrown form.

Mold Forming

A mold is a matrix, a tool for imparting a new shape to a material. Molds are excellent tools for creating ceramic form. Because clay has no form of its own, it can be made to take the form of the mold quite easily. There are two different strategies for doing this. The first is the press mold process in which the ceramist uses "normal" moist clay; the second is slipcasting where the ceramist pours a thin clay and water mixture called a casting slip into the mold.

Press Mold Forming

Press mold forming is the simplest mold-forming process. To use this method you force a moist coarse clay body over or into a mold. As the clay dries, it releases from the mold; at this point you remove it from the mold, clean, and finish it.

Slipcast Forming

Slipcast forming is more complex and takes longer to learn. The principal underlying the slipcast forming process is quite simple, however - that plaster of Paris will absorb the moisture in a clay slip. When this happens, the casting slip in contact with the plaster mold begins to dry, thus creating a form which is in effect a replication in clay of the inside surface of the mold. It is this clay replication which becomes the mold-formed piece.

Bowl, The Teco Pottery, ca. 1908, height 2½".

Ram Press Forming - An Industrial Mold Forming Method

In recent years a number of studio ceramists have begun to adopt an industrial tool, the ram press, to their creative work. The ram press is a mold forming tool that allows the ceramist to form clay using great pressure. The machine is composed of a positive and a negative die. Clay is placed in the bottom die and the top die is forced into the bottom die. This gives the clay the form the ceramist desires. After a period of use the dies become quite moist and air is blown through tubes in the mold to force out the moisture. The method is most appropriate for making pieces with open forms such as bowls and plates. Studio ceramists are beginning to find ways to exploit this tool to create unusual and striking imagery.

Slip Forming

To create a slipcast piece you pour the slip into the plaster mold. A layer of slip adheres to the mold wall and some of its water is absorbed. In this way a wall of clay is built up on the

Angelo diPetta, "Rock Garden," 3½" x 4" each piece, 1999. diPetta says of these: "In these pieces the outer form becomes the 'mold' for the inner forms. The outer form is shaped and carved from a red earthenware with sawdust additions. I fire it to bisque to cone 010 and then wet sand it to create a smooth, polished surface. These forms then become molds for the inner forms. I bisque fire these pieces and glaze them with stained transparent glazes to cone 06. I smoke fire the outer forms and seal them with an acrylic floor wax diluted with water. I then glue the inner and outer parts together with an epoxy." Photo by the artist.

inside surface of the mold. In the middle of the mold cavity, however, the slip remains wet. When you decide that the clay wall is of sufficient thickness, you pour out the still wet slurry. You allow the clay form inside the mold to become firm and then take it from the mold, ready to finish, dry, and fire.

You begin the slipcasting process by making a model and then casting this model in gypsum plaster (plaster of Paris) to make the mold. We use plaster because it very effectively absorbs the water in a clay slip. Depending on the form of the piece, the mold will be one part or segmented into two or more parts. Studio ceramists tend to work with one- or two-piece molds rather than more complex multiple-part molds that are difficult to manage.

Making the Mold

Use only fresh plaster of Paris - if it is more than six months old it will be lumpy and not set well. Mix the plaster in flexible plastic buckets (it will stick to other types of containers). *Note:* Unused wet plaster should not be washed into the sink drain or the toilet for it will clog the plumbing. Let unused plaster set completely before discarding it.

Make the model from wet clay, avoiding undercuts (places where the model is formed in such a way as to impede the removal of the mold). You are now ready to make a mold from this model.

Mixing Plaster

Sift plaster into a flexible bucket containing water. A successful plaster-to-water ratio will be approximately 1.25 to 1 by weight. Sift the plaster into the water (never the

reverse) until small "islands" of plaster stick out above the water. After a few minutes agitate the mixture vigorously. It is now ready for use.

Making a Simple One-Piece Mold

➤Rub petroleum jelly on a sheet of glass and place the clay model upside down on the glass.
➤Make a container to hold the wet plaster around the model using four separate greased plywood walls. Adjust the size to the size and shape of the model, leaving plenty of room so that the plaster walls will be thick enough to absorb the water in the slip (at least 2½").
➤Pour the plaster into the containing structure.
➤Jostle the container to release any air bubbles and allow the plaster to set.
➤Separate the mold from the glass sheet.
➤Remove the model from the plaster.
➤Allow the mold to dry a few days before using it.

Making a Simple Two-Piece Mold

To keep this process simple, the model is cut in half in this version of the mold making process. While this can be very effective, other strategies are used in more complex and sophisticated versions of the process.

➤Make the model and cut it in half.
➤Place half of the model on a sheet of thick glass that has been greased with petroleum jelly.
➤Use plywood "dams" to build a container around the model.

Slyvia Netzer, "Torus - Life Saver - Safety Net," 1999, slipcast, low fire. The photo shows part of an installation of this work at the AIR Gallery, New York City, at an exhibition called The Miasma Morph Museum (Sylvia Netzer, Director, C.O.O.) Netzer uses imagery from sources such as scientific illustration and photographs of the building blocks of nature as seen in the microscope. She uses these forms to create large installation pieces. Netzer made the Life Saver-like shapes using a slipcasting strategy. She says of this: "I was never interested in slipcasting because it seemed boring to make the same form over and over. I also wasn't interested in its 'dead, anonymous' surface. When I wanted to make 'Torus - Life Saver - Safety Net,' I decided that I needed to make forms that were both large and lightweight. I decided that slipcasting was the most promising technique for this. I made six molds all at the same time. Each mold was slightly different and distinct from the others. I also distorted each form in cleaning up the mold. Slipcasting turned out to be a very efficient way to produce a large sculpture. Furthermore, the surface was perfect for accepting the 'encaustic (wax and pigment) glaze' that I've been using for the past several years."

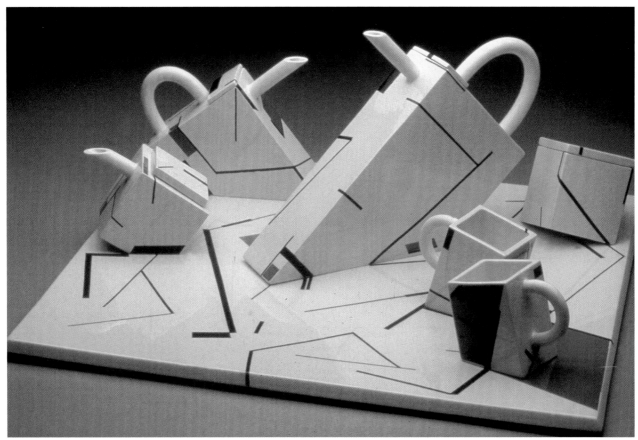

Marek Cecula, "Interiors, Cup II," 10" x 10" x 8", 1992, high-fire porcelain and gold glaze. Photo by Bill Waltzer.

➤Pour plaster over the model and allow the plaster to set.

➤Remove the plywood dams.

➤Release the mold from the glass and turn it to reveal its face. Leave the model embedded in the plaster.

➤Carve two or three small inverted domes into the wall on the face of the mold. These will act as keys for the other half of the mold.

➤Place the second half of the model on the cast half that's still in the mold.

➤Apply petroleum jelly or mold soap to the face of the mold.

➤Build the plywood dams around the bottom half of the mold. These will hold the plaster for the top half of the mold.

➤Pour the plaster into the plywood dam over the other half of the mold. Allow the plaster to set.

➤Remove the plywood dams.

➤Separate the two halves of the mold.

➤Remove the model from the mold.

Casting Slip

A normal clay/water slip mixture cannot be used as a casting slip. It contains so much water that it would quickly saturate the mold. Therefore the ceramist uses a slip that is specially formulated for the slipcasting process. Casting slip contains a deflocculant. The deflocculant breaks the bonds that hold a clay together and changes a stiff clay or clay body into a liquid slip.

It is a complex task to make a casting slip. It is often best to take up the slipcasting process by using a slip supplied by a ceramic supply house. These slips are consistent and reliable. Even ceramists who are very familiar with the casting process often prefer to use such prepared casting slips. In the explanation given below the slip referred to is one that has been purchased from a clay supplier.

Using the Mold to Make a Piece

➤It is important to note that you will need to "season" the mold and that the first few casts may not be entirely successful.

➤If the mold is a multi-piece type, bind the sections together with industrial belting (available at a good hardware store).

➤Pour the slip into the mold, let it set a few minutes, and pour in more if the slip has receded to a point where you can no longer see it.

➤Wait 30 minutes and measure the thickness of the slip layer adhering to the sides of the mold. When this slip layer is satisfactorily thick, pour out the rest.

Leslie Strong, "Welcome Home," 8" x 5" x 5", low-fire terra cotta and cactus quills. Organic materials such as cactus quills can be very effective when accompanying clay forms. The cactus quills are thin and spiky while the clay is a heavy and often ponderous material. The two form types work together very well.

➤Let the slip layer become firm, then remove the clay form from the mold.
➤Clean the piece with a sponge.
➤Trim the lip and any mold lines with a sharp knife.
➤Smooth the surface of the piece with a sponge.

The mold-forming process has many similarities to printmaking. Just as printmaking first became popular as an economical way to create two-dimensional images, slipcasting began as an economical way to create three-dimensional forms. Since the slipcast process allows for the easy duplication of complex forms, it can be very economical. Even today many pieces are formed using slipcast methods for this reason. Clay artists, however, are beginning to explore the slipcast medium as a way to produce form and imagery that they cannot achieve in any other way. The Teco ware piece illustrated on page 95 is an example of American Art Pottery. The job of making the complex and precise sculptural form employed in this piece would have been very awkward using other forming methods.

Note: For a more thorough examination of the mold-making process, refer to *Mold Making for Ceramics* by Donald E. Frith.

Gillian Lowndes, "No. 3 Sieve, Scroll, Fork," height 15 cm, 1998, porcelain and nonclay materials. Fiberglass, indigo porcelain slip, crazed glaze, fork with bristles. Fired to 1240°C. Small sieve with Egyptian paste and wires pushed through the surface, 995°C. Lowndes assembled the parts after firing. For many years Lowndes has been very interested in exploring the nature of the ceramic medium and pushing it to its limits and beyond. In recent years she has combined her ceramic forms with nonclay materials. These experiments have resulted in forms that are interesting and exciting visually and somehow steer away from any expected imagery.

Experiments in Form Creation

Ceramists sometimes become fascinated with the process of forming and may wish to experiment with forming methods that, in one way or another, are on the frontier of our understanding of the way clay can be formed.

Fiona Ross, "Helios," 19" x 10" x 10", 2000, concrete and porcelain. In her work, Ross explores the nature of ceramic materials and the way they react to the fire. The objects that come from her kiln attest to more than the energy of the fire, they attest to her ability to set the stage, to assemble the required materials and tools so that the results can be looked at as objects of art.

She has said of her work: "The brutal character of the fire makes me intensely curious about the changes that occur inside the kiln. Transformation is compelling and contains elements of creation as well as destruction. I am interested in sculptures that have this sense of inception and subsiding, that record and mirror the passion and forces that created them.

"I have worked out a way to make my pieces from powdered clays and minerals. I pack these as dry materials in clay-lined firebrick saggers and the materials fuse at high temperatures to form a ceramic aggregate. I use several different aggregate bodies in my work, from semi-porcelain to a combination of feldspars and local clays. Each firing teaches me something new, so I find that careful records are necessary.

"Dozens of body tests, some kiln mishaps, and experimentation with firing variables have led me to discoveries about the potentials of this medium. When I began this work I found that the sculptures took the shape of their saggers during the firing. I modified the sagger interiors with clay and began adding porcelain, stoneware, and refractory concrete inclusions to get better forms and compositions, but still was not satisfied. First, sagger firing interfered with the intimate relationship between flame and clay. Also, larger pieces were difficult to fire to fusion because of the amount of aggregate and the insulation of the saggers. Then, in a breakthrough, I began refiring my work in looser saggers and discovered that they began to deform and skew in response to time, gravity, and the flame path, demonstrating the unaffected grace of the inanimate. I now fire work two or more times after the initial firing, using bag walls that I have designed to encourage and control the movements of the forms in the fire. In my mind these forms exist at a point between creation and destruction. It is the tension between these two forces that at once sustains my interest and satisfies my personal aesthetic." Photo by Taylor Dabney.

Modular Forms

The ceramic sculptor may work with a multi-form piece in which all the forms are made separately and assembled after firing. These assembled pieces can be held together with wire, bolts, or other fasteners or cemented with mastic or glue. This technique allows the ceramist to build a large complex piece from small, easily handled forms.

Mixed Media

The use of mixed media techniques has attracted interest in recent years. It allows the ceramist to use materials such as wood, plastic, or metal along with clay. These materials are generally not finally brought together to complete the piece until the ceramist has fired the clay forms. In this way the positive characteristics of clay as a material are maximized and its limitations are minimized.

Combining Metal and Clay in the Fire

A number of ceramists have experimented with the firing of clay forms that have metal elements embedded in them. The difficulty here is that the metal does not shrink while the clay generally does. This will cause the clay elements to crack around the metal. This may be dealt with in two ways - the ceramist may wish to integrate the cracking into the imagery of the piece or may use a clay that shrinks very little. Illustrated are two pieces in which the cracking is integrated into the imagery. Deborah Sigel has taken the first path while Gillian Lowndes has taken the second. *or Over- size the hole...*

Using Melting to Create Form

Many ceramists are interested in bringing their materials close to the point of melting in order to create forms that attest to the unique behavior of ceramic materials in the fire. These experiments are especially interesting when carried out by ceramists who have a love for ceramic materials and an understanding of their behavior in the fire.

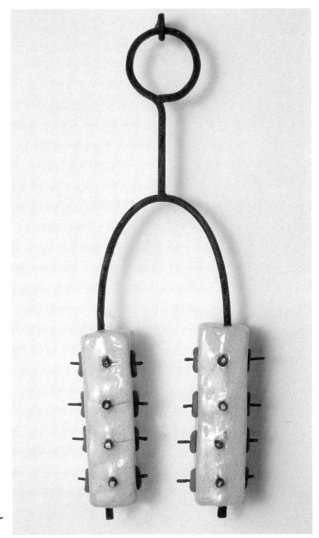

Deborah Sigel, "Gravitational Transformation," 12" x 5" x 3", 1996, ceramic and steel. Sigel is very interested in the behavior of materials in the fire. In this piece she has combined ceramic with metal elements. The metal is a heat resistant steel. As you can see, the metal/clay interface can cause cracking. This is because the clay shrinks and the metal does not. Sigel is interested in this phenomenon and sees it as an enhancement in the character of the piece. She says of her work: "I use Egyptian paste and steel rods. I use basic blacksmithing techniques to shape the steel. I then weld the pieces together. I fire the pieces (both steel and Egyptian paste) in positions in the kiln that will enhance the final result. I often fire pieces suspended in the kiln so that heat, gravity, and time can be used as a transformational tool in the creation of the pieces. In essence I set up a situation for the process to complete." Photo by the artist.

6

Clay Imagery

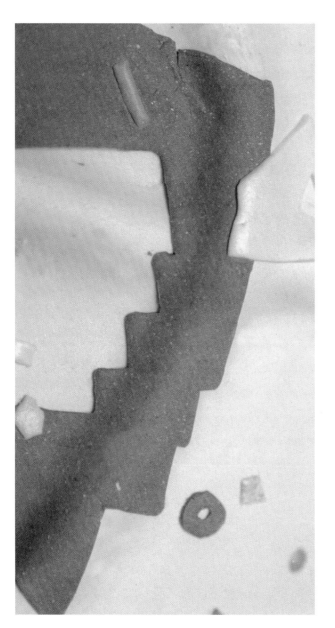

One of the best ways to create imagery on the surface of ceramic pieces is with clay: a good deal of our imagery is created in this way. Just as clay lends itself easily to the creation of form, it also lends itself easily to the creation of surface imagery. Some of the earliest potters excelled in their use of clay imagery: the potters of the Jomon culture of ancient Japan took this approach in their large modeled and carved coil vessels. Strategies for creating this kind of imagery are usually very simple and straightforward. There are a number of different ways of creating them.

Sprigged Imagery

The ceramist makes this from clay elements and applies this to the surface of the form. In the application process the ceramist simply presses clay elements upon the surface of the piece. These elements are usually slipped so they will bond effectively.

Applying Sprigged Imagery

➤Cut and form the clay elements.
➤Apply slip to the surfaces that will make contact with the form.
➤Press the clay elements into the form.

Here we see a thin slab of dark clay applied to a light clay body. We also see other small colored clay elements applied using a sprigging strategy.

Don Pilcher, "Porcelain Vase," height 12", 2000, thrown with extruded and sprigged porcelain elements, cone 10 reduction. Pilcher's use of sprigging with no slip or glaze creates a rich and yet spare bas-relief imagery on the surface of the piece.

Marc Leuthold, "Porcelain Wheel," diameter 12", 1996, carved porcelain fired to cone 9.

David MacDonald, "Carved Jar," height 16", 2000, thrown on the potter's wheel, carved relief, fired to cone 9/10 in a reduction atmosphere. MacDonald carves patterns composed of parallel lines into the surface of his pieces. This kind of imagery is reminiscent of the imagery used by the potters of Nigeria. MacDonald, an African American, is very interested in this imagery. Photo by Brantley Carrol.

Carved clay imagery.

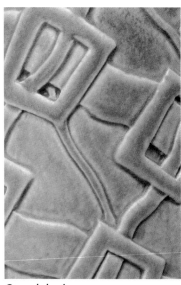

Carved clay imagery.

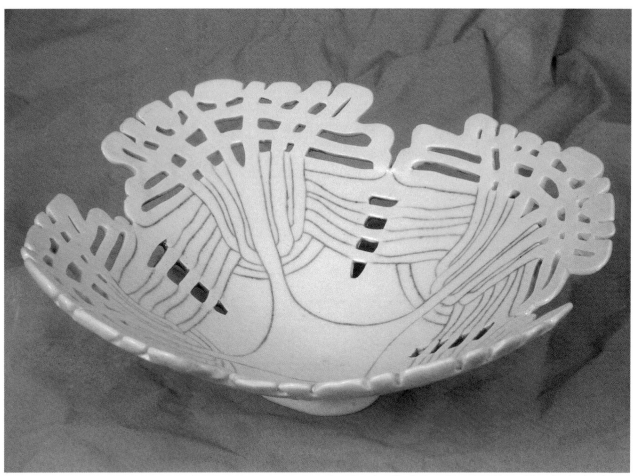

Ann Ransier, "Reticulated Bowl," 1997, white clay body, slump formed over a bisque mold. Ornamented with reticulated areas and engraved imagery. Intaglio glazed with a black glaze and finished with a white glaze. Fired to cone 3 in an electric kiln. Ransier carves and engraves the surfaces of her pieces to create a rich and introspective imagery.

Left: Stamped imagery with intaglio glazing.

Carved and Engraved Imagery

This is imagery which is carved or engraved into the surface of the clay. Scalpels are excellent tools for precise carving - they are slim (and therefore do not get in the way of carving) and very sharp. You may also find that you need scraping and smoothing tools to clean and refine the image.

Carving an Image in a Ceramic Form

➤Create and finish a form.
➤Draw the imagery on the surface.
➤Carve the imagery into the clay.
➤Finish the image with smoothing tools and fine sponges.

Regis Brodie, "Oval Form #1."

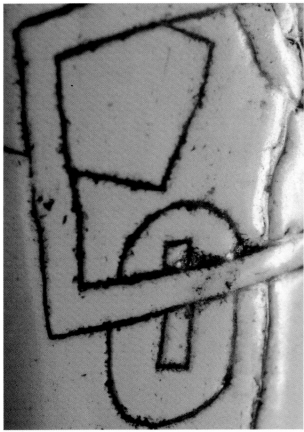

Engraved imagery with intaglio glazing.

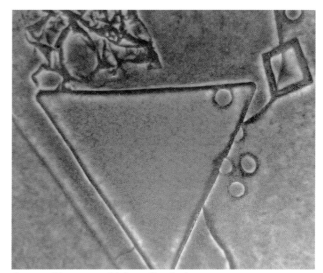

Stamped imagery with intaglio glazing.

Stamped or Pressed Imagery

Stamped imagery is created by pressing into the clay with stamping tools made from bone, wood, metal, rubber, cork, etc.

Using Stamped Imagery on a Slab Form

➤Make slabs for a ceramic piece.
➤Stamp the slabs with various stamping tools.
➤Assemble the slabs, being careful not to damage the imagery.

Press Molded Imagery

Press molding is related to stamped imagery. Small press molds can be used to create elements which are applied to the form. Decorative handles and emblems have long been treated in this way.

Making an Applied Press Mold Element

➤Start with a block of plaster which has set.
➤Carve an image into the plaster.
➤Blow out any plaster dust and press clay into the plaster.

➤Clean the clay element.
➤Apply the element to the surface of the piece.

Sandblasting

In this technique the ceramist directs a stream of sand, under pressure, on the surface of the piece. The surface affected by the sand is abraded and engraved. Areas of the piece may be masked to retain their original surface while the unmasked areas are modified.

Slip Trailing

In slip trailing the ceramist creates a raised line imagery with a thick slip. This is done with the aid of an application device called a slip trailer - usually a flexible plastic or rubber bulb with a narrow nozzle at one end. Slip-trailed imagery is generally applied to a piece when the body is leather-hard. It requires a steady hand and some experience: it is a good idea to practice on test slabs before using this technique on a piece you hold in high regard.

In the past, low-fire domestic wares were decorated with slip trailing and then covered with a clear glaze. Now this method is used at all points of the firing spectrum. As in the past, transparent or translucent glazes are often applied over this imagery.

Using a Flexible Slip Trailer

➤Prepare a thick slip.
➤Immerse the nozzle of a slip-trail device in the slip.
➤Squeeze the bulb and fill it with slip.
➤Squeeze the bulb to apply slip over the piece. This creates a raised, linear design.
➤You may wish to cover the piece with a transparent glaze.

Yoshiro Ikeda, "#3 Teapot," 17" x 10" x 7", 1998, fired to cones 02 and 03. The slip-trailed line has a unique look. It is raised, often shiny, and has the look of a liquid material caught in mid pour (which in a sense it is). Here we see it applied over a smoky, dark background. The whole effect is strong and highly patterned and marked by a sense of visual logic.

7

Ceramic Surfaces

Introduction

From clay we derive form: once that form is created, however, we usually manipulate it in some way in order to enrich the surface. To a degree unmatched by any other artistic medium, we ceramists manipulate both form and surface - it is our job to balance the two as best we can. This is a difficult task, rendered even more difficult by the fact that form and surface in ceramics are almost always created at two separate times using very different methods for creation. The intertwining of form and surface is the engine that drives our medium and gives the best ceramic pieces a tension, a restless energy, and a sense of resolution. In our time, with its emphasis on the experimental and the personal, there is a great deal of interest in the wide range of surfaces open to the ceramist.

No one ceramic surface finish is universally useful or "good." The rule is, if it meets our needs, it's good and should be used. Each ceramist's needs are unique - for one the most desired characteristic will be the ability to withstand the stress of cooking and cleaning, for another, a rich texture or color, and for a third, exciting application possibilities. The potter who wishes to create durable, useful, and easily cleaned vessels will have a very different idea of what constitutes a good surface than the ceramist who wants to apply a complex, highly textured surface on a sculptural nonfunctional form. The ceramist has to give weight to the character of the form, the purpose of the piece, and the nature of the materials and tools at hand. The ceramist can also use the choice of surface finish to convey intangibles, such as adherence to a particular artistic creed. Surface treatments go in and out of fashion; the surface treatment on a piece may follow the current fashion or perhaps be in the advanced guard of contemporary practice. Or it may harken back to a traditional practice or more rarely be completely independent of both fashion and tradition. There is no one standard we can all accept, nor should there be.

Ceramic finishes intended for application to the surface are perhaps the most complex and interesting part of our technology, rooted in our medium's past and at the same time constantly evolving and shifting direction. Most of our surface finishes are fired and are unique to our medium.

Clay Surfaces

It is possible to leave all or most all of the clay surface showing - free from any application of a surface finish. This is especially appropriate for sculpture or sculptural pottery in which form is at the heart of the piece. An applied surface on a piece of this sort may seem to be an unwelcome distraction. Such simple clay surfaces can also be useful for work with a clay body whose color or texture is interesting enough to require no added coating.

Applied Surfaces

Most ceramic pieces, however, are finished by covering them with a mixture that modifies the surface of the piece. This may be made from paints, which are composed of a colorant and a glue binder that dries in contact with air. Paints do not have the durability of most fired materials, nor do they bond with the clay body as intimately as fired mixtures. On the other hand, they are easily controlled and flexible in use.

Most often, however, the ceramist uses mixtures that are fired on the piece. These create durable surfaces that are tightly bonded to the clay body. Ceramic surfaces are divided into two main types, those which are vitreous or glassy, and those which are nonvitreous and essentially clay-like. The vitreous surfaces are further divided into glazes, vitreous slips and engobes, and the nonvitreous surfaces into washes, slips, engobes, and terra sigillatas.

Paula Winokur, "Segments Erraticus," each segment 22" x 22" x 5", 1999. Three segments of nine. Winokur made these segments with a slab formed, porcelain clay body, unglazed and fired to cone 10. Photo by John Carlano.

Richard Notkin, "Legacy," 1999. Notkin says of this work: "I made the ears from about 50 different stoneware bodies, with all kinds of aggregates mixed in, like sawdust, vermiculite, perlite, chunk feldspar (up to 20 mesh), eggshells, etc. I made these pieces in two-piece press molds (I made the molds from carved clay originals). There are more than 20 different ears, right and left, they range in size from 1" to 24". I tumbled some of the ears with gravel, sand, and water in a cement mixer (with the blades removed) after firing to give them a worn, eroded look. There is no glaze or wash or stain added to any of the surfaces. I fired these at cone 10 in a reduction atmosphere." Courtesy of Garth Clark Gallery, New York City.

Richard Notkin, "Legacy" detail.

Nonvitreous Surfaces

Vitreous means glassy. Some of our most interesting and exciting ceramic surfaces are not glassy. The most common of these are colorant washes, slips, and engobes. Generally these surfaces are not glassy, nor do they run and flow in the fire. Some ceramists use these surfaces under glazes to create imagery that would not be possible using glazes alone. The combination can be used to create an imagery which is quite graphic and hard edged; unlike that from glazes used alone, it will not blur or run. Other ceramists use nonvitreous surfaces as the final finish for the piece. There are times when a normal glassy surface finish is not

quite right. Many pieces don't require the durable, smooth surfaces we get from glazes and don't look well when they are used. The dry, mat surface of an unglazed engobe can be far preferable to the shiny surface of a transparent glaze or even the satin surface of a glaze which is translucent. We have a number of alternatives open to us, surfaces whose character is very varied. We benefit if we are familiar with these alternate possibilities. We should not fall into the trap of using a glaze finish just because "this is the way it is supposed to be done."

Washes

Washes are made from dark-colored clays, stains, or oxide colorants. They are very thin and reveal a great deal of the character of the clay beneath them. They are easy to use and quite durable. Their surface tends to be mat (sometimes with a barely discernible sheen). Their color tends to be darker than the body they are applied to in a manner similar to wood stains. These surfaces work well when used by themselves or in conjunction with other surfaces such as glazes.

Finishing a Piece With Glazes and Washes

This is a very useful method for finishing a piece whose clay surface has been ornamented with intaglio and/or relief imagery. The glaze is used in the interstices of the piece and the colorant wash is then sprayed over its surface. It is an especially useful method for beginners because it is essentially WYSIWYG, meaning what you see before firing is pretty much what you get after the firing is complete.

You Will Need
➤Bisque-fired piece whose surface has been modified with scratched, impressed, or relief imagery
➤Small amount of glaze(s)

Barbara Frey, "Let's Go Teapot #2," 5¾" x 9" x 3", 1999, cone 6 porcelainous, colored clay body. This piece is on the frontiers of utility/nonutility. It is a working teapot. It has, however, not been created with the intention of use but rather its identity is in the inventive character of its imagery. Photo by Harrison Evans.

➤Wash solution
➤Sponge
➤Sprayer
➤Turntable to turn the piece during the spraying process

The Procedure
➤If you want the interior of the piece to be glazed, do so at this point.
➤Dip a sponge in the glaze and daub the glaze in the interstices created by the intaglio or relief imagery. Allow the glaze to dry for a few minutes.
➤Wash off any excess glaze from the surface of the piece, leaving the glaze only in the interstices. Let the piece dry for 30 minutes.
➤Place the piece on the turntable and spray the wash solution over its surface.
➤Clean the foot of the piece.
➤The piece is now ready for firing.

Slips and Engobes

Slips and engobes have little of the flowing characteristics and the active visual textures which distinguish glazes. Both slips and engobes are high-clay formulations. If a recipe has a high proportion of clay, it will have a high viscosity and will not flow and blur during the firing. Furthermore, it will not be marked by visual texture. These characteristics insure that high-clay surfaces look very different from glazes. There is some confusion as to the differences between slips and engobes. Many contemporary ceramists have found it useful to define the two in the following manner. If the clay materials comprise 21% to 50%, it's classified as an engobe; if 51% or more, it's a slip. Engobes, having a higher percentage of nonclay materials, are more refined in character than slips.

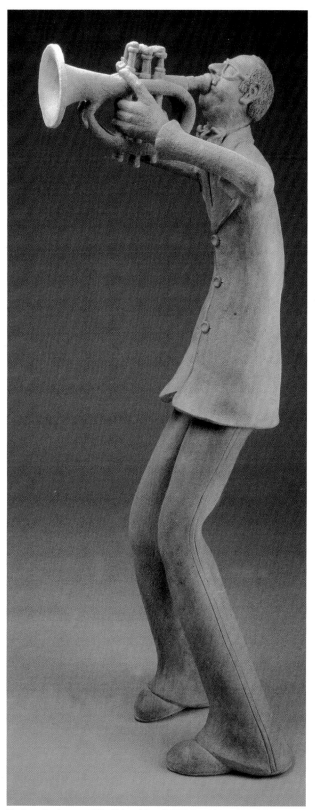

Turker Ozdogan, "My Friend Dr. O," 52" x 18" x 11", 1984. Ozdagon made this piece with a stoneware clay body. Quite often ceramic sculpture requires no glaze. Forms and textures vary a great deal and this alone creates a rich surface. Glazes may cover the clay surface unnecessarily. Furthermore, we identify glazes with the vessel form, unless very carefully handled they may not look "right" on a sculptural form.

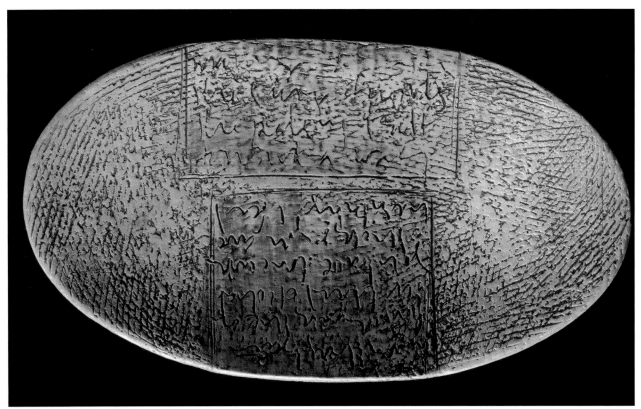

Mary Barringer, "Conversation Platter," 9" x 15½", 1999, stoneware clay body. Barringer uses washes to enrich the surfaces of her pieces without shrouding any of the details of the clay surface. She creates these surfaces layer by layer, they are a very important part of the piece and go well with her highly resolved forms. Photo by Wayne Fleming.

Mary Barringer, "Conversation Platter" detail. Photo by Wayne Fleming.

Using Slips and Engobes

Because slips and engobes do not flow in the fire they can be used for complex, graphic images which, if they were painted with glazes, would not survive the firing. To take advantage of the image creation possibilities of slips and engobes, they are generally applied in ways that would be inappropriate for glazes. Brushes are the most frequently used application tool for these surfaces but airbrushes and airbrush and stencil methods are also used a great deal. In fact, any strategy that can be used to create imagery is appropriate for the application of slips and engobes.

Finishing a Piece With a Nonvitreous Surface - Brush Application

You Will Need
➤ Leather-hard or dry clay piece
➤ Nonvitreous surface mixture (wash, underglaze stain, slip or engobe, or group of slips or engobes)
➤ Brush or group of varied brushes
➤ Turntable to turn the piece during the slip painting process

The Procedure
➤ Apply the nonvitreous surface(s) to the piece. You may find it useful to vary the size and type of brushes to achieve different brush effects. It can

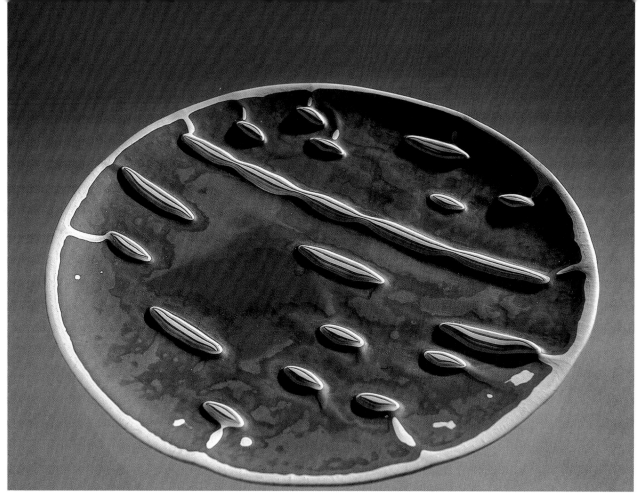

Kathryn Lawrence, "Drifted," diameter 30 cm, 1999. Lawrence used Jasper slips to create the imagery we see here. These are slip bodies pioneered by the English ceramist Josiah Wedgwood. They contain melting materials that create a durable slip. (Wedgwood used barium as a flux, now different fluxes are used.) The surface is rock-like and the color is rich and saturated.

also be useful to use sgraffito techniques with the slips. The linear imagery of the sgraffito line works well with the brush-applied nonvitreous surface. The engraved sgraffito line contrasts well with the softer brush effects.

➤When the piece is completely dry, it is ready for firing.

Applying Glazes Over Nonvitreous Surfaces

Often washes, stains, slips, and engobes are covered with a glaze: this protects their surfaces which otherwise are not as durable as glazes. Furthermore, because nonvitreous surfaces do not run in the fire, they allow for imagery that is difficult to achieve with glazes used alone. You may apply the glaze over the dry nonvitreous surface or fire the piece to bisque and then apply the glaze. The results combine advantages from each surface type.

Finishing a Piece Using Engraved Slip Imagery Covered by a Clear Glaze

You Will Need
➤Leather-hard or dry clay piece with light or medium light body color
➤Dark-colored slip that contrasts with the body color
➤Brush or group of varied brushes

➤Sprayer (an atomizer sprayer will work well for most pieces - see page 232)
➤Turntable to turn the piece during the slip painting process

The Procedure
➤Apply the slip to all or part of the surface of the piece.
➤Carve into the surface of the slip using engraving and sgraffito techniques. You will be able to create detailed drawings in the slip using these techniques.
➤You now have a choice: you may single fire the piece or use a bisque fire to ready it for the glaze. If using a bisque fire, when the piece is completely dry, fire it to bisque, then glaze the interior and spray the slip painted areas with a coat of glaze and fire the piece to maturity. If using a single-fire procedure, pour the glaze into the interior of the piece while it is still moist. A dry clay piece may break apart when filled with wet glaze.
➤While the piece is still moist, pour the glaze into its interior. Cover the interior with glaze and pour out the excess.
➤Allow the piece to dry and apply the slip. Allow the piece to dry again.
➤Spray the piece with a light coating of glaze and fire it.

once-firing technique

Joanne Hayakawa, "Spine," 22" x 6" x 28", 1993-4, made from a stoneware clay body and bones. Hayakawa does not like to shroud her forms and clay surfaces with thick surface coatings so she avoids thick glaze surfaces. Here she has colored the clay with a series of stains and washes. They work very well with the sculptural form.

Nick Starr, "Verdigris Bowl," diameter 17¼", low fire vitreous engobes with a very light coating of a clear glaze. The artist states that vitreous engobes give him an excellent level of control over the imagery on his pieces and that he values this greatly.

Vitreous Engobes

Vitreous means glass-like. A vitreous engobe is an engobe with a glaze-like surface: however, it still will have the smooth surfaces and nonflowing character of a normal engobe. The principal behind vitreous engobes is very simple. The refractory quality of these high-clay recipes is offset by powerful melters. Vitreous engobes are hybrid formulations - they look and act like slips. They do not act like glazes, nor do they look very much like glazes, but they do have the shiny surface of glazes. Furthermore, they have much of the durability of glazes. In other words, there are many good arguments for using them.

Like normal engobes, vitreous engobes should contain from 25% to 50% clay. The rest should be frits, feldspars, and fluxes. Make sure these materials encourage strong melts at the firing temperature you are using (for guidance on this see the fluxing power notations in the section on intuitive glaze analysis, pages 222-224).

If these surfaces are applied exactly like glazes they will rarely be successful: their surfaces will seem flat and lifeless. If, on the other hand, they are applied like an engobe or a slip, perhaps with a brush or a painting knife, they are likely to be very lively and successful. (A painting knife is a tool that looks like a miniature trowel used by artists to apply heavy layers of paint.)

The ceramic artist Susanne Stephenson has worked with vitreous engobes for many years. In the essay on page 120 she explains her work with these surface treatments.

Vitreous Engobe Recipes: Cones 04/03

Material	R1	R2	R3
Ferro Frit 3124	38	44	50
Nepheline syenite	12	11	10
Tenn ball clay (OM4)	31	28	25
Flint	19	17	15
	100	100	100

Problems Posed by Slips and Engobes

Slips and engobes (including vitreous slips) are prone to pinholes and crawling. Pinholes are very small openings that appear on the surface of the glaze or engobe and reveal the clay body. They are artifacts of reactions at the height of the fire - openings in the surface that have not melted and healed. They are far less likely to heal in high-clay, vitreous slips and engobes than in glazes because of clay's high

Allan Rosenbaum, "Pipeline," 24" x 23" x 26", 1997. Earthenware, finished with stains and glazes. Rosenbaum has said of his work: "These sculptures are hand-built from terra cotta clay using a coil-pinch and slab construction process. I stain the pieces with oxides and paint with slips and underglaze stains before the initial firing. After this firing, I apply a wide variety of earthenware glazes in layers. I then fire the pieces up to four times to achieve a rich and varied surface, applying more glaze layers as I go. I am especially interested in the manner in which glaze color and texture interact with the form. I hope that the relationship between form, color, and texture adds to the metaphoric possibilities of my sculptural pieces." Photo by Katherine Wetzel.

A close-up view of a dark wash. This kind of imagery can be created by applying a wash made with a dark-colored clay. It darkens the clay and in the process livens the color and texture.

Georgette Zirbes, "Manoa Conversations #7," 27" x 23" x 8", 1995. Zirbes made this piece with a cone 6 stoneware clay body. She treated the surface with slips and washes and coated it with a very thin coat of transparent glaze. Photo by the artist.

Susanne Stephenson, "Spiral Dance II," 18½" x 16" x 14", 1997, terra cotta. Photo by John Stephenson.

Vitreous Engobes

By Susanne Stephenson

In my work I want the surface and the form to be interdependent. My goal is to make color express three-dimensional form, for color to actually be perceived as that form. Soft clay forms are thrown and altered to begin the development of the expression. In order to help bring color and form a step closer together, I began working with vitreous engobes.

With the single application of a vitreous engobe on greenware one can achieve the rich color and thickness of a slip but, unlike the slip, it will also develop the gloss or sheen of a glaze.

I arrived at two base recipes which would work for most colors. The percentage of stain added to each base varies from color to color. For instance 20% for blacks, 25% for greens, yellows, and blues, and 30% for crimsons, peaches, and pinks.

Of the hundreds of tests I made, approximately 36 were selected as suitable for my studio use. These tests were evaluated for color quality, for surface, and for the way the vitreous engobe fit on several different clay bodies. I was also looking for vitreous engobes which could be considered practical to use for single-firing application. An unexpected discovery as the result of this research was that some of the same vitreous engobes could be used on already fired bisque ware and also as overglazes.

When a vitreous engobe is applied thick, it has a shine; when it is applied thin, it has a dry appearance. Working with applications of varying thicknesses, therefore, produces surfaces of rich variation but without the complication of the two-step process of slipping and glazing. Testing and combining engobes has expanded my understanding of what is possible in ceramic surfaces, and I have also been able to expand my palette of color.

In order for the surface and form to be interactive, I rely on clay slips (not engobes) in high relief. Thick applications produce a surface in high relief that ranges in contrast from blacks to grays to whites. I use vitreous engobes to produce intense hues such as yellows, reds, greens, and blues to suggest certain light qualities and strong contrasts in a landscape context. These hues are used in the low relief areas. Since I have been working with more intense color, I have focused more on vertical forms. It has been exciting to discover the flexibility I get in a painting medium as I use these engobes.

Angelo diPetta, "Tumblers," finished with a simple terra sigillata surface. Terra sigillata gives a rich, waxy surface and, as we see here, it effectively lends itself to simple applications.

viscosity. To counter pinholes you should use low viscosity fluxes in the recipe. Both sodium and boron frits are effective for this purpose.

Crawling is caused by shrinkage. During the early stages of the firing, high-clay recipes shrink a great deal and, as the clay shrinks, fissures open in the surface coating and pieces of it may flake away. There are two ways to deal with this problem: either by applying the slip or engobe to an unfired clay body or by modifying the recipe. If a recipe which shrinks is applied to a clay body which also shrinks (in other words, an unfired clay body), then there is little trouble with crawling resulting in bare spots. If the recipe is applied to ware that has already shrunk a good deal, such as bisque ware, a good part of the clay in the recipe should be calcined (fired to bisque temperatures). For example, if the recipe contains 35% clay, 25% of it should be calcined. The calcined clay is compatible in shrinkage with the bisque-fired clay body. Calcined kaolin can be purchased from ceramic supply firms. However, if you only need a small amount you may find it best to calcine your own clay by placing it in a bowl and firing it to cone 010 or 08.

Unfortunately slips and engobes are not as durable and abrasion-resistant as glazes. However, materials can be added to a slip or an engobe that will make them more durable. Especially useful is the flux titanium: when it is

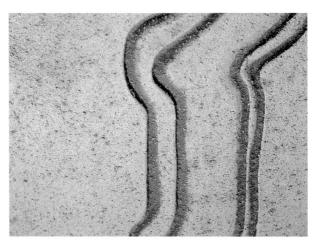

A close-up view of a gritty slip. Note the highly textured surface associated with gritty slips. In this piece the white slip was applied to the unfired clay. The piece was fired to bisque and a dark wash was applied to the surface. The piece was then fired to maturity.

used in additions of 2% it will harden the recipe and make it much more durable. While such recipes are still not as durable as glazes, they are far more durable than most other engobes or slips. Titanium's only drawback is that it bleaches the color of some of the brightest stains; if this is the case, 2% additions of zinc or tin instead of the titanium will enhance durability, though neither is as effective a hardener as titanium.

A close-up view of terra sigillatas and sgraffito imagery. The terra sigillata was applied to the dry, unfired clay with brushes and its imagery is quite soft. The sgraffito imagery was then carved into the surface to reveal the light color of the clay body. The sgraffito imagery contrasts with the terra sigillata in its hard-edged geometric character.

A close-up view of a glaze and terra sigillata combination. The dry greenware piece was first covered with a thin layer of terra sigillata and the piece was fired to bisque. A thin white glaze was poured over the piece in numerous layers. The sgraffito line was carved into the surface, revealing the red color of the terra sigillata. The white glaze is soft and flowing while the sgraffito line is hard-edged and geometric.

Gritty Slips and Engobes

The surface of slips and engobes tend to be smooth and mat surfaced. Gritty slips are formulated with coarse clays and have a rough surface. They are easily formulated by substituting a coarse fire clay for other (finer) clays in a slip recipe. This kind of coarse surface is particularly appropriate for sculptural pieces.

Terra Sigillatas

Terra sigillatas are highly refined clay slips: all their crude sediments have been removed. This desedimentation process is accomplished by a deflocculation of the slip. Deflocculation is a process in which alkaline materials are added to the slip: if the correct amount is added, the clay particles in the slip no longer attract each other and the slip loses much of its viscous character. Under these conditions the cruder and heavier particles begin to sink to the bottom of the container. Once this happens you may decant the mixture; save the fine particles, and discard the crude particles.

Three ingredients are necessary to make a terra sigillata: clay, water, and an alkaline deflocculant. The clay is first weighed and placed in a container, then the water and the deflocculant are weighed and added to the mix. Sodium silicate is the most commonly used deflocculant.

Deflocculant Amounts

If you are using sodium silicate you will need to add 0.5% by weight (multiply by .005) and three times as much water

as clay to deflocculate most dark-colored clays. Most white and buff clays need 0.3% sodium silicate (multiply by .003) and four times as much water as clay to deflocculate them.

Stir the mixture thoroughly and pass it through a sieve (30 mesh or finer). In about half an hour it is ready for its first desedimentation. This is accomplished by pouring the slip from its container into another: when most of the slip has been poured out you will see a coarse sediment at the bottom of the container. This sediment is fairly easy to recognize because it is grainy in texture and generally somewhat darker than the rest of the slip. During the decanting process this sediment is allowed to remain at the bottom of the container until all the fine material has been poured off, then the coarse material is discarded. Continue the process by pouring the slip back and forth between the two containers (wide-bottomed containers work best). There should be a short period of rest between each pour, perhaps 20 minutes.

Occasionally (especially the first few times you try to make a terra sigillata) you may have difficulties with under- or over-deflocculated mixtures. If you have very little sedimentation, you probably need more deflocculant, if you have no sedimentation you probably have used too much deflocculant.

As the process continues, the sludge becomes finer and lighter in color and finally reaches a point where all the dark, coarse particles have been removed. At this point, halt the desedimentation process. Now test the sigillata by applying it to a bisque tile, allowing it to dry and rubbing it lightly. If the sigillata is good, it will take on a perceptible shine and

Terra Sigillatas

By Gail Busch

I started to use terra sigillatas in 1979, my junior year at the Kansas City Art Institute. I was making small Yixing-esque teapots from terra cotta clay, putting a lot of attention into the surfaces of the pots and small details on handles and spouts. I did not want to use a glaze that might conceal the best parts of my teapots, so I decided on terra sigillata as the next best thing to wet clay. I have always liked to let fine details in the construction of my pieces draw the eye of the viewer; for example, to places where a spout or handle is attached. As my work has become more refined, these attachments have become smoother and more delicate, and I prize terra sigillata because it does not obscure these details.

At first I simply dunked the bone-dry pots into the thin terra sigillata, but I was disturbed by the way the top surface of the clay liquefied into the terra sigillata and I was afraid to try to burnish the delicate spouts and handles after the sigillatas dried. I began to experiment with using sigillatas on bisque-fired pots. I made terra sigillata from many different clays, and found that any clay with a high iron content would work well in sigillatas for bisque application, but white terra sigillatas consistently peeled, blistered, and shivered off the pots when I used them on bisque.

Twenty-one years later I am still using terra sigillatas on bisque ware, and have been using a white terra sigillata base made with added fluxes for the last ten years. I mix the white terra sigillata with stains and oxides to make various blues, greens, and other colors. I especially enjoy combining colors with similar values, lulling the eye of the viewer into seeing them as the same color, letting the discovery of their differences come as the reward for longer study.

Terra sigillata is an ideal surface for ceramic artists who like to work with color, but want to add it in a thin skin on the surfaces of their work, instead of the thicker blanket and reflective surfaces of many glazes. It is the surface sheen of

Gail Busch, "Cups," 1995, terra cotta clay body with painted terra sigillatas plus small glazed areas.

terra sigillata that distinguishes it from other clay slips. Some terra sigillatas I use remind me of satin, and others of velvet. I also like the way terra sigillatas respond to proximity to glazed areas. I use commercial glazes in small areas adjacent to the terra sigillatas. Flashing, in this case the darkened areas of terra sigillata which sometimes halo glazed areas, is one of my favorite ceramic special effects.

little if any of the sigillata will come off on the polishing cloth. On the other hand, if it is mat as it dries and if it leaves a layer of clay on the polishing cloth, it is not yet a true terra sigillata. It is a good idea to test fire the terra sigillata: small test kilns are well suited to this task.

You can create a very wide range of color using only a red and a white clay plus colorants or stains. For example, if a bit of the white sigillata is added to the red clay, the result is a pink-orange color. If you add cobalt instead, the result is a brown or black. Stains added to the sigillatas are used to create the rest of the color spectrum. Stains will look much the same in the unfired state as the fired and can be added by eye, which lets you avoid complex measuring procedures.

Locally found clays can make excellent terra sigillatas. Their deflocculant requirements vary; to find out the proper amount of deflocculant, set aside a few hundred grams of the slip as a test batch. First try no deflocculant, then add deflocculant to the slip in increments of .1%. Wait 20 minutes each time and check the mixture. One of these mixtures should produce more sigillata than the others. This indicates the best percentage of deflocculant.

If you attempt to make the sigillata with too little water it will not desediment. Use plenty of water in this process. Your mixtures should be quite thin, use four times as much water as clay. This excess water, however, must be removed before you can work with the terra sigillata. Evaporate it either by exposure to air or by simmering (do not allow the mixture to boil). Do not let the terra sigillata get too thick; these very fine particle surfaces crack and flake off when applied heavily.

True terra sigillatas are low-fire surfaces (fire them in the range of cone 04 to cone 1). Sigillatas lose their smooth surface and their unique waxy quality when fired above cone 1. They show every detail of the clay surface and tend to look as if they are bonded to the clay rather than constituting a separate and distinct coating, as glazes often do. It is best to apply terra sigillatas to fine-grained, low-fire clay bodies; red terra cotta bodies are excellent.

Application

Terra sigillatas are usually applied to greenware. They may be applied by brushing, spraying, dipping, or pouring. Their stability in the fire means that sigillatas lend themselves especially well to brush application: with care and a bit of practice even broad areas of flat color may be applied. Terra sigillatas are high in alumina and do not flow or blur in the fire. It is possible to develop strategies that can be used to produce complex imagery which would not work at all well if used with glazes. Terra sigillatas are often used with sgraffito (engraved) imagery on greenware pieces. The Greek vase painters used this technique extensively. Sigillatas lend themselves to multiple-fire and refire techniques (which are possible but difficult when used with glazes) and such procedures can become a normal part of working with terra sigillatas. After firing, finish the terra sigillatas by burnishing or waxing.

Using Glazes and Terra Sigillatas on the Same Piece

Low-fire glazes (cone 04 or 03) may be used alongside terra sigillatas. You can contrast painted areas of terra sigillata with poured, splashed, or sprayed glaze applications. The satin mat or semi mat surfaces of the sigillatas contrast nicely with the glassy surfaces of low-fire glazes.

Using Terra Sigillatas as Underglazes

Terra sigillatas need no glaze and are generally left unglazed. However, they can be finished with a glaze, sometimes to very good effect. In recent years a number of ceramists have begun to use terra sigillatas under glazes. The darker-colored terra sigillatas are especially effective in this role. They can be used throughout the entire firing range, including the mid and high fire. A particularly interesting example of this strategy is the application of a barn red terra sigillata under a translucent glaze in order to create a rich earth red color in an oxidation firing.

8

Glazes

Introduction

Most ceramic pieces are finished with glazes, for of all ceramic surface finishes, these, more than any, combine beauty with durability. Glazes vary a great deal in surface quality, color, visual texture, and richness of effect. This variety is another reason for their popularity: ceramists like the wide variety of choices they have when using glazes.

Glazes resemble glass and indeed they are chemically similar to glass. Glass, however, does not have a crystalline structure whereas glazes almost always do. It is this structure that marks glazes with visual textures and with satiny, inviting surfaces.

The earliest glazed pieces seem to have come from Egypt: they derived their glazed surfaces from the presence of alkaline salts in the clay body. Lead glazes were developed next in Babylon. This work was low fired. Then, in Han Dynasty China (206 B.C. to 220 A.D.), high-fire glazes derived from the wood ash byproduct of the fuel were developed. By the 18th century an understanding of chemistry was emerging and ceramists were able to employ a much larger group of glaze materials. Their experiments gave ceramists access to a wider array of materials than had been available to them before. While we may not be superior to ceramists of the past, we have many more ways to affect the durability, behavior in the fire, visual texture, and color effects of glaze recipes than our forebears.

The Influence of Firing Temperature

One of the most important factors influencing the look of a glaze is its intended firing temperature. Firing temperature influences the durability, color, and visual texture of the glaze. These influences are profound and firing temperature is one of the most important decisions the ceramist must make.

John Stephenson, "Spool," 17½" x 14½" x 14½", 1999, low-fire terra cotta clay body and low-fire glazes. In this piece Stevenson shows a fine, highly personal sense of low-fire color. Photo by the artist.

Note: Contrary to what might seem like common sense, firing temperature does not influence glaze flow very much - the alumina content of the glaze is a far more influential factor in this important glaze attribute.

David Pendell, "Another View," 28¼" x 21" x 2". Pendell finishes his pieces with various underglaze stains, terra sigillatas, commercial glazes and stains, fired several times to cones 04 to 1. He sometimes uses vitreous enamels for particular color effects and fires these at cone 018. Pendell has mastered a wide variety of low-fire color strategies.

Cone 04

Cone 04 is equivalent to 1060°C/1940°F. In recent years a great many studio potters have taken up work at this temperature. Many aspects of this lower part of the firing spectrum are very pleasing: glaze character and visual texture can be very varied, glaze color can be extremely vivid. Ceramic stains play a big part here for they work very well in low fire.

Many who work in the low fire use commercially prepared glazes. They are purchased already mixed and ready for use. Studio potters who use them benefit from a very elaborate infrastructure already in place, which is established to distribute these glazes. Originally they were intended for use by those working in low-fire slip ware (often called "hobby ceramics"). Commercial glazes are sold in a wide variety of colors and textures, so many in fact, that it takes considerable expertise to exploit their very wide possibilities. Most commercially prepared low-fire glazes contain ingredients (such as gums and colloids) that make them suitable for brush application. Their use is subject to some controversy and there are many who never use them. Some object to their flamboyant colors and textures, others simply object to

the idea of buying glazes made in a mass production setting. Other ceramists love them, delighting in their wide color range, their reliability, and their interesting textural possibilities. Most of the ceramists who use them feel that they are still exploring the craft. For them, however, the emphasis has shifted from the creation of new glaze recipes to new strategies for glaze application.

Ceramists should remember that many of these glazes contain lead compounds which can leach into foods. Avoid any use of lead glazes in pieces which might conceivably be used to hold food.

Mixing Cone 04 Glazes in the Studio

There are advantages in making low-fire glazes in the studio. Economy is one of these - commercially prepared glazes are fairly expensive, whereas a glaze made in the studio can be quite inexpensive. Many ceramists working in the low fire use studio produced glazes along with commercially produced glazes. In this way they can combine the economy of studio made glazes with the exciting colors and textures of commercially prepared formulations. Spray, dip, and splash techniques work well when applying these

Victor Spinski, "Box With Paint Cans," 16" x 14" x 10". Spinski is a master of low-fire color. He has chosen this subject as a way of challenging his skills in the matching and use of colors in our everyday environment. Photo by Tom Stiltz.

Paul Sherman, "Hydnocerus Series IV #2," 4' x 24" diameter, 1993, coil-formed earthenware clay body, low-fire color. Color for Sherman is very personal and expressive. He uses it to challenge the viewer.

Antonella Cimatti, "Sole," height 30 cm, diameter 10 cm, 1998, earthenware bowl with engobe and glaze, decorated by brush and airbrush. Realized in the studio "Fabbrica Casa Museo G. Mazzotti" in Albissola, Italy.

glazes. With the addition of gums or colloids they can be made suitable for brush application.

What to Look for in Cone 04 Recipes

Cone 04 glazes should have significant amounts of silica and strong melters. Look for the bulk of the recipe to come from frits with perhaps a little soda feldspar, small amounts of powerful melting materials (which contain no silica), and 3% to 12% clay. High-impurity clays are quite appropriate at this temperature.

Cone 02

Cone 02 is equivalent to 1120°C/2048°F. Cone 02 is considered to be an unusual firing temperature: at present very few ceramists work in it. However, it has much to recommend it. At cone 02 the ceramist still has access to all the advantages of the low fire without needing to use lead fluxes. Cone 02 glazes are brilliant in color and rich in surface, and they are surprisingly durable.

What to Look for in Cone 02 Recipes

Cone 02 glazes should be high in silica and strong melters. Look for recipes in which frits and soda feldspar make up most of the glaze, with smaller amounts of powerful melting

materials (which contain no silica) and 3% to 14% clay. As in cone 04 recipes, high-impurity clays are quite appropriate at this temperature.

Cone 3

Cone 3 is also an unusual firing temperature for the studio ceramist. It is, however, often used in the ceramic industry. Cone 3 is equivalent to 1168°C/2134°F. Glaze character is excellent and very versatile: it can be based on glaze stains and exhibit brilliant color effects or it can be based on iron-bearing clays and natural colorants, in which case the result is an earthy color balance. The result is a kind of split personality in that it can be used to give either a low- or high-fire look.

Among the most useful glaze types for cone 3 are those which are smooth and enamel-like and which rely on color for their impact: these remind one strongly of the low fire. Also, very useful at this firing temperature are earth-colored glazes and glazes with a great deal of visual texture. The earth-colored glazes derive their color from high-impurity clays; the highly textured glazes from lithium or titanium. These are strongly reminiscent of the high fire. Cone 3 glazes may be dipped, sprayed, poured, or applied with a brush.

Leopold L. Foulem, "Abstraction 1701 (yellow)," 9¼" x 6½". This piece was thrown on the potter's wheel, finished with commercially produced yellow glaze and fired to cone 06. This piece is in homage to Art Deco ceramic pieces. Photograph courtesy of Garth Clark Gallery, N.Y. Photo by Pierre Gauvin.

What to Look for in Cone 3 Recipes

Cone 3 glazes should be fairly high in silica-containing materials. These should include at least 10% to 15% frit to insure a good glaze melt and stability in the fire. If earth-colored glazes are desired, the use of iron-bearing clays in the recipe is recommended. Small amounts of zinc or titanium are useful in these glazes to harden and further stabilize them.

Cone 6

Cone 6 is equivalent to 1222°C/2232°F. Cone 6 is valued for its stability and its compatibility with work intended for firing in the electric kiln. Many recipes intended for cone 6 have been published. In recent years cone 6 has become very popular; many ceramists work at this firing temperature. Clay bodies are widely available and many are very plastic and very durable.

While cone 6 color is not as rich as that of the lower temperatures, its color range is still quite wide. Both normal colorants and most glaze stains work well at this temperature. Most cone 6 glaze surfaces are not marked by the rich flow patterns and textures of the higher temperatures but the glazes can look quite appealing and they can be highly durable and stable. These are practical virtues and it seems that this is the way we have come to think of this firing temperature. Cone 6 glazes may be dipped, sprayed, poured, or applied with a brush.

What to Look for in Cone 6 Recipes

Look for recipes that encourage moderately strong melts such as frits and feldspars together in the same recipe. Keep calcium/magnesium melting materials below 15% as they are quite stiff at this firing temperature. Wood ash is particularly useful in that it encourages rich glaze textures.

There are a number of glaze types which are useful at cone 6. These include glazes with strong visual textures derived from wood ash or lithium, earth-colored glazes with color derived from high-impurity clays, glazes whose mat surfaces and high viscosity creates a stone-like look, and glazes whose low viscosity heightens the effect of carved or relief imagery.

Commercially Prepared Cone 6 Glazes

In the past few years we have seen a number of commercial suppliers come out with a line of glazes meant for cone 6. They seem to be trying to emulate the success of their low-fire preparations with ones suited to higher-fired work. Their potential market is significant and there is no reason why these glazes should not also find favor with many ceramists.

Cone 9

Cone 9 is equivalent to 1280°C/2336°F. The glaze color is muted and reserved but quite rich. Many cone 9 glazes are highly figured, their surfaces marked by complex patterns of glaze texture and flow. These glazes are durable and stable and the bond between glaze and body is intimate and strong. Cone 9 is often associated with reduction firing: reduction-fired cone 9 glazes are marked by robust, earthy color and dark mottled patterns coming from the reduced clay body. These add texture to the glaze surface.

Most ceramists who glaze at cone 9 apply their glazes by dipping the piece in the glaze or by splashing or pouring the glaze over it. These methods work well with cone 9 highly figured glazes.

What to Look for in Cone 9 Recipes

Many of the classic glaze types were developed for cone 9 and 10. Cone 9 recipes are rarely very complex; generally they contain a few materials in good balance. Their activity comes from the character of the fire rather than from complex interactions of highly powerful melting materials. Look for high percentages of potash feldspar in these glazes; frits and the more powerful feldspars are less often needed or used. Calcium/magnesium melting materials dominate the flux category. The glaze clays of choice are kaolin or ball clay though the higher impurity clays may be used as well.

Cone 9 Glaze Types

This temperature lends itself very well to tough, durable clay bodies and glazes. Encouraged by this a great many of the ceramists who create utilitarian ware work at cone 9.

Useful glaze types at cone 9 include those which contain significant amounts of calcium/magnesium: this encourages hard-surfaced glazes, some of which are highly figured with visual textures, others, such as celadon, have smooth, unmarked surfaces. Other useful glaze types include those which contain titanium, lithium, wood ash, and bone ash, all of which encourage highly figured glazes.

Glaze Recipe Types

We encounter so many glaze recipes that it is difficult to keep track of them. In order to deal with this variety more effectively, they are organized here by recipe types. We ceramists use impromptu systems of glaze classification all the time, for they are very useful. The idea here is that glazes have significant attributes and that these may be used to place a glaze in a category. These categories are useful tools to help us understand the nature of each individual glaze. We deal with a long list of significant attributes including their appearance, important ingredients, the way they are used, and the way they are fired.

Glazes Classified by the Amount of Silica, Alumina, or Modifiers in the Recipe

Balanced Recipes

These are recipes with a good balance of silica, alumina, and fluxes. The most reasonable way to insure this is to look for a glaze which contains from 55% to 85% feldspar and 6% to 10% clay: the rest can be materials that are not glassmakers and modify the glaze (this allows for 15% to 35% of these materials). Recipes that fall within these perimeters are likely to be stable, useful, and reliable.

High-Silica Recipes

High-silica recipes are quite glassy, very durable, stable, and smooth. Such glazes derive their silica from ground silica (flint), feldspars, frits, and silicates. An example of a glaze that would be high in silica would contain 60% to 70% feldspar, 5% to 8% clay, perhaps 8% to 12% flint or a silicate, and the rest 10% to 27% materials that modify the glaze.

High-Alumina Recipes

High-alumina recipes are durable, stable, and nonflowing. Their surfaces may be very dry and mat or if strongly fluxed, smooth and enamel-like. Their color is somewhat bleached. Alumina is derived from clays, feldspars, and many frits (though not all, some frits are very low in alumina). In a glaze of this sort clays should comprise 12% to 20% of the recipe and feldspars (or frits with an alumina content more than 8%) 60% to 70% of the recipe.

Recipes High in Modifying (Nonglassmaking) Materials
(containing little silica or alumina)

These recipes tend to be florid with a great deal of visual texture. They are plagued by poor durability, instability, excessive and erratic glaze flow, and crazing. Ceramists use them because they can be very exciting and rich looking. A content of 38% to 45% of these materials is appropriate for recipes of this type. Such a glaze recipe might look like this: 40% to 50% feldspar/frit, 5% to 10% clay, and 40% to 50% materials that are not glassmakers and are there to modify the character of the glaze.

Glazes Identified by the Influence of a Material

Another way potters distinguish among glazes is by characterizing the glaze according to its ingredients. This strategy is especially useful because strong similarities exist among glazes with similar ingredient combinations in terms of how they look and fire.

Wood Ash

The ashes of wood - the products of an open fire - may be

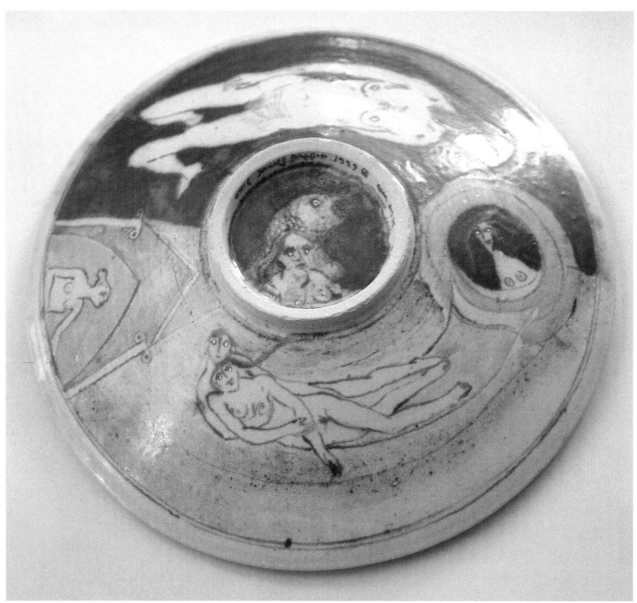

Eric James Mellon, "Theme of Tenderness," diameter 10", elm ash glaze fired to 1300°C in a gas fire. Mellon uses ash glazes to create a rich glaze effect. He carefully studies the behavior of these glazes to obtain these results and yet control glaze flow.

added to glazes to modify their character. They can strongly enrich glaze surface and color and are a wonderful glaze material. Though they seem very simple, wood ashes are a complicated mixture of coarse minerals, including significant amounts of calcium and potassium. Their coarse particle size causes them to melt unevenly in the glaze fire. They leave a telltale "calling card," that is, the glaze melt has an uneven texture, marked by runny and comparatively refractory areas in close proximity. This results in the instantly recognized wood ash texture.

Wood ash derives its character, including its flux content, from the tree it came from. Trees absorb minerals from the earth. These minerals vary from tree to tree, depending on the environment and species. Wood ash, therefore, varies from batch to batch. Wood ash glazes derive their strong visual textures from ash's crude, granular particles and from its phosphorus content. While its ingredients do not vary much (silica, alumina, calcium, phosphorus, and trace elements), their proportions can vary a great deal so wood ash can never be counted on to work in any particular way, nor can this year's batch be counted on to act like last year's. Consistency may be the most important factor: if the ceramist is consistent in the material accumulated for ash making, gathering it at the same time of the year from the same kind of plant or tree in places similar to each other, then the ash is likely to give more consistent results.

All ash varies greatly depending on its source, the season, and the place it was gathered.

Sources of Wood Ash

Some ceramists insist upon using ash only from hardwoods, while others will happily use the much more

Louis Katz, "Bowl With Ash Glaze," 9" x 22" diameter, 1997, soda-fired stoneware. This piece is a fine example of the rich, varied surfaces one can obtain from wood ash glazes. This surface is highly compatible with Katz's rich, pitted, clay body surfaces.

common softwoods. Many potters claim that certain fruitwoods give the best results. Still others do not use the ashes of wood at all but rather the ash of reeds and straw.

Wood ash from wood taken in the spring can be very different from that taken in the autumn or winter because the tree has had a chance to absorb a different grouping of minerals.

The nature of the fire also affects the nature of the ash. Wood ash from an efficient airtight stove is quite different from that of the old-fashioned fireplace and not as effective. This ash contains a lower percentage of the fine particle, water-soluble fluxes that contribute so much to wood ash's strong texture. It still contributes texture, though somewhat less noticeably than wood ash from an open fire.

It is perhaps best to see wood ash not as a glaze but rather as a supplemental glaze material. It works very well as a material to use for adding visual texture to already formulated glazes. In this way it takes on the congenial role

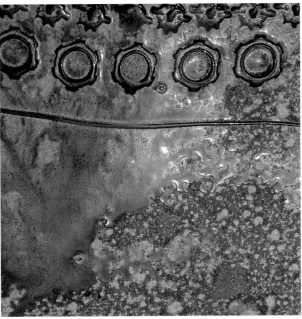

Wood ash glazes fired in oxidation combine the terrific wood ash texture with high key color.

of a supplemental flux; wood ash can modify and enrich the glaze while deriving the benefits of stability and consistency from the basic glaze formula. Add the wood ash to glazes you are familiar with, in amounts that vary from 5% to 30% of the total glaze weight. If the addition does not texture the glaze as much as you would like, simply add more wood ash. If the glaze is unstable, running and flowing too much, add more of the basic glaze formula.

Because it is unpredictable, it is unwise to treat wood ash like other glaze materials, which are more uniform and consistent. It is best to test this material before applying it on a piece. If it is to be used as an additive to a known glaze recipe, it is best to add it to a number of different glazes (in test amounts) with the idea that at least one of the mixtures will work well.

Appropriate Work Strategies for Wood Ash

Lung irritations from wood ash or any other caustic material can be prevented with a good dust mask (a number of excellent ones are on the market). Make sure you use filters appropriate for the job and change the filters often. Protective outerwear should also be worn when dealing with caustic dusts such as wood ash. These are easy to find at industrial suppliers, they fill a real need, and are quite inexpensive.

Wood ash is also hazardous in the wet glaze because it is highly caustic. Ceramists who use wood ash glazes a great deal will find that their skin will crack and bleed from exposure to this material. Care should be taken; ideally rubber gloves should be worn.

A Wood Ash Testing Program

Gather enough wood ash to make the experiment worthwhile. Dry mixing wood ash is a very dangerous proposition if carried out in a careless manner: please follow the safety directions in the previous paragraph.

Add samples of wood ash in amounts of 10 grams and 40 grams to 100 grams of the following glazes:
➤ a high-silica recipe
➤ a high-alumina recipe
➤ a recipe with a high percentage of materials that do not contain silica or alumina
➤ a dark clay recipe

In a sense this is the ceramist's version of a material's assay: it is an effective way to find out which glaze types will work with a particular batch of wood ash.

Recipes That Contain Dark Clays

Excellent glazes may be made from dark clays. Dark clays are high in fluxing and coloring impurities; they will form a glaze with little help from added fluxes if they are fired to stoneware temperatures. They can enrich glaze surfaces and color in a significant manner. This is especially true of glazes

fired in oxidation because these benefit greatly from the richness imparted by dark clays. The most important impurities in a dark clay are iron, titanium, and calcium. The iron content darkens the glaze significantly. The titanium content encourages some visual texture and makes the glaze more durable. The calcium content encourages glaze flow and visual texture. Many glaze recipes in this book call for a dark, iron-bearing clay. Glazes of this type have been great favorites of Chinese and Japanese potters for a thousand years and their work has been very influential for potters in our time. Many beautiful examples of this oriental glaze type are found in museums and collections, one of the most famous of which is the glaze known as "Hare's Fur."

In the United States and Canada, potters have access to many dark clays that may be used in glazes. A fine source of these dark clays are locally available clays. Dark clays contain such fluxing oxides as calcium, magnesium, manganese, iron, and titanium. High-impurity clays are almost complete glazes in themselves; the addition of only a small amount of flux (about 10%) is enough to turn this material into a fine glaze at cones 5 to 10. Glazes rich in a dark clay may be brown, green, or mustard, and, with the addition of colorants, soft green, blue, burnt orange, and black.

Below are the analyses of a dark clay and, as a contrast, a light-colored clay - a kaolin. Note the difference in the silica and alumina contents, as well as the difference in the amount and type of impurities.

A Comparison of a Dark and a White Clay

	Redart Clay	Kaolin
Silica	64%	48%
Alumina	16	37
Iron	7	.6
Potassium	4	.2
Magnesium	2	.3
Titanium	1	
Sodium	.4	
Calcium	.2	.1
Loss during firing	5	12

These dark clays are much lower in alumina than other clays. Glazes made with a lot of dark clay are therefore also low in alumina. The amount of alumina in a glaze profoundly affects its color, texture, and behavior in the fire.

These clays are complex compounds. They may be used in the glaze as sources of silica, flux, and colorant; they are somewhat plastic and therefore help keep the glaze in suspension. These clays are valuable additions to any muted color glaze in proportions varying from 10% to 90%. In small amounts they serve to darken and flux the glaze; in large amounts they dominate the character of the glaze, muting its color and smoothing and hardening its surface.

Glazes made with more than 15% dark clay often have some shrinkage. If they are applied to the bisque-fired piece, the glaze may shrink enough to flake and crack, or it may even fall off the piece and onto the kiln shelf. Therefore, when using glazes containing more than 15% clay, the potter should calcine some of the clay. In the calcining process, the potter fires the dry slip clay in a bisque bowl to a temperature of 700°C. In a sense, calcined clay is preshrunk, which prevents glaze from shrinking and flaking on bisque. It is a good idea to leave 5% of the high flux clay uncalcined. The uncalcined clay, which is somewhat plastic, keeps the glaze in suspension.

Sodium and Potassium Glazes

Glazes containing sodium and potassium derive these elements from feldspars and frits. Their feldspar/frit content should be between 60% and 70%. These recipes tend to be strong, durable, stable, and reliable, with strong, unbleached color. Soda and potash feldspars are quite similar. Both contain sodium and potassium; the soda spars merely contain more soda than potassium while the potash spars contain more potassium than sodium. Sodium is a somewhat stronger flux than is potassium; it is especially useful in low- and mid-fire glazes. It does, however, encourage crazing. In high-fire glazes potassium is favored.

Boron Glazes

Now that Gerstley borate is becoming hard to find, the most useful source for boron in glazes is one of the boron frits. Recipes which contain boron frits in amounts from 30% to 80% tend to have strong durable glaze surfaces, stable melts, and good color. Boron is a very strong flux which melts at a low temperature: it is very useful in low-fire recipes and in amounts up to 20% in high-fire glazes as well. High-fire glazes that contain too much boron may be overmelted; these glazes lose most of their character and take on a hard, glassy look.

Titanium Glazes

Small amounts of titanium (.5% to 2%) cause very strong melts (see eutectics page 15), larger amounts (6% to 12%) are usually quite refractory and encourage mat surfaces. Small amounts of titanium encourage extremely durable glazes and fine color. Larger amounts of titanium encourage rich visual textures (see the section on high titanium flowing mat glazes). Unfortunately, titanium also encourages pinholing, especially in the mid and low fire. If titanium is used with materials that contain sodium (soda feldspars and frits) and other low-viscosity materials, this can be minimized. The sources for titanium in glazes are titanium dioxide and rutile. Some high-impurity clays contain small amounts of titanium as well.

Flowing mat glazes are unusual and extremely striking. At the beginning of the 20th century they were very highly regarded but they have become rare because they are difficult to use. Their strong glaze flow and brilliant color is the result of their low percentage of alumina. They readily flow off the piece and onto the kiln shelf, welding the piece to the shelf. The ceramist must fashion a receiving cup to catch the glaze overflow. Their unusual character and great beauty make them worthy of attention.

In 1905 *Grand Feu Ceramics* by the French ceramist Taxile Doat was published in an English version in Syracuse, New York. The title, a blend of French and English, means "High Fire Ceramics." Doat was especially fond of two glaze types: crystalline glazes and flowing mats. Many of his recipes contain significant amounts of titanium. The titanium encourages crystals (when fired appropriately) and rich mat glazes which flow a great deal and which he called "flowing mats." Here is a Doat recipe adapted for current use:

Mat Ivory Yellow (a flowing mat glaze, cone 9 oxidation)

30 soda feldspar
12 kaolin
36 ground silica (flint)
14 whiting
8 rutile

Glazes Containing Opacifiers

The ceramist adds opacifiers to a glaze to make it opaque. While a number of materials may be used to opacify glazes, tin oxide and zirconium dioxide are the most reliable. Neither of these materials are glassmakers (though zirconium opacifiers contain a bit of silica as an impurity).

Zirconium is highly refractory and its use is somewhat limited in the low fire. In the higher fire its effects are varied. In mat glazes zirconium encourages surfaces marked by a finely divided visual texture; in shiny and transparent glazes it tends to encourage surfaces which are very shiny and lack depth. Zirconium opacifiers work well in the reduction fire.

Tin is useful at all parts of the firing spectrum, but is especially useful in the low fire, for it does not hold back the melt and it also discourages crazing. It is less useful in the high fire, particularly in reduction, which may affect it adversely. Tin is far more expensive than zirconium and this too limits its use.

Tin and zirconium may be used together quite effectively. Opacity is improved and the surface quality can be as good or better than tin's when used alone.

One category of opacified glazes contains no colorant. Such glazes would be clear if they were not opacified but with this addition they take on a white color.

High-Clay Recipes

High-clay recipes tend to be mat, nonflowing, durable, and highly stable. They are plagued with pinhole problems, but these can be moderated by including soda feldspar: its low viscosity compensates for the high viscosity of the clay. High-clay glaze recipes contain from 14% to 20% clay.

Spodumene Glazes

Spodumene is a lithium feldspar. It is a very strong glassmaking flux and very useful in the low fire. It encourages rich visual textures and highly saturated alkaline color. For example, copper, which is normally green in the oxidation fire, will be a strong blue in the presence of spodumene. Spodumene is low in viscosity and discourages pinholes. Because of this, it is an admirable partner for titanium if used in the following percentages: spodumene 12% to 24%, titanium 6% to 12%.

We derive lithium not only from spodumene but also from lithium carbonate. Of the two materials spodumene is far preferable because the lithium in spodumene is locked into the compound in such a way as to minimize inhalation and ingestion problems. Lithium carbonate should be handled with care as it can cause organ damage and can have a strong effect on the ceramist's mental state.

Interesting results may be obtained with a family of glazes formulated from combinations of calcium, phosphorus, and lithium, often in a glaze containing a slip clay. Though these formulas fired at cones 3, 6, and 9 are not identical in appearance, they all have a visual texture called orange peel (light and dark diverse patterning). The texture of these glazes is shown best when they are applied by spraying. Some of these recipes are unstable, especially those intended for cones 3 and 6 and work best as overglazes.

Zinc Glazes

Zinc contains no silica and is a material that is not a glassmaker. It is a prime example of a material which is a strong flux in small amounts and a weak flux in large amounts (see eutectics). Small amounts (1% to 2%) are often added to transparent glaze recipes to insure a good melt. Larger amounts are usually quite refractory and encourage mat surfaces. Zinc is used in amounts of 8% to 20% to create mat, opaque glazes. If fired in the appropriate manner zinc encourages the growth of crystals in the glaze (see the section on crystal glazes, page 148).

Lead Glazes

Lead produces very beautiful results; unfortunately it is toxic and cumulative in its action. Lead glazes may release lead into foods, especially acid foods, in a slow and insidious manner. This toxicity can be a problem for both the ceramist and those who use our work. Lead's toxicity can, to some extent, be managed but it will always be a problem. The use of lead frits reduces the danger but does not eliminate it. Even fritted glazes may leach lead under certain conditions. Lead should never be used by studio potters in glazes that could conceivably be used to contain food. It is important to acknowledge that people will sometimes press a piece into service as a food container even if it never was intended for that purpose. In its unfritted form lead is not a glassmaker. When fritted it contains alumina and silica and is in the glassmaking category.

Substitution Strategies for Lead in Glazes

High boron and high sodium frits will substitute for lead-containing materials. You may also wish to add .5% to 1% zinc oxide or titanium as these materials enrich the glaze surface and enhance melting. In the low fire you may find that these substitutions work best if you raise the firing temperature to cone 02 or cone 1.

Barium Glazes

Barium-containing recipes are quite dangerous to both the potter and consumer. While barium can be fritted, barium frits do not encourage the highly valued, soft mat surfaces of unfritted barium. Barium encourages the growth of very small crystals in the glaze. The result is a glaze surface which, under high magnification, reveals a corrugated surface. Barium glazes are soft looking and mat surfaced rather than shiny. This is because their broken surface scatters light instead of reflecting it. Barium is strongly alkaline and has a strong effect on color, especially copper, which is turned a strong, saturated, royal blue. Barium is not a glassmaker.

Dangers for the Potter

Unfritted barium is a dangerous material. Dr. Michael McCann has stated that the dangers from inhalation and ingestion are especially high; its effects can be cumulative and chronic symptoms can develop. For the consumer, barium glazes (especially the ones with the beautiful mat surfaces) can be the source of chronic symptoms that are difficult to isolate and identify.

Substitution Strategies for Barium Glazes

Tin oxide is a fine substitute for barium. It encourages the rich waxy surfaces which are a hallmark of this material. If used in amounts of 10% to 14% it will produce soft satiny surfaces. Unfortunately, it is one of our most expensive ceramic materials.

Both zinc and titanium may be used in amounts of 6% to 10% to achieve effects somewhat akin to barium. These are relatively inexpensive materials. *Note:* See the sections on zinc and titanium glazes for more suggestions on using these materials.

William Brouillard, "Majolica Platter." Brouillard pays homage to the majolica of the Renaissance in this piece. It is wonderfully drawn and shows a love of detail.

Calcium/Magnesium Glazes

These two oxides have a dual nature in that they are quite refractory (nonmelting) until cone 8, at which point they become strong melters.

High calcium/magnesium glazes are usually meant for firing at cone 8 and higher; amounts of 15% to 30% calcium/magnesium or 25% to 50% calcium/magnesium silicates are commonly used. These glazes are often marked by a rich pattern of rivulets playing over the surface of the glaze. In the lower fire, high calcium/magnesium glazes tend to be chalky and bleached in color.

Calcium/Magnesium Materials

Material	Contents	Type
whiting	calcium	influences the melt
magnesium carbonate	magnesium	influences the melt
dolomite	calcium and magnesium	influences the melt
talc	magnesium, calcium and silica	silicate
wollastonite	calcium and silica	silicate

Linda Arbuckle, "Square Upright Bowl," 7" square x 6" high, 1998, majolica painted on terra cotta. While we tend to identify majolica with complex linear patterns, we see a very effective use of large, swiftly painted sections in this piece.

Copper Reds

Copper can be used to create red glazes in the reduction fire; the red color will develop in reduction with 1% to 3% copper carbonate. A wide range of glaze types will work; typically they are high in silica and low in alumina. The most desirable type of copper red glaze will have a ruby color, but this is somewhat hard to control. If too much copper is present, the glaze may take on a more liverish tone.

Glaze thickness is also an important factor in the production of good color. If too thin, reds will not develop; if too thick, the colors will be muddy. Tin encourages bright copper red colors. Copper reds are at their best when applied to light-colored and white bodies because the darker bodies tend to darken the color. Experiment is necessary for the consistent creation of good copper reds.

Strontium Glazes

Strontium has been put forward as a substitute for the toxic material barium carbonate. It too is said to have toxic effects but much less than barium. It is not as stable as barium and its surfaces are not as rich or velvety. It is, however, a useful material and worth exploration.

High Zirconium Glazes

While zirconium is generally used as an opacifier, glazes rich in zirconium (15% to 20%) can have durable, rich looking mat surfaces. It is quite refractory and should be used with materials that encourage strong melts such as soda feldspar. Though it may have some silica content as an impurity, it is not a true glassmaker.

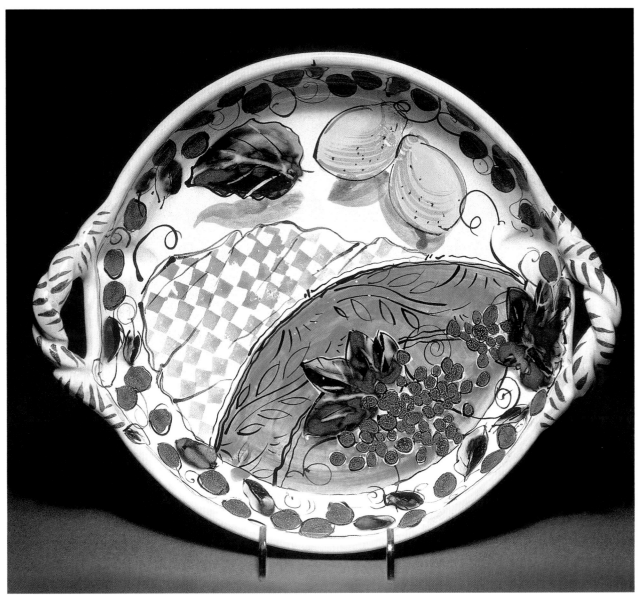

Ann Tubbs, "Grapes, Lemons," cone 04 majolica, stoneware, thrown with hand-formed additions. Tubbs has worked in all sorts of ways over the years. She seems recently to have found a home in majolica. She says she likes it because she loves to draw and you can see this is true. The images we see here, associated with the table, are drawn with verve and communicate enjoymet.

Glazes Classified by Appearance

Transparent Glazes

These come closer to true glass than other glazes. Like glass they have no crystalline character: their character is that of a frozen liquid. Transparent glazes should contain between 55% to 70% feldspar and perhaps some ground silica or silicates: all these are sources of silica which is our main glass forming material. They should have just enough clay to insure that they do not flow readily (3% to 6%). They should not have high percentages of nonglassmaking materials, over-reliance on fluxing materials is a "brute force" strategy for creating transparent glazes, a strategy that results in weak, unstable recipes. Keep the percentage of these materials below 30%.

Transparent Mat Glazes

These glazes are very low in silica and high in flux. Owing to this low silica percentage, they are not as durable or stable as other transparent glaze recipes but their surface is soft and appealing. Their mat character is accentuated by slow cooling.

Majolica

Classical majolica is both a glaze type and a glazing

Matthias Ostermann, "Wall Plate: Phineus & the Harpies," 1997, 27 cm diameter, drape mold formed, majolica glaze with applied stains and sgraffito. Ostermann has explored many of the possibilities of majolica, color, texture, brushwork, and sgraffito. The sgraffito work is especially interesting. He uses rich, saturated color and liquid, flowing brushwork. He contrasts this with an energetic, bright white sgraffito line. He uses these strategies in the service of a complex narrative imagery. Photo by Jan Thijs, courtesy of Prime Gallery.

strategy. The glaze is low fire; it derives its white color, its characteristic opacity, its smooth surface, and its reactions to applied color from a significant tin content. In the majolica strategy, coloring oxides and stains are painted directly on the glaze surface. These stain the glaze and create the color imagery. At its best the majolica imagery is rich in surface and saturated in color.

The name "majolica" comes from the medieval name for Majorca, an island off the coast of Spain and at one time a source of Moorish pottery for Italy and the rest of Europe. This Islamic/Spanish pottery tended to rich flat pattern and highly stylized imagery. It was soon imitated, especially in Italy and Holland. The Italian work was often quite complex and featured imagery which was strongly spatial, in imitation of Renaissance and Baroque painting.

Traditionally these glazes were fluxed with lead, which encouraged rich glaze surfaces and good color reactions. Now, due to our heightened awareness of the problems

Karen Koblitz, "My Obsession Series #1," 18½" x 11" x 10", 1998, low-fire clay and glazes. In her majolica work Koblitz reminds us of the brilliant color and complex painted imagery of Renaissance painted pottery from Northern Italy. She combines superb drawing skills with wonderful color and a feeling for the history of the medium. Photo by Susan Einstein.

James Lovera, "Black & White Bark Vessel," 6¾" x 10", 1993, wheel thrown, fired in an oxidation atmosphere. Lovera created this visually textured glaze effect by layering glazes. He applied the refractory white glaze over the highly active dark glaze. In the early part of the firing the dark glaze broke through the white glaze. Later in the firing the two melted together, creating the rich imagery we see here. Photo by Lee Hocker.

associated with lead, other fluxes are often used.

A number of contemporary ceramists have taken up experiments in majolica. Some of them use techniques which are as authentic as possible. Others try to create a modern version of this way of working. There is interest in lead-free and in mid- and high-fire majolica glaze strategies. These cannot exactly duplicate the character of the low-fire, lead-containing, majolica glazes, but they still can be quite rich and are more suitable than the lead-containing glazes for application to utilitarian pieces.

Luster Glazes

The luster effect is that of a metallic surface applied over all or part of the glaze. It is the result of the conversion of some of the oxides in the glaze into a thin metallic film. This is accomplished in a reduction atmosphere in the low fire; during the reduction process carbon monoxide is created. Carbon monoxide lacks an oxygen molecule and will take it from wherever it can. Coloring oxides contain oxygen molecules (which is why they are called oxides): the carbon monoxide pulls the oxygen from them. When they lose their oxygen molecules the metallic oxides are transformed into pure metals. The surface of glaze is converted from its normal state (and color) to a film of pure metal. Metallic oxides that can be used to create lusters are gold, platinum, bismuth, copper, and tin.

Luster reduction can be accomplished in two ways: by firing in a reducing atmosphere or by adding a reducing agent to the glaze recipe.

Those lusters fired in a reduction atmosphere can be made by the studio ceramist. Low-fire recipes rich in melters and containing an appropriate colorant are used. The kiln is reduced very heavily once the maturation point has been reached. Reduction is continued until the kiln atmosphere loses its color (approximately 500°C/1000°F). In the great lustered pieces from Iran and from Islamic Spain, ceramists employed this method to produce work of real intensity and beauty.

There are commercially prepared lusters that contain a reducing agent (usually an organic binder such as oil of lavender). This burns out during the firing and in doing so creates a localized reduction. Commercially prepared lusters may be applied to the piece directly from the container. They are generally applied to an already glazed and fired piece and then fired to a point just above red heat: 600° to 700°C (1200° to 1300F).

Visually Textured Glazes

These glazes are marked by often pleasing visual textures. Some of these derive their visual texture from a reduction atmosphere in the kiln firing (see page 173). Others do not require reduction. The following materials produce visual

Nina Hole, "Danish Teapot," 24 x 18 x 10 cm, cone 06, oxidation atmosphere in the electric kiln. The highly bubbled surface on this piece significantly enhances its character.

texture, especially in mat and satin mat glazes: bone ash (calcium phosphate), calcium containing materials, spodumene, wood ash, zinc oxide, and zirconium.

Bone ash encourages mottled effects such as soft spotted patterns to form in the glaze. Like lithium, it encourages glaze to pull away from the edges of the form.

Calcium containing materials, whiting, and dolomite encourage patterns of running glaze above cone 8.

This is a Rookwood piece from the 1920s. The glaze was low viscosity, probably due to a low alumina content. As a result we see a halo-like imagery at the edges of the relief imagery.

Spodumene, with its significant lithium content, causes a pattern of light and dark modulations on the glaze surface. These modulations are similar in pattern to salt glaze. It encourages running patterns and also causes the glaze to pull away from the edges of the form. The result is a halo-like effect around the corners of the piece and around any manipulated imagery in the clay. It contains silica and alumina and is a glassmaker.

Titanium encourages light-colored spots and patterns of running glaze and in a long cooling cycle, crystal patterns. It is not a glassmaker.

Wood ash causes a modulated pattern of light and dark rivulets, blooms of color, and small spots.

Zinc oxide, in a long cooling cycle, encourages crystal patterns to form within the glaze. It is not a glassmaker.

Zirconium compounds cause a tight pattern of light-colored spots and a small crystal pattern to form on the surface of the glaze.

Dry, Highly Textured Glaze Surfaces

In recent years some ceramists have become quite fascinated with glazes marked by a "decaying wall" character that many find evocative of the fire. These surfaces are desiccated: they are dry textured, deeply fissured, parched, and curdled. Often the body is partially revealed where the glaze has pulled or flaked away. These desiccated surfaces are partially vitrified formulations. This is often achieved by using recipes abnormally high in melters that are not glassmakers (they may total as much as 60%) and that contain a great deal of calcium, magnesium carbonate, or a zirconium opacifier. To insure extremely dry surfaces they should be fired below cone 8.

Industrial (Smooth Surfaced) Glazes

These glazes are just the opposite of the highly textured recipes: they are smooth and enamel-like glaze surfaces. They are often associated with the oxidation fire and the low and mid fire because smooth glaze surfaces are easy to create under these conditions. Glazes of this type are generally well balanced in their silica/alumina/flux ratio. Their significant flux tends to be sodium or potassium derived from feldspar or frit (55% to 65%): they encourage good melts while not bleaching colorants or stains.

These glazes are best applied with the sprayer, which can be used to blend two or three colors. They lend themselves to novel color combinations and the use of some of the more unusual stain colorants. At their best, the results, while not speaking much of the earth, are serene and elegant examples of the ceramist's art.

Low Viscosity Glazes

Low viscosity glazes are valued because they run in the fire. Though this can make them difficult to work with, ceramists can use the phenomenon to emphasize raised and engraved imagery on the surface of the piece. If a dark low

Opposite: Rick Malmgren, "Twisted Vase," height 11", 1999, lava glaze, fired to cone 6 in a reduction atmosphere. Malmgren's reduction experiments at cone 6 show us that this kind of firing can result in highly successful work of great appeal. He says of this: "All my traditional cone 10 glazes work just as well at this temperature. Only minor adjustments to the recipes are needed." He includes a recipe that he likes for creating highly textured surfaces:

Marilee's Lava Glaze C6
This glaze works extremely well in oxidation and reduction. The slower cooling in reduction tends to make for smaller volcanic eruptions. Fine silicon carbide seems to work best. This is a very rough glaze and is not intended for food surfaces.

Custer feldspar	*45*
EPK	*12*
Flint	*12*
Whiting	*21*
Titanium dioxide	*0.1*
Silicon carbide	*0.3*

For gray to black add:
Black Mason stain 6600	*7.0%*

Gary Grosenbeck, "Two Platters," 13" square, 1999, slab formed, hand-carved porcelain, fired to 10 oxidation. This is an example of porcelain fired in the oxidation atmosphere. The ware is durable and glaze colors are clear and saturated.

viscosity glaze is applied to a light-colored body with added or subtractive imagery, the glaze will run off the sharp edges of the form and the imagery. This will encourage the formation of a light-colored line around the edges of the imagery, emphasizing it and encouraging the formation of a rich visual pattern.

The small vase pictured on page 144, from the American Art Pottery firm of Rookwood, is an example of low viscosity glaze application. The piece was mold formed in 1923. The designer placed a mold-formed relief imagery of stylized cattails on the surface of the piece. This softly raised relief imagery was designed with a low viscosity glaze in mind. Note the way the glaze strongly runs away from the edges of the imagery while other areas of the imagery remain covered with the dark-colored glaze. The dark glaze contrasts with the strong white color of the porcelainous body. While any kind of glaze application may be used with low viscosity glazes, the subtlety of the effect is perhaps most consistent with the simple surfaces of dipping or spraying. In this case a spray application was used.

Glazes Classified by Intended Use or Purpose

Utilitarian Glazes

Ideally, glazes meant for utilitarian work should look no different from other glazes: they should merely be very durable and easily cleaned. This means they should have ample silica sources (55% to 85% feldspars/frits) and little of the nonglassmaking materials (no more than 30%). Such stable and reliable glazes may not always have the strong visual textures that characterize less stable glazes but sensitive glaze application can compensate for this.

Glazes for Outdoor Use

Glazes intended for work to be placed outdoors should be very durable and well suited to withstand the rigors of the weather. The two most successful surfaces for such work are those with high amounts of silica and those with a high alumina content. Both contribute good durability. Vitreous engobes, with their high alumina content and great durability, are particularly appropriate for this use (for more on vitreous engobes, see page 117). Such surfaces are likely to contain 25% to 45% clay and 45% to 65% feldspar or frit. They should contain between 10% to 30% of nonglassmaking materials. Their feldspars, frits, and nonglassmaking materials should powerfully encourage melting.

Glazes for Porcelain Bodies

Cone 9 is the firing temperature of true porcelain. Owing to the brilliant white base of the porcelain clay body they rest upon, porcelain glazes have a rich character. The same glaze applied to a stoneware body and a porcelain body will take on a very different look: glazes applied to porcelain are not grayed by the buff or brown undertones of stoneware and are more brilliant in color.

Porcelain glazes may be fired in either oxidation or reduction; often the differences are not great. Color can be quite similar (except in the case of copper, which is green in oxidation and red in reduction). The black spots that mark reduction-fired bodies and glazes that we associate with reduction, do not appear here because porcelain bodies contain only a very small percentage of iron.

A number of very famous glaze types are strongly identified with reduction-fired porcelain. Among them are celadons and copper red glazes. While both glazes may be applied over stoneware bodies, they are at their best over porcelain. When applied to porcelain the celadons can take on a watery, cool blue-green marked by a feeling of depth and the copper reds produce a rich scarlet red color.

10

Glaze/Firing Combinations

This is an interesting topic because it deals with complex combinations of special recipes, firing techniques, kilns, and firing strategies. In this way ceramists have developed strategies that insure a rich and personal imagery.

Crystal Glazes

Crystal glazes require special recipes and firing strategies. They are characterized by metallic crystals that float on the surface of the glaze.

Glaze crystals are created when the ceramist combines a low alumina glaze recipe that contains titanium or zinc with a special firing technique. The first part of a crystal fire is quite normal but once the desired firing temperature is reached in the latter part of the fire, the temperature (after being allowed to drop for a few minutes) is held steady in a long soaking period. It is during this period that the zinc or titanium crystals have a chance to form and develop. Appropriate amounts are 6% to 10% titanium and 2% to 8% zinc.

Below is a crystal glaze recipe from Taxile Doat, a French ceramist who specialized in crystal glazes at the beginning of the 20th century (from *Grand Feu Ceramique* by Taxile Doat).

Mat Crystalline Yellow Brown
(crystal glaze, cone 9 oxidation)

Feldspar	26
Kaolin	10
Ground silica	37
Whiting	12
Rutile	8
Red oxide of iron	7

Diane Creber, "Vase," height 6½", crystal glazes with copper colorant fired in a reduction cooling environment. Creber says of her firings: "The kiln is taken to 1320°C then shut off and cooled quickly to 1100°C. The kiln is turned on again and the temperature is held or allowed to drop slightly for the next four hours. It is during this time that the crystals grow. The kiln is then turned off and allowed to cool naturally." Photo by the artist.

Raku

Raku requires special recipes, special firing and after-firing strategies, and special kilns. Raku is a specialized variety of low-fire work. It belongs to a category of ceramic work which embodies not one strategy or even two but rather a whole group of strategies and recipes that, when used together, create a distinctive entity and take on a kind of life of their own.

Raku is unusual among glazed ceramic work in that it is a

Steven Branfman, "Raku With Glass Inlay," height 15", wheel thrown, fired approximately to cone 08. During the forming the artist inlaid colored glass and during the firing he brush applied a raku glaze. Branfman postfired in a metal container with organic materials (pine needles, sawdust, wood shavings). Photo by the artist.

quick-firing technique. Its bodies, forms, and glazes must be designed to withstand the shock of very abrupt heating and cooling. It is a low-fire technique. Raku glazes are often crackled or otherwise unstable due to their quick cooling. Though unstable, their character can be complex and exuberant. Examples of this are glazes with metallic flashing or richly crazed surfaces. Those ceramists who fire in raku a great deal are generally looking for these effects and their glazes are most often brilliantly colored and applied with great energy.

These brilliant surfaces contrast with the clay body, which turns a soft, velvety black due to smoke reduction. Smoke reduction also affects the glazed surfaces of the piece: coloring minerals such as copper take on a strong metallic appearance and craze lines are blackened and strongly emphasized.

Raku has encouraged the development of specialized recipes and work strategies, dictated by its quick firing and its rich unstable glaze surfaces. Clay bodies tend to be very coarse, forms to be quite burly and compact, glaze recipes very simple (visual complexity comes from the fire and not the recipe itself). Raku glazes are most often dipped, sprayed, or applied with a brush. Glaze imagery tends to be strong and direct, reflecting the character of the medium.

The idea of raku is originally derived from the Japanese. The word raku means enjoyment; its connotations are that of quiet, reflective pleasure. In Japan it was most often associated with the aristocratic amateur or the tea master, rather than with the professional potter. Before the 1930s and '40s it was unknown outside of Japan. It has evolved a great deal since its introduction in the West, to the point where it has become one of the most inventive of our ceramic techniques.

It did not exist in the way we know it until some time after World War II. We in the West were first introduced to the concept by Bernard Leach in *A Potter's Book*. In a wonderful section of this book Leach talked of his introduction to raku: it was also his introduction to ceramics:

"One day in 1911, two years after I had returned to the Far East, I was invited to a sort of garden party at an artist friend's house in Tokyo. Twenty or 30 painters, actors, writers, etc. were gathered together on the floor of a large tea room; brushes and saucers of color were lying about, and presently a number of unglazed pots were brought in and we were invited to write or paint upon them. Almost all educated Japanese are sufficient masters of the brush to be able to write a decorative running script of, to Western eyes, great beauty, and many of them can paint. I was told that within an hour's time these pots would be glazed and afterwards fired in a little portable kiln, which a man was stoking with charcoal a few feet beyond the verandah in the garden. I struggled with the unfamiliar paints and queer long brushes, and then my two pots were taken from me and dipped in a tub of creamy white lead glaze and set around the top of the kiln and warmed and dried for a few minutes before being carefully placed with long-handled tongs in the inner box or muffle. Although this chamber was already at dull red heat, the pots did not break. Fire clay covers were placed on top of the kiln, and the potter fanned the fuel till the sparks flew. In about half an hour the muffle gradually became bright red, and the glaze could be seen through the spy hole, melted and glossy. The covers were removed and the glowing pieces taken out one by one and placed on tiles, while the glow slowly faded and the true colors came out, accompanied by curious sharp ticks and tings as the crackle began to form in the cooling, shrinking glaze. Another five minutes passed and we could gingerly handle our pots painted only one short hour before."

The process Leach describes is one in which the decorator paints an image with monochrome slips, which are then covered with a clear lead glaze. Not only the process but the look of raku was very strongly modified when it was taken up by Western ceramists. They were most excited by the speed with which the whole process could take place, by its direct quality, and by the flamboyant color and texture effects they could achieve with it. This was very impressive and raku became a very popular way of working almost overnight.

In some ways the method remains the same as the traditional Japanese method: we still place the glazed piece in an already heated kiln, watch the glazes melt, draw it from the fire with tongs, and still have an opportunity to examine the completed piece about an hour after it has gone into the fire. Finally, the sense of excitement which Leach conveys in such rich language is still with us and raku's devotees remain obsessed by it (see pages 151-153).

The Toronto ceramist Michael Sheba uses raku as his primary method for finishing his pieces. He takes a very interesting approach to raku - one that has allowed him to create controlled and elegant imagery. He has developed a strategy in which he carries out preparatory firings in an electric kiln and then a final firing in a raku kiln. This gives him the control that makes his work special.

Safety/Toxicity Problems Associated With Raku

During the firing, raku is potentially quite dangerous; it is common for the ceramist to be exposed to fumes during the firing and cooling process. This exposure is, however, somewhat moderated because most raku firings take place out in the open (raku firings should never be sited indoors). Many materials commonly used in the past are avoided today as we've become more aware of the dangers they pose. Lead glazes should be avoided. Many colorants are quite dangerous, including chrome, tin chloride, manganese, and vanadium. Some potters spray solutions of materials such as tin chloride on the surface of the heated piece as it is taken out of the kiln. This practice is potentially a source of danger.

Physical safety is also important. During the raku process the ceramist is working very close to the fire, so there is a real danger of burns. Raku firings pose environmental problems. The smoke produced during the smoke reduction process makes it very difficult to fire raku in a city or built up area, so the raku process is much more suitable to open country.

The ceramist who works in raku must also worry about the way the consumer will use the piece: raku pieces should never be used for preparing or containing food. Raku clay bodies are porous, and even lead-free glazes are likely to be soft and liable to break down in the presence of highly alkaline or acidic foodstuffs (fruit juices etc.).

Though not without its dangers and drawbacks, raku has been a very valuable addition to ceramics. It is unique and encourages a vibrant personal imagery and a very direct approach to our materials and processes.

Michael Sheba, raku bowl with crackle glaze, 8" x 2¼". Most glazes will craze from heat/cooling stress when raku fired. Carbon from smoke enters the craze lines, creating various crackle patterns. Photo by Peter Hogan.

How I Work With Raku

By Michael Sheba

Raku is a very alluring process. Its immediacy and hands-on directness have universal appeal because we witness and direct clay body and glaze transformations before our very eyes. It has the power to evoke a sense of mystery and ritual and conveys the feeling of ancient artifacts or relics that show the patina of age and timelessness. A kind of magical alchemy takes place as we work with the basic elements of fire, air, water, and earth. Even with little or no background, attractive (if not totally reproducible) results will typically show the three basic characteristics of raku: 1. a blackening or carbonization of unglazed clay areas, 2. crackle patterns on glaze surfaces, and 3. metallic lusters with glazes that contain suitable metal oxides such as copper oxide.

Because it is disengaged from its original Japanese traditional and cultural context, and because its results often seem unpredictable, raku North American style is regarded by some as just a fun recreational activity. Raku appears to be too serendipitous and too process-dominated to allow for artistic intent. Contrary to popular misconceptions, a remarkable degree of control of the raku process is possible and in the right hands raku has become a serious form of artistic expression.

Most study of raku goes no further than a simple look at glaze formulation, oxidation, and reduction. Many ceramists overlook other important and essential factors that would allow them to achieve successful and predictable results. A thorough understanding of raku processes

Michael Sheba, "Carved Raku Bowl," 4½" x 4". When raku fired, unglazed clay becomes various shades of gray to black from carbonization (reduction) by smoke. Photo by Michael Sheba.

Raku kilns are rapidly fired to 1000°C/1830°F, opened, and the pots removed one by one with the tongs and special gloves. Photo by Michael Sheba.

Pots are placed on a bed of combustible materials which instantly burst into flame. The degree of reduction (smoking) is controlled by smothering the fire with a metal pail. Timing sequences largely determine the various effects that result. Photo by Michael Sheba.

enables the meaningful evaluation of results and the implementation of successful strategies to achieve intended artistic aims. Relationships such as that between the thermal mass and cooling rate of each pot and the threshold temperature at which glazes become "responsive" must be considered in order to develop successful timing sequences that determine what to do and when. Even a study of combustible materials (such characteristics as quickness and length of burn, resin content, degree of dryness, and particle size) will determine what kind of reduction intensity we can expect and when it will happen.

A basic understanding of the raku process allows us to vary the amounts of carbonization from white through various greys to black, and to control the size and placement of crackle patterns and lusters. Though many consider effects such as copper mats and Soldner-type halos particularly unpredictable and elusive, I have found that with the proper approach they can be obtained at will.

From experience I have seen that by first studying the basic underlying theoretical principle of raku, even my beginning students are able to achieve their intended practical results remarkably quickly. With further experience a good theoretical background acts as a springboard from which we can work more intuitively and release the full potential of our creativity.

Today, explorers of raku have expanded its standard repertoire by incorporating color, terra sigillata, silver nitrate based gold lusters, fuming glaze surfaces with metallic salts, using slip resists and peel-away "shadow crackle" effects, etc.

An infinite number of permutations and combinations are possible. The "happy accidents" discovered along the way are more than enough to keep anyone's involvement with raku fresh and engaging.

My work is mostly hand built, often with wheel-thrown additions. I impress or incise marks and textures. I use a large variety of glazes, underglazes, and slips. I alter these recipes to achieve specific effects from the raku process. I apply these surfaces in layers with an airbrush and inlay some areas with low-fire enamels. I multi-fire all my pieces in an electric kiln to cone 08/06 as I build up the glaze layers before a final raku firing to cone 06 in a front-loading propane kiln.

Raku is a fast firing process done in specialized kilns that withstand rapid heat change and are easy to load and unload. Front-loading, top hat (the whole body of the kiln can be raised or lowered), and car kilns are best and these are fuel fired with propane or natural gas. Although top-loading kilns are popular, they are not the best choice because they lose heat quickly when opened and are most dangerous to unload. I use a kiln made from insulating firebricks with a lightweight ceramic fiber top and door.

I use the raku process as a subtle modulator and supportive unifying force for my strong geometric imagery. Because I cannot rely on a hit-and-miss serendipitous result and still achieve my artistic aims, it is essential for me to thoroughly understand and be able to direct the raku process. For example, the location and intensity of crackle patterns must be managed so as not to compete with or overwhelm my imagery. To this end I have developed complex strategies that

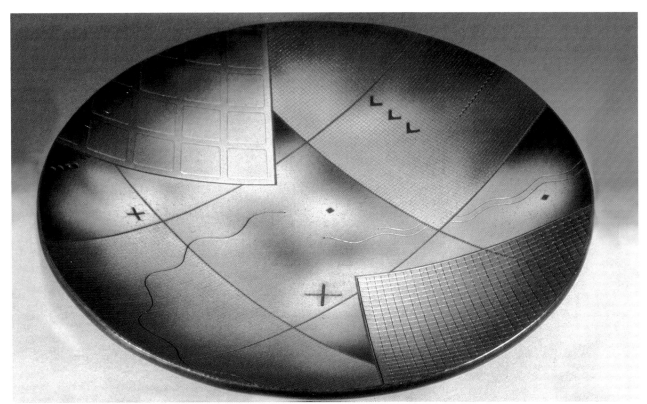

Michael Sheba, "Synergy Series: Raku Plate," 18" diameter, hand built with a wheel-thrown foot ring attached. Impressed and incised textures. Airbrushed slips, underglazes, and glazes. Multi-fired at cone 06 with postfiring reduction. Photo by Michael Sheba.

include glaze formulation and special handling to achieve a level of control that allows a reasonable expectation that I will be able to achieve what I desire.

A Raku Firing

Raku is a fast firing process. It is often a group activity because several firings are done in one day, with constant loading and unloading. Often one person manages the door while another removes the pots with tongs and sometimes a third is available to help with smoke reduction.

During the firing the pots are heated to 1000°C/1830°F in 30 to 60 minutes. Raku is different from all other ceramic firing methods in that the kiln is opened at this time and the glowing pots are removed with tongs. Those working at or near the kiln should wear fireproof gloves, protective clothing, and eye protection.

The glazes are molten and very responsive to changes in atmosphere. After the piece is drawn from the kiln the potter places it on a bed of combustible materials such as sawdust or leaves. This instantly bursts into flames. Now a member of the team smothers the fire by covering it with a metal pail. This creates an intensely smoky atmosphere inside the pail. Using predetermined timing sequences of uncovering (allowing oxygen in) and covering (creating an oxygen deficiency), the atmosphere around the responsive molten glazes can be manipulated to achieve the various effects that give raku its distinct character. After 20 minutes, the pots are usually cool enough to handle, any grime or soot is washed off, and we get to see what the piece really looks like.

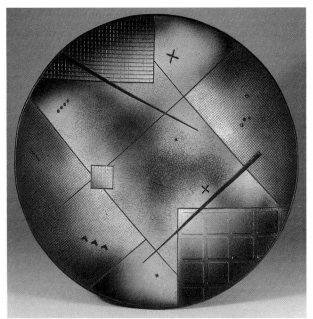

Michael Sheba, "Counterpoint: Raku Plate," hand built with a wheel-thrown foot ring attached. Impressed and incised marks and textures. Airbrushed slips, underglazes, and glazes. Multi-fired at cone 06 with postfiring reduction. Crackle patterns deliberately located to not interfere with the geometric imagery. Photo by Michael Sheba.

11

Glaze Making and Testing

Glaze Making

For most ceramists the first experience of the technical side of ceramics takes place during glaze making. The process of glaze making is easily mastered if you have the right tools, follow an ordered procedure, and take the work seriously.

You Will Need
- ➤An accurate scale calibrated in grams (for more information on scales see, page 231).
- ➤A clean pan or bucket in which to weigh the glaze materials (your scale may come with such a pan). This is called the measuring container. Stainless steel salad bowls come in various sizes and make excellent measuring containers.
- ➤A clean bucket in which to mix the weighed glaze materials. This mixing container must be large enough to hold the entire recipe.
- ➤A good dust mask (with government safety approval).
- ➤Water (for suspending the glaze).
- ➤A fine sieve, either 50 or 80 mesh (50 or 80 strands to the inch).
- ➤If you are making up a large amount of glaze (more than 2,000 grams) you will also need a coarse sieve (the type you can buy in the supermarket).
- ➤A clean bristle brush (for pushing glaze through the sieve).
- ➤A waterproof marker (for labeling the glaze container).

The Glaze Making Process
- ➤Put on the dust mask.
- ➤Locate each material in the recipe and make sure you have enough of it.
- ➤Clean the scale and make sure it's properly balanced before you begin work.

Glaze tests by Angelo diPetta.

- ➤Place the measuring container for weighing your materials on the scale. With no materials in the container, the indicated weight should be set at zero point. If not, adjust the tare compensation of the scale so that it reads zero (for information on scales and setting tare, see page 231).
- ➤Weigh your first material.
- ➤Place it in the container that you will use to mix and store the glaze.
- ➤Weigh out each successive material and place it in the mixing container.
- ➤Add enough water to make a mixture the thickness of cream.
- ➤If you have a propeller mixer, use it at this point. Otherwise, mix the glaze with a stirring stick or a wire whisk. Once the glaze is properly mixed with water, you may remove your mask.

Glaze tests by Richard Zakin.

➤Place a sieve supported by two sticks on top of another mixing container.

➤Pass the glaze mixture through the sieve (you can use a stiff brush to force the glaze through the sieve). This homogenizes the mixture and gets rid of any lumps. If you have made up a large amount of glaze (more than 2,000 grams) it greatly speeds up the process to pass the mixture through a coarse sieve before using the fine sieve.

➤Move the sieve over to the original mixing container and pour the glaze through the sieve once more. Double sieving insures a smooth mixture.

➤Make a waterproof label for the glaze and place it on the container.

Glaze Testing

Unlike paint, glazes must be fired. Furthermore, glazes are transformed by the fire and do not have the same surface or color before they are fired as after. The kiln firing changes the characteristics of the glaze in a most profound way. The best way to track these transformations is to fire glazes first on a test tile. This will allow you to see what a glaze's surface, color, and texture are after firing. The test tile should be fairly large and should have a character that is similar to your normal work. It is especially important to use the same clay and firing as you normally use in your work. Both of these strongly influence the character of the glaze.

The Testing Process

➤Prepare a test tile.

➤Thin the glaze with water to the appropriate consistency. For single color application this is liable to be the thickness of heavy cream. If you plan to use the glaze in a multiple-layer glazing strategy, the glaze (or glazes) should be thin and milky.

➤Apply the glaze to the tile by dipping, pouring, or spraying.

➤Fire the tile in a way consistent with your normal firing methods.

➤Label the completed glaze test. Include its name, recipe (including colorants), firing cone, and the date. In a classroom or group situation include your initials for identification.

Glaze Application

When we talk about a glaze or a finish or the look of a ceramic work, we are really talking about a whole "orchestra" of recipes and strategies that together make up the identity of the piece. A glaze must be applied and the application must work with the clay piece it rests upon. It is affected by the intention of the artist, by ideas of use and purpose, by the clay body, the form type, and the other slips and glazes applied along with it. The rich, fabric-like, poured glaze application that works so well on a full-bodied vessel piece will probably look very wrong on a sculptural form. By the same token, the carefully painted, brush applied, low-fire glaze may not be appropriate on the full-bodied form but may be perfect on the sculptural form. A simple dip application may suffice for a complex form, whereas a complex multi-layered application may be just right for a simple form. In the past we ceramists have talked a great deal about glaze recipes but perhaps not enough about application strategies. Glaze application requires an understanding that the ceramist has to orchestrate form, surface, materials, and processes to create a coherent whole.

The ceramist must also have a feel for the transformations the glazes go through in the firing. After the firing most glazes do not look the way they did before they went into the kiln. The transformation of the glaze from a dry powder to a glassy surface bonded to a clay form is very unsettling at first. Color and visual texture change as well. Thus, an area that was gray will turn blue or green in the fire and an area that seems smoothly covered with glaze before the firing may, after it is fired, reveal an active, complex, broken texture. As ceramists we have all needed time and experience to get used to this phenomenon. The transformations that glazes undergo during the firing make the job of developing or improving a glaze application strategy much more difficult. Therefore, ceramists generally employ carefully worked out strategies for applying glazes. The business of learning to develop and carry out glaze applications is an exciting and demanding challenge. There are few aspects of ceramics as crucial as this.

Application Methods

There are a great number of strategies for getting the glaze on the surface of the ware and each may be varied in many ways. The discussion that follows is a short precis of the many possibilities open to the ceramist. The strategies for application are simple but they allow many variations. You may dip your work into glaze, you may apply it with a sprayer, or you may pour the glaze over the piece. You may even apply the glaze with the painter's classic tool, the brush.

Dipping

Dipping is the easiest and most common glaze application method. The method encourages smooth surfaces, good in themselves and excellent as a ground for other applications. Since enough glaze must be available to allow you to immerse the piece, you must make a good deal of the glaze when preparing for a dip application.

➤Fire the piece to bisque.
➤Wet or wax the base of the piece.
➤Grasp the piece at the top and dip its bottom half in the glaze.
➤Wipe away the glaze from the bottom of the piece and let it dry.
➤Grasp the piece at the bottom, being careful not to smudge the glaze, and dip the top half in the glaze.

Dipping With Glaze Tongs

Glaze tongs look like a set of metal claws. They are useful for glazing small and medium sized pieces.

➤Fire the piece to bisque.
➤Wet or wax the base of the piece.
➤Grasp the piece with the tongs and dip it in the glaze.

Pouring a glaze.

➤ Dip a fine brush into the glaze and fill in the claw marks.
➤ Wipe the glaze off the bottom of the piece.

Splash and Pour

Splash and pour applications are classic methods for applying glaze. They are simple and direct. When fired, the imagery reveals a pleasing flow pattern.

➤ Suspend the piece over the glaze bucket (either holding it or setting it on a rack or on sticks).
➤ Fill a cup with glaze.
➤ Splash or pour the glaze over the piece, making sure the runoff pours back into the glaze bucket.

A piece may be glazed with this method alone but more often we use it in conjunction with dip or spray application techniques. Splash or pour glaze applications may be used under or over another glaze.

Spraying

Spraying is a very effective glazing technique. It requires little glaze and it can produce very beautiful results. Spraying tends to smooth and soften the look of the glaze. It is, therefore, especially useful in the oxidation fire of the electric kiln which can often be characterized by harsh transitions. For more information on sprayers see pages 231-232.

➤ Place the piece on a revolving turntable.
➤ Spray the glaze over the whole surface of the piece. Keep the sprayer moving to allow the glaze to dry before you apply more. In this way no one area becomes so saturated that it will drip and smear.

The Atomizer-Sprayer

Spraying may also be accomplished with an atomizer. This simple machine runs on the lung power of the ceramist (see page 231 for a photo of an atomizer).

Brushing

Brushes are fine tools for applying glazes but they can be frustrating. We are used to applying paint with a brush and may expect similar results when brushing on glaze. You must remind yourself that this is not possible. If you try to apply large, unbroken areas of solid glaze color with a brush the results will not have the smooth, unbroken surface they had before firing.

Some ceramists like the textured brush applied surfaces they see after the firing and enjoy creating many of their surfaces in this way. Others prefer to limit their use of brushes to the creation of linear imagery because this imagery changes much less in the fire. Still others use glazes that have been prepared using a very fine grinding process and have additions of glues and binders to aid in the creation of broad, fairly smooth surfaces. Most of the commercially prepared low-fire glazes are of this type. In this way glazes can be specially prepared for the application of smooth glaze coatings over large areas of the work.

Complex Application Strategies

One of the most effective ways to insure a rich glaze surface is to combine a group of varied surfaces and application strategies. Complex application strategies will typically require you to use a number of glazes together or perhaps a mixture of washes, slips, engobes, and glazes. Such strategies may also require you to employ a variety of application methods such as brushing, pouring, and spraying. Examples of such strategies can include combinations of such creation strategies as clay relief, stains, slips, and glazes. While strategies of this sort might seem to promise a long, labor-intensive activity, they can, with practice, be accomplished deftly. Though such applications may take a bit more time than others, they allow you to create your own "language" of glazing.

Intaglio Glazing

An intaglio image is one that has been incised or engraved. Many ceramists like to combine it with "sprigged" or added clay ornament. Once the piece has been fired to bisque this kind of imagery can be glazed in a way that accents the intaglio imagery.

➤ While the piece is in the greenware state, engrave the imagery into its surface. Fire it to bisque.
➤ Daub the glaze in the incised areas of the piece.
➤ Wash off the excess glaze, leaving the glaze only in the interstices (the corners and low places which catch the glaze).

William Hunt, "How to Make Your Fortune in Ceramics," diameter 22", porcelain fired to cone 7 in an oxidation atmosphere. Hunt has used brush painted underglaze to create the lettering on this piece. Looking at this piece we are reminded of how pleasing text can be as ornament on ceramic work.

Elaine O. Henry, intaglio glazing detail.

➤You may fire the piece with no further application of glaze, or you may apply a stain or another glaze over the surface. A dark-colored intaglio glaze will "come through" light-colored glazes applied over it. The intaglio imagery shows up quite well and the effect can be quite pleasing.

➤*Optional - Finish the piece by applying a light-colored dipped glaze:*

➤Prepare a light-colored glaze.

➤Grasp the piece at the top and dip its bottom half in the glaze.

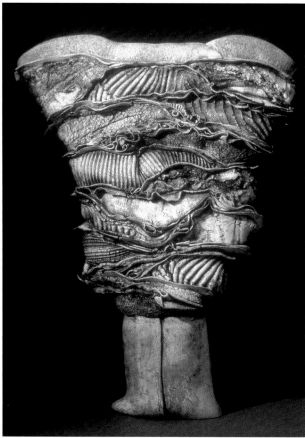

Elaine O. Henry, "Footed Cup," 1997, porcelain clay body with intaglio glazing strategy. This strategy is very effective in part because it results in blended color changes. These graduated color changes can have great appeal.

➤Wipe away the glaze from the bottom of the piece and let the glaze dry.
➤Grasp the piece at the bottom, being careful not to smudge the glaze, and dip the top half in the glaze.
➤Clean the base of the piece to ready it for firing.

Painted Imagery

1. The Process for a Dip Application
➤Fire the piece to bisque.
➤Wet or wax the base of the piece.
➤Prepare a light- or mid-colored glaze.
➤Grasp the piece at the top and dip the bottom half in the glaze.
➤Wipe away the glaze from the bottom of the piece and let it dry.
➤Grasp the piece at the bottom, being careful not to smudge the glaze, and dip the top half in the glaze.

2. The Process for a Brush Application
➤Prepare a dark-colored stain or glaze.
➤Use a brush with fine soft hairs, such as a Japanese brush, to apply the dark glaze to the surface of the dipped glaze.

Regis Brodie. This piece is an example of engraved imagery. Brodie threw the piece using a porcelain clay body. After a bisque fire, he applied a black engobe over the surface of the piece, then removed much of it with a sponge, leaving it mostly in the engraved recesses. He added thin calligraphic marks to the surface. Brodie fired the piece to cone 9/10.

Using a Brush to Apply a Textured Surface

1. The Process for a Brush Application
➤Prepare a dark-colored stain or glaze.
➤With a very stiff bristle brush (a well-used house painting brush works well), apply the dark glaze to the surface using broad motions to create a highly textured imagery.

Ginny Marsh, "Garden Vessel," diameter 20", reduction fired, cone 9. Marsh used intaglio glazing at the rim of this piece. The method works well and produces very pleasing results.

2. The Process for a Poured Application
- ➤Fill a cup with glaze.
- ➤Suspend the piece over the glaze bucket (either holding it or setting it on two sticks resting on the lip of the glaze bucket).
- ➤Splash or pour the glaze over the piece, making sure the runoff pours back into the glaze bucket.
- ➤Make sure to leave some of the textured, brush applied areas free of poured glaze.

A Multiple-Layer Glaze Strategy

- ➤Dip half of the piece in the base glaze and let it dry.
- ➤Dip the other half of the piece in the base glaze and let it dry.

- ➤Apply additional layers using one of the following methods:
  1. Pouring another glaze over the base glaze, covering only part of the surface.
  2. Pouring a strongly textured glaze (such as an ash glaze) over part of the piece.
  3. Spraying a dark glaze over the lip of the piece.

Combining Stamped, Sprigged, or Carved Imagery and Glazes

Many ceramists combine imagery created in the clay with glazes. Because clays are two-dimensional and clay imagery

Jack Troy, "Giraffe Bottle," porcelain, slips painted over a wax resist and finished with a transparent glaze, fired in cone 9 reduction atmosphere. The complex, highly patterned imagery complements the full, rounded form of this ceramic bottle.

Alan Lerner, "Wheel-Thrown Pitcher," 11" x 5". Lerner used an earthenware clay body to make this piece. He applied a mat black glaze and drew linear imagery with a wax resist medium. He then applied lithium glazes colored with stains. The wax resist areas created the black line. He fired the piece to cone 06.

Rimas VisGirda, "Woman with a Knit Cap," height 18", 1996, coil formed, stoneware clay body, white engobe (dipped), inlay drawing, stain applications, and a clear glaze fired to cone 10. VisGirda then covered the piece in a black glaze and washed it off, leaving the glaze in the interstices. He added details in underglaze pencil and fired to cone 05/04. He then painted imagery with lusters and china paints and fired these to cone 018. VisGirda combined high-fire and low-fire strategies in this piece. He created much of the linear imagery by engraving through a layer of wax resist, then daubing a black glaze into the engraved line.

Jeff Irwin, "Moving in Two Directions," diameter 10", 1999. This plate is made from a recycled porcelain plate (already fired to maturity and glazed). Irwin applied a satin black glaze with a wide brush, let it dry overnight, and engraved the imagery through the glaze, revealing the white color of the porcelain. Irwin's method has much in common with the Tzu Chou method of creating imagery. The difference is that here he works on a piece already fired to maturity.

is three-dimensional, this works well and encourages complexity. Because glaze flow is influenced by clay imagery, the glazes will flow from raised imagery into depressed imagery. This encourages color and thickness variations.

➤ Create the stamped, sprigged, or carved imagery on the greenware piece.
➤ Let the piece dry completely and fire it to bisque.
➤ Use an intaglio method of application by applying the glaze over the imagery and wiping it away so that it stays only in the depressed areas and edges.
➤ Apply a thin glaze or glazes over this imagery to finish the piece. The carved imagery and the intaglio glaze will come through this layer to complete the imagery.

"Tzu Chou" Imagery

This strategy is an adaptation of work made in China during the Sung Dynasty. In this strategy the ceramist applies a slip or nonrunning glaze to an unfired clay body of a contrasting color. The ceramist then carves through the glaze to the underlying clay body. The result is engraved imagery with an appealing graphic character. This method is particularly suited for use in the oxidation atmosphere of the electric kiln.

➤ Lay a dark slip over the surface of a light-colored, unfired piece.
➤ Carve a sgraffito line through the slip to the light-colored clay.
➤ Apply a light coat of a clear glaze over the slip.
➤ Fire the piece.

A close-up view of Tzu Chou imagery. A nonflowing black glaze was applied to the surface of the piece. The sgraffito lines were carved into the surface.

Combining Engraving and Glazing

1. The Process for Tzu Chou Imagery in the Greenware State
➤ Apply a stain or slip using spraying, brushing, or pouring methods.

James McKinnell, "Porcelain Bowl," diameter 10", wax resist and glazed engobe surfaces, cone 9/10 firing in a reduction atmosphere. This use of wax resist imagery is effective and sensitive to the medium. Photo by the artist.

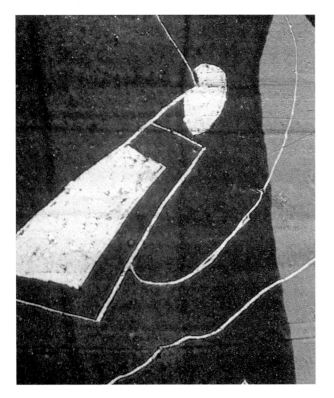

A close-up view of a surface in which glaze and sgraffito have been combined. This piece was first fired to a soft bisque. Thin and thick layers of a black glaze were then poured over it. The sgraffito was carved into the surface, revealing the white body.

➤Use a needle tool to engrave imagery into the surface of the application.
➤Fire the piece to bisque.

2. The Process for a Splash Application
➤Fill a cup with glaze.
➤Suspend the piece over the glaze bucket (either holding it or setting it on two sticks).
➤Splash or pour the glaze over the piece, making sure the runoff pours back into the glaze bucket.

3. The Process for a Dip Application
➤Wet or wax the base of the piece.
➤Grasp the piece at the top and dip the bottom half in glaze.

Giovanni Cimatti, "Plate," 38 x 31 cm, 1999, terra sigillata, glaze, and raku. This is a unique combination of terra sigillata and raku. The result is extremely elegant and reminds us that the Italian ceramists have the advantage of working from the background of a long and powerful tradition. Photo by the artist.

➤Wipe away the glaze from the bottom of the piece and let it dry.

➤Grasp the piece at the bottom, being careful not to smudge the glaze, and dip the top half in the glaze.

4. The Process for a Localized Spray Application

➤Place the piece on a revolving stand.

➤Prepare a dark glaze. Transfer it to a small cup. Add enough water to make it as thin as skim milk.

➤Spray part of the piece with the thin stain or glaze using an atomizer sprayer.

➤Clean the base of the piece to ready it for firing.

A Sample Strategy for Combining Carving and Glazing

1. In the Greenware State

➤Carve imagery into the surface of the piece.

➤Fire the piece to bisque.

2. Use a sponge to apply a dark glaze over the surface of the piece.

➤Clean off most of the glaze, leaving it only in the interstices (the crevices and sunken areas that catch and hold the glaze).

Pouring glaze on the interior of the pot.

Pouring the glaze back out. The result is a glazed interior.

Applying a black glaze on the surface of the piece.

Wiping the glaze off, leaving it only in the engraved lines on the surface.

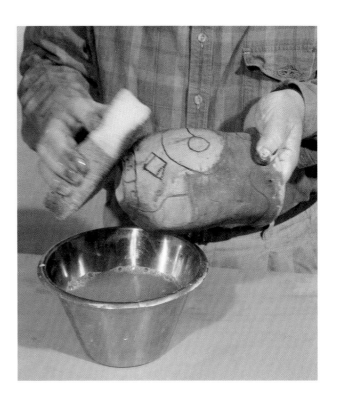

Continuing the wiping process.

Finishing the wiping process.

Dipping the piece into a base glaze.

Dipping the top of the piece in the base glaze.

Spraying the lip of the piece with a dark glaze.

Mary Jane Edwards, "Memorial Urn," 10½" x 7" x 7", 2000. In her new work the artist combines terra sigillata with a metallic glaze to create a convincing and appealing imagery. Photo by the artist.

➤Place the piece on a revolving turntable in a spray booth.
➤Spray the glaze over the whole surface of the piece. Keep the sprayer moving to allow the glaze to dry before you apply more to avoid drips and smears.
➤Fire the piece.

Combining Terra Sigillata and Glaze Applications

Many contemporary ceramists have come to rely on terra sigillatas at low-fire temperatures to create durable, lustrous surfaces. In recent years a number of ceramists have noticed that they also may be used at higher firing temperatures. At these temperatures the surface loses its lustrous sheen but becomes even more durable.

Dark-colored terra sigillatas are most effective when combined with glaze surfaces. They hold their color and contrast nicely with the shiny or satin surfaces of glazes. You may use sgraffito to engrave complex imagery onto the surface of the piece. You may use dip, splash, or brush application. Brush application is particularly appropriate for sigillata. It contrasts well with the dip and splash applications that are most appropriate for glazes.

1. **Use a brush to apply a dark terra sigillata imagery to a dry but unfired piece.**
➤Use a needle or chisel-shaped tool to engrave imagery on the surface of the piece.
➤Fire the piece to bisque.
2. **Apply glazes using pouring methods over parts of the**

Angela Fina, "Vase," height 13", 1999, barium copper glazes. Fina works with thrown porcelain and applies multiple glaze layers. She dips the first layer, then applies subsequent layers with a sprayer. She fires to glaze temperature, cone 11 in a reduction atmosphere, only once (multiple glaze layers - one firing).

surface of the piece. Leave some of the terra sigillata areas unglazed.

Firing at Multiple Temperatures

This is the process of firing a piece to different temperatures during successive firings. The ceramist starts with the highest temperature and moves on down the temperature scale. This process was developed because, at one time, no one part of the firing range was effective for the production of the whole spectrum of glaze color. In firing at multiple temperatures the whole color spectrum could be covered.

Though the color spectrum of the mid and high fires has been very effectively extended, the multiple-firing strategy is still quite useful. This is because each part of the firing spectrum can produce very different results. Combining them results in work of almost symphonic complexity. The process requires patience and skill. The ceramist must be willing to spend time and energy on each piece. The best work of this sort, however, is very rich.

Testing a Glaze Application Strategy

Just as a test tile is the best tool for testing the surface, color, and texture of a glaze, so too is it the best tool for

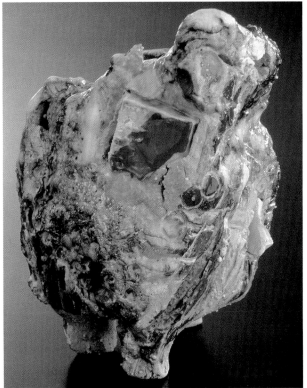

Itsue Ito, "Kyo Yu #1," 25 x 20 x 20 cm, 1994. Ito fires her pieces a number of times at multiple firing temperatures to create a complex layered imagery with strong roots in nature. The construction is massive and Ito feels that inner supports are necessary to support the overall weight and size of the piece. She prefers this to making clay pieces look light and airy because she wants to show how clay really looks and feels. She wants to leave all the marks she made while making the piece. She wants her clay work to have a natural look. She feels that this is because of her Japanese background with its emphasis on natural things.

Peter Beard, "Thrown and Altered Vessel," height 27cm, 1999. Beard works with a stoneware clay body, and impressed stamps and wax resist to isolate the glaze layers and uses multiple firing techniques to create rich patterns. These complex work strategies are a very central part of the identity of his pieces. Photo by P. Beard.

testing a glaze application. The test tile is a surrogate for a finished piece: if the application works with a glaze or a glaze combination, a similarly glazed piece should be satisfactory as well. In order to see what a glaze application will look like on your work, the test tile should be fairly large and should have a character similar to your normal work.

For Hand-Built Work

Only if you work with flat slabs should your test tiles be flat; if you work with curved surfaces, curve your test tiles.

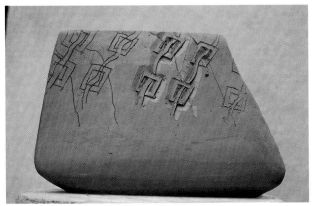
Beginning the carving process.

Defining the first carved layer and working on the second.

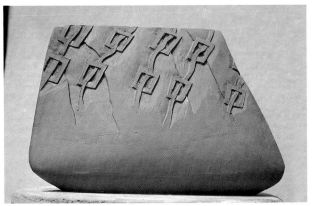
Cleaning and refining the results.

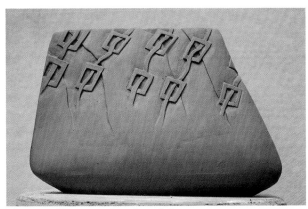
The carved imagery after the refining process.

Applying a glaze after the bisque firing.

The fired and finished piece.

After the glaze has been wiped away, leaving it only in the interstices of the carving. The piece is now ready for the covering glaze.

Glazes, multiple layers, sgraffito, and resist areas.

Richard DeVore, "Vase," 15½" x 12¼", 1996, stoneware clay body, multiple firings at various temperatures and firing atmospheres. DeVore has worked out a firing strategy that results in complex and very rich surfaces. He builds up layers of surface with each firing, creating a dappled, stone-like imagery.

Engobe tests: stone-like surfaces.

For Wheel-Formed Work

If you usually use the wheel to make your forms, throw a large cylinder and cut it into three or four tiles; in this way your test tile will have the same throwing lines and form sense as your normal work.

Make sure the tile is dust free. If you prepare your work for glazing by first firing to bisque, fire the test to bisque. Use your normal glaze application and firing methods. In every way try to make the test tile a good surrogate for your normal work.

13

Kilns and Kiln Designs

A kiln is a chamber made from refractory (nonmelting) materials. The ceramist places ware in the chamber. Heat created in this chamber (or in a firebox close by) is contained there and so builds up to high temperatures. The ceramic ware undergoes the firing and cooling process. While clay can be fired in an open fire and does not require a kiln, kilns must be used to attain high temperatures. Furthermore, they allow the ceramist excellent control of heat rise and fall and protect the ware during the rigors of the fire. Therefore, almost all contemporary potters use them.

The kiln designer's job is to make a kiln that keeps its structural integrity over a period of many firings while being efficient and keeping heat loss to a minimum. The kiln must allow the ceramist to efficiently control temperature rise and fall inside the kiln. It must be carefully designed for safe and efficient use of the fuel and must protect the ware during the firing. It must allow the ceramist access for loading and unloading and must have a "spy hole" to provide a view of what is going on inside the kiln during the firing.

Kiln Atmosphere

This term refers to the oxidizing or reducing properties of the fire. These properties strongly influence the character of the ware.

Reduction Firing

In the reduction process the ceramist reduces the amount of oxygen allowed to enter the firing chamber. A fuel-burning kiln demands a great deal of oxygen: it is very natural for the atmosphere inside a fuel-burning kiln to become depleted of oxygen during the firing. Reduction leaves its mark on both clay bodies and glazes. It modifies color and visual texture. Clay body color is deepened, sometimes moving to rich oranges and reds and sometimes to gray colors. A strong visual texture is created by dark spots

David MacDonald. Here we see the rich surface of a sawdust-fired smoke reduction piece.

that occur in a random but pleasing manner over the surface of the piece. These are caused by particles of iron oxide which have been changed to black iron oxide in the reduction process. Glaze texture and color are also modified. The dark spots that mark the surface of the clay come

John Neely, "Teapot," reduction cooled. Neely maintained reduction conditions in his kiln during the cooling period. In this way he was able to produce the black body color we see in this piece. A glaze would be redundant here.

through to the glaze and mark it as well. Glaze color can be strongly marked by reduction: for example, copper will turn a blood red, white glazes take on a cream color with a broken texture of dark spots, iron greens and ocher colors become burnt oranges and brick reds; sky blues become slate blues.

Flashing

Flashing occurs because fuel-burning kilns allow the ceramist to subject the work to direct flame. In the flashed area, color will be deepened and the transition from one color to the other may be marked by unpredictable visual effects. Flashing occurs naturally in fuel-burning kilns. The ceramist may heighten the effect by modifying the flame path inside the kiln or by strongly reducing one or two burners in a multiple-burner kiln.

Reduced and flashed work is valued for its rich and unpredictable character.

Low-Fire Reduction

We often associate reduction with the high fire but it is also used in the low fire and can result in very effective surfaces. Low-fire reduction lets us darken and enrich clay surfaces while leaving the surface of the clay completely revealed so that it may speak for itself.

The black pottery of African village potters and the similar work of the Pueblo potters of the Southwestern United States are examples of low-fire reduction. So too are the carbon blackened surfaces we see from some raku firings and sawdust firings.

To carry out a sawdust firing the ceramist packs the work in sawdust in a simple kiln structure, sets the sawdust on fire, and allows it to burn until combustion ceases from lack of fuel. As the sawdust burns, rich patterns of carbon smudging are left on the surface of the piece. Pieces fired in sawdust have a natural and direct quality that can be very appealing. Sawdust firing has the advantage of being economical - sawdust is usually free for the taking. The firing is carried out in a simple firing container rather than in a true kiln. These only require a top and a wall with small openings to allow air to enter and smoke to leave during combustion.

A Sawdust Firing

Applying a stain to the surface of the piece.

Placing the piece on a bed of sawdust. More sawdust will be added to cover the work.

Placing wadded up newspapers on the sawdust to start the fire.

Setting the newspaper on fire.

Covering the fire with sheets of metal after the sawdust has been ignited.

Removing the cooled work a few hours after the four to six hour firing is finished. The darkened work can now be cleaned and waxed.

The best thing about the sawdust fire, however, is that the work that comes from it is marked by the fire and this can be very appealing. Furthermore, sawdust firing is very appealing to students new to ceramics, it is spontaneous and can be quickly learned.

Pieces intended for the sawdust fire can be painted first with stains or terra sigillata. The sawdust fire is very effective with these surface coatings and the fire markings are emphasized.

Making a Sawdust Kiln

The sides of the structure should have openings to allow ready access of air to all parts of the densely packed sawdust. If the kiln is made from bricks (common red brick will do) they should be laid without mortar and with openings to allow air to enter. If using a metal garbage can (which works well) pierce the sides with a sharp tool to allow the entry of air.

Firing a Piece in the Sawdust Fire

You Will Need
- ➤ Piece suitable for sawdust firing (strong and compact in shape and you may wish to bisque fire it first)
- ➤ Sawdust kiln
- ➤ Sawdust to fill the kiln
- ➤ Metal lid for the kiln

The Procedure
- ➤ Place a layer of sawdust in the base of the kiln.
- ➤ Place the pieces to be fired in the kiln and surround them with sawdust. If you wish the fire to proceed fairly slowly (the safest option), pack the sawdust fairly tightly around the pieces.
- ➤ Cover the pieces with a layer of sawdust.
- ➤ Place the metal lid over the kiln, temporarily leaving a gap of a few inches to create a bit of a draft.
- ➤ Start the fire with pieces of paper and let this burn for a few minutes.
- ➤ Close the lid of the kiln.
- ➤ During the first hour check the fire periodically and restart it if necessary. After 30 minutes the fire should be well enough established to stay lit until all the sawdust has burned.
- ➤ Unload the pieces the next day and brush off any burned sawdust.
- ➤ Lightly wet the pieces and wax and buff them. If a piece is too delicate to wax and buff, spray it with a transparent acrylic medium or a liquid wax.

The Pottery of African Village Potters

African village potters create a low-fire reduction ware whose surface is a rich, lustrous, dark black. The work is fired in the open in impromptu firing structures composed of the pots plus shards and fuel. Firing takes place over a very short period - perhaps an hour or two. The method differs from sawdust firing in that at the end of the firing, the potters pull the still hot work from the fire and pour oil over it. The oil quickly burns and stains the surface of the piece carbon black. This is polished and the piece is done. The surface color is more uniform than that from a sawdust fire. Although this method is very simple, the resulting surface is very elegant and effective.

Oxidation Firing

In this kind of firing oxygen is allowed free access to the kiln chamber. In the past this was not so easy, wood-fired kilns naturally went into reduction during the firing. Even then not all ceramists fired in reduction. For example, lead glazes boil and bubble in reduction. Ceramists who finished their pieces with lead glazes took the trouble to control their kiln firings and avoid reduction. With the advent of modern kilns it became very easy to fire in oxidation. Fuel-burning kilns, whose burners are fan driven, lend themselves to oxidation firing. The very popular electric kilns not only lend themselves to the oxidation fire; most of them are not designed to be fired in reduction at all.

The contemporary ceramist must decide whether to use an oxidation or reduction firing atmosphere. This will dictate the choice of a kiln. Neither oxidation nor reduction is superior; both are tools to be used by the ceramist when appropriate.

Fuel-Burning Kilns

Fuels are organic and carbon based, they burn readily. Until recently, all kilns were fuel burning; even now when we have ready access to easily fired electric kilns, many ceramists continue to use fuel-burning kilns: this kind of firing has an enduring appeal. Very simply, there are certain kinds of visual effects that can only be obtained from a fuel-burning kiln.

Fuels can be divided into solid, liquid, or gaseous. Until the late 19th century only solid fuels were available. Animal dung, wood, and coal are all solid fuels. In kilns fired with solid fuels the unburned ash residue must constantly be removed. Only one solid fuel - wood - finds a great deal of use among contemporary ceramists in the developed countries. Now most fuel-burning kilns are fueled with a liquid such as oil, or a gaseous fuel such as natural gas or propane.

Fuel-burning kilns may be very simple structures; sawdust kilns fall in this category. More sophisticated fuel-burning kilns are designed around a concept of heat flow and they can be categorized in this way. As a result, we call the various designs updraft, crossdraft, and downdraft.

In updraft kilns the firebox is at the base of the kiln: the flame moves up through the ware to an exhaust and a chimney at the top of the kiln. In kilns of the crossdraft design the flue is on the side of the kiln - the side opposite the burners - so the heat travels through the ware and is then drawn up the chimney. In downdraft kilns the flame begins at a firebox in front or on the sides of the firing chamber. It

Mary Roehm, "Punctuated Bowl," 6" x 11", 1999, porcelain, natural ash glaze, wood fired to cone 12. Roehm's approach to the wood fire is exuberant and inventive. While based on tradition it is highly experimental and innovative.

is directed up over the ware and then back down again through the ware. The flame is exhausted into an underfloor chamber and from there is drawn up the chimney. The crossdraft and downdraft designs are the most complex and efficient: it is much easier to reach the high temperatures required for stoneware and porcelain temperatures using kilns of the crossdraft and downdraft type.

Most fuel-burning kilns are built by the ceramist rather than a commercial firm. To build them requires knowledge, time, and skill. Many kilns are the result of innovative and creative thinking and have a real impact on the life and work of the ceramist.

The Wood Kiln

Wood is a surprisingly versatile fuel; in many places in the world it is the most economical and widely available fuel.

There it still may be used for low-fire work in simple updraft kilns. In the developed countries, however, wood is mostly used for high-fire work in complex downdraft kilns.

Firing a wood kiln to high temperatures is physically demanding and requires constant attention: it calls for an instinctual understanding of what is going on inside the kiln. Almost all high-fire wood kilns work on the crossdraft or downdraft principal. These require a firebox in the front or bottom of the kiln with supports (made from either clay or metal) to hold the burning wood. There must be an outlet for spent gases; this outlet is usually placed near the bottom rear of the kiln. Finally, the outlet is connected to a chimney rising above the kiln which pulls the spent gases from the kiln and exhausts them into the atmosphere.

High-temperature wood firing is still used today by ceramists who value the richness of its wood ash, flashing, and reduction effects. During the firing the ashes of the wood

Paul Soldner, "Sculpture." Soldner fired both of these pieces in the wood kiln. Other than the glaze that settles on all pieces in the wood kiln, this piece is unglazed and testifies to the effectiveness of this way of working.

Pat Oyama, "Thrown Porcelain Bowl," wood fired at cone 14. In its luminous color, rich textures, and translucency we see the result of this very high-temperature wood fire. Photo by Bob Hsiang.

Janet Mansfield, "Anagama Fired Jar," height 45 cm. This piece was made from local clay and glazed with the ash naturally generated during the firing. The fuel was eucalyptus wood. The firing took three to four days in Mansfield's anagama kiln.

fuel fall naturally upon the ware, and if the firing temperature is high enough the ashes are volatilized and become a glaze. These glazes have a soft dappled imagery which covers the top surfaces of the piece and falls gently away toward the foot of the piece. The richness of these surfaces is the main argument for using wood as a high-fire fuel. The high temperatures necessary to create these effects were first attained by the Han potters in China (200 B.C. to 200 A.D.).

A special variant of the wood kiln is the hill-climbing kiln (known to the Chinese as the Dragon kiln and the Japanese as the Anagama kiln). In this very old design the ceramist

Charles Hindes, "Wood-Fired Tea Bowl," 1998. A classical interpretation of what the wood fire can do. Hindes has focused on this aspect of ceramics with great emotional and intellectual intensity.

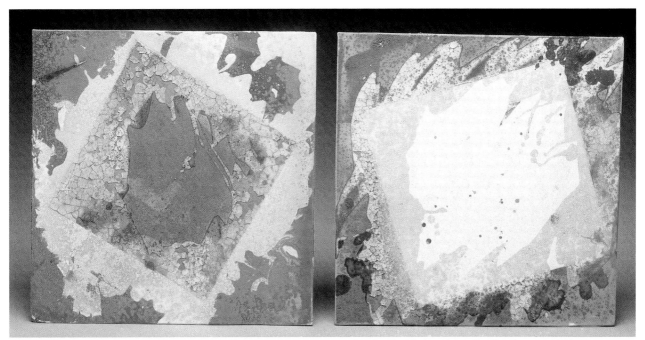

Kathryn Holt, "Shifting Planes," 18" x 18", tile form, earthenware, once fired with a light salt application in an oxidation atmosphere. For a number of years Holt has engaged in a group of very absorbing experiments with unusual materials and firing strategies. These explorations are neither purely scientific or purely aesthetic but rather combine both approaches to create a group of very special objects.

relies on the height of the top part of the kiln to act as a natural chimney. This is a multiple chamber design; each chamber is connected to the next. The flame passes from one chamber to the next, moving up the hill until it exits at the last chamber at the top of the kiln. In this way a draft is created and the kiln can reach high-fire temperatures.

Oil and Gas as Fuels

Liquid and gaseous fuels have become highly favored among contemporary ceramists. This is because they do not require constant stoking and they create no unburned ash residue that must be periodically removed. These fuels include oil, kerosene, natural gas, and propane. Modern kilns fired with these fuels are very flexible instruments and allow the ceramist to use a wide variety of glaze types and rich visual textures.

Oil is widely available, inexpensive, and has many advantages. Those who fire with oil maintain that pieces fired in the oil kiln are apt to be a bit richer and a bit more highly reduced than those fired in the gas kiln. On the other hand, it is difficult to keep an oil flame lit until the temperature inside the kiln is above 1000°F. Oil-fired kilns must have a burner system which compensates for this characteristic. Oil kilns are also apt to be a bit smokier than gas kilns.

Kilns fueled with natural gas or propane (a derivative of natural gas or petroleum) do not have combustion problems and so are used more in highly populated areas than oil kilns. The burners used to fire these fuels are quite efficient and have only a moderate impact on the environment.

Natural gas, delivered in pipes, is popular in the United States and Canada. Its price is moderate but its availability is limited to populated areas. Propane, while more widely available, is more expensive. Because these fuels have very little residue and no ash they do not encourage as much visual texture as do wood or even oil kilns.

Oil and Gas Kiln Design

Many high-fire oil and gas kilns are downdraft designs. These kilns have a firebox at the front or the sides of the firing chamber (most often at the sides). These kilns are very similar in design to those meant for firing solid fuel with the exception that since there is no unburned ash residue, the firebox can be smaller and need not have a door for the removal of ash.

There are gas kilns that are updraft in design and employ very powerful blower-driven burners. These rely on the efficiency of the fuel and the power of the burners to reach high temperatures. This design type is commonly found in commercially manufactured gas kilns.

The Salt Kiln

Salt firings require fuel-burning kilns that are specifically designed for the salt-firing process. They are constructed from refractory materials high in alumina (relatively unaffected by the salt that covers everything in the kiln). Special ports are built into the side of the kiln. At the point when the kiln is nearing the highest part of the fire (generally near cone 9 or 10), the ports in the kiln wall are

Robert Winokur, "The Italian Hill Town," 40" x 9" x 16" (in two parts), 1996, salt glazed, Pennsylvania brick clay with slips and engobes. Winokur shows that salt fire can be very persuasively used to create architectural, highly thought out, imagery. Collection: Los Angeles County Museum. Photo by John Carlano.

opened and salt is forced into the kiln. The salt reacts very strongly to the heat of the fire and breaks into its component parts, sodium and chlorine. The chlorine is expelled as a gas (see sidebar on chlorine). The sodium is deposited on the surface of the ware with such force that the silica and alumina of the clay unite with the sodium from the salt to create a glaze on the surface of the piece. This surface is marked by a strong visual texture, called "orange peel," a very active pattern resulting from the violent chemical reaction produced as the salt is exposed to the heat of the kiln. It is this surface which distinguishes salt firing from all other glaze treatments.

Colored slips may be applied to the body before firing; the salt will cover these without obscuring them but will enrich these surfaces to create a unique effect. Salt firings are particularly effective when used with pieces made with porcelain or porcelainous clay bodies. These bodies bond well with the salt and their white color is complemented by the salt glaze. Salt firings typically are taken to cone 9/10.

Toxic Side Effects of the Salt Fire

Salt is composed of sodium and chlorine. In the fire the two break apart and the chlorine becomes a gas. This gas is toxic (chlorine was used as a poison gas in World War I). Salt kilns should be located outdoors or in a well-ventilated kiln room.

A close-up view of a salt-fired surface. This photo clearly illustrates the light/dark patterns associated with the salt fire.

Soda Firing

Soda firing (sodium carbonate) is similar to salt firing (sodium chloride), but it differs in that it is nontoxic (the chlorine in sodium chloride becomes a potentially toxic gas when the salt burns in the kiln). Soda firing also makes less residue inside the firing chamber. Most important, soda has its own unique and subtle character. The soda glaze surface is thin, nicely textured, durable, clear, and tightly bonded to the clays and slips it rests upon. As is the case with salt, it

Maren Kloppmann, "Box," 4½" x 4½" x 4½", 1998, porcelain thrown and altered, finished with terra sigillata and glaze, then soda fired. These pieces are fine illustrations of what soda firing can do to enrich ceramic surfaces. Photo by Peter Lee.

Peter Pinnell, "Jar," height 9", 2000, grey porcelain, wheel thrown and altered, coated with terra sigillata and fired to cone 8 in a reduction soda fire. This piece is a fine illustration of the character of soda-fired work. The color is rich and the surface is highly modulated and marked by some visual texture but not the strong overall light and dark pattern known as orange peel that we see in the salt firing.

takes a good deal of heat to bring out the best of the soda. Therefore, most soda firings are to cone 9 or 10.

At the height of the firing the ceramist introduces soda (sodium carbonate) into the kiln. The soda unites with the alumina and silica in the clay to form the clear surface finish. Many glazes react especially well to soda firing. The application of soda encourages these otherwise stable surfaces to become active and highly flowing and the colors to brighten. In some sections of the work the glazes pool and run off the edges of the form. They lighten these edges, highlighting those areas where the form changes direction.

Soda firing is very effective when used with slips and glazes that have a mat surface. Where the soda affects them most they turn shiny, while elsewhere their surface stays dry or mat. Soda enriches the surface of unglazed areas of the piece and they take on a slight sheen. The contrast of these unglazed areas with those that are glazed is very appealing. Many ceramists who work with soda prefer spraying it rather than scattering it inside the kiln because in this way the soda diffuses over the ware most effectively (this is

Lisa Ehrich, "Amputees," 66" x 48" x 12", 1999, thrown and hand-formed pieces assembled, stoneware clay body sprayed with white slip, iron oxide (in local areas), then soda fired. Photo by Tracy Hicks.

important because soda does not explode and scatter in the heat of the fire in the same way as salt).

Soda firings are different from salt in that the salt firing results in an overall light and dark pattern (often called orange peel). Soda does not really do this. Instead, it causes the glazed surfaces to react to the soda by intensifying color and by encouraging highly flowing and pooling glazes. Though this was a 17th century technique, many contemporary ceramists have been active in reviving it. They were looking for a kind of firing that produced gases that seemed to be somewhat less dangerous than the chlorine gas that is a byproduct of salt firings. They wanted a look similar to salt fire, however. They ended up with a look that was in some ways similar and in others quite different from that of the salt fire.

Electric Kilns

Electric kilns are used by contemporary ceramists more often than kilns of any other type. They are produced in large numbers and are sold at relatively low prices. Their economy, simplicity, reliability, and relatively benign impact on the environment guarantee their great popularity. They are somewhat limited in the eyes of many ceramists because they do not lend themselves to the rich effects of reduction and flashing that characterize fuel-burning kilns. On the other hand, they have many virtues - they lend themselves to a wide color range, are simple to load and fire, and are reliable and efficient.

Electric kilns are very simple structures. They are essentially closed boxes made from soft, porous, highly insulating bricks. Inside the kiln, running along channels grooved into its walls, are coils made from a special alloy. Heat is produced by forcing a great deal of electric current through these tightly wound coils. The result is friction and the result of the friction is heat. This heat is even, easily controlled, and quite reliable.

Electric kilns may be fired manually or with the aid of control mechanisms. Older models are limited to terminating the firing when the kiln reaches maturity. Newer, computer-controlled designs can be used to control the firing from the beginning till its end, raising and lowering the temperature as required.

Though electric kilns are useful at all parts of the firing spectrum, they are particularly suitable for low- and mid-fire work. They are not quite as well suited for work at the highest part of the firing spectrum: coils that are used for high firings tend to wear out more quickly than those used only for low-temperature firings. However, if careful glazing

A front-loading electric kiln. Courtesy of the Fredrickson Kiln Co.

and cleaning procedures are used this need not be an insurmountable problem. At present the manufacturers of coils for electric kilns recommend that they not be fired above cone 8 (1263°C/2305°F) but if care is exercised they will last fairly well even if fired to cone 9 (1280°C/2336°F).

Purchasing a Commercially Made Electric Kiln

Most electric kilns are purchased completely assembled and ready to plug in. Their design and construction vary a great deal: it is no easy matter for the ceramist to make an intelligent purchasing decision.

At one time most electric kilns were front loading. Kilns of this design are highly durable for they must be heavily braced. This makes them very heavy and bulky. While front-loading kilns are expensive, this design results in a kiln that

Sara Radstone, "Sculpture," hand formed, fired to cone 7 in an electric kiln. Fired in sections and joined after firing. Radstone works with pinched out slabs, which are marked with the texture of this pinching process. She forms large slabs, then cuts them into sections when they are leather-hard (she is using a small electric kiln at present and this dictates the maximum size of each section). She then applies various ceramic surface finishes to the slabs. She combines oxide washes, very thin mat glazes, and/or vitreous slips. After the firing she reassembles the sections and joins using a metallic glue. The look of the work is strongly influenced by the process of its creation.

A test kiln with a test tile load.

A test kiln with a load of small test pots (colored clay body tests).

lasts a long time and can be loaded quickly and easily. Top-loading electric kilns have been very popular for years because they are relatively inexpensive. These kilns must be carefully designed for they are subject to mechanical and heat stress, particularly in their roof and hinge areas. If you choose a top-loading kiln, make sure the roof is replaceable. The flat roof of a top-loading kiln will eventually crack under the stress of normal use. The roof hinges, also points of stress, should be designed with strong elongated arms to keep them away from the heat path. Many newer top-loading electric kilns are segmented. The electrical connections between each segment can be a source of real problems. Look for connections made with industrial grade cables which can withstand the stress that results when the heavy segments are assembled and disassembled.

The gutters that hold and support the coils should be deep and set at an angle to hold the coils securely. The coils should be pinned to the soft brick with refractory metal pins to insure that they will not come loose and sag during the stress of the high fire. The coils should be made from an alloy that resists high temperatures (such as Kanthal A1); they should be easily replaceable and fairly thick (thin coils burn out very readily), and should be consistently wound to avoid hot spots. The switches, wiring harness, and connecting wires should be heat resistant and of the highest quality. Connections to the power source should be secure: a poorly connected coil will soon burn out. The insulation should be effective and durable.

Look for kilns that fire evenly. Floor-mounted coils help keep an even heat throughout the kiln. They add to the expense of the kiln but are a mark of a professional design. Computer-controlled zone firing has proved very effective in assuring an even firing. Each zone is furnished with its own pyrometer and the computer is programmed to direct current to those coils that need it most. Originally computer control was envisaged as a way to automate the firing. An even firing was an unanticipated benefit.

Electric kilns are high current devices and they require special, high quality, high capacity fuses, cables, and outlets. For the installation of an electric kiln there is no substitute for the services of a qualified electrician.

Small Test Kilns

Most small test kilns are very simple devices and they can be easily built or purchased. They are electric fired and work from normal house current (110 volts U.S., 100 G.B.). They have small firing chambers, usually under a square foot in area, are portable, quick firing, and inexpensive. Because of the quick pace of the firing, pieces fired in these kilns are likely to crack or explode. Furthermore, their quick cooling adversely influences the look of the glaze. In a normal firing cycle, glazes have a chance to develop a crystalline pattern during the cooling period. Most glazes derive a great deal of their character from the process of crystallization, a process which opacifies and modulates their surfaces. A glaze fired in a test kiln that has been allowed to cool quickly will not only lack character, it will also not look the same as a glaze fired in a standard kiln. To control the firing cycle and encourage rich glaze surfaces, the current flowing to the test kiln must be controlled so that the coil runs only part of the time. This can be done with a reliable and inexpensive device called a "current interruption" switch. If you purchase a test kiln, you

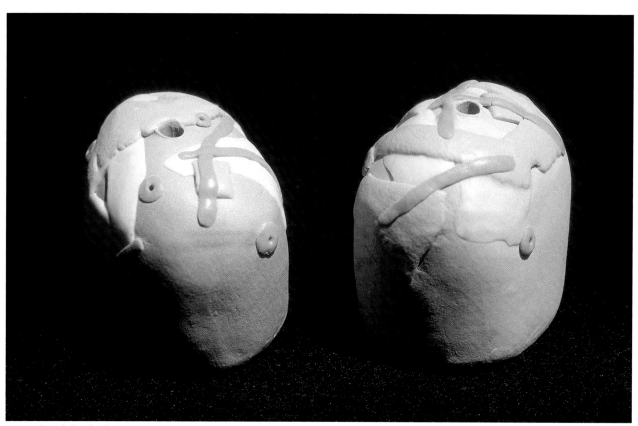

Two colored clay body test pieces.

may be able to find one with the controller already installed.

The following firing cycle is recommended for test kiln firings: 10 minutes on very low current with the kiln lid open, then close the lid. After 20 minutes, turn up the switch. Continue to turn it up every 20 minutes, switching the current from low to medium to high. Leave the kiln at the high setting until the cone bends and the kiln has reached the desired temperature. Now the kiln must be fired down. Turn the switch down every 30 minutes, switching the current from medium to low to very low. At the end of this procedure turn the switch off and allow the kiln to cool. An hour later, partially open the lid. Forty minutes later take off the lid and empty the kiln.

You can fire finished pieces as well as tests in these tiny, quick-firing kilns. While you must tailor the form and size of the piece to the limitations of the kiln, in many cases this presents an interesting challenge. Small-scale ceramic objects such as jewelry are perfect for this kind of kiln. Since the kiln is so portable and may be installed anywhere, it is conceivable that a ceramist who is on the move might find it a useful tool.

14

Kiln Loading

Kiln Furniture - Kiln Shelves and Posts

As contemporary ceramists we often take for granted tools that make our working lives much more convenient and give us more control over our work. Kiln furniture falls into this category. This is a system that allows the ceramist to construct a temporary structure inside the kiln to support the ware intended for firing. At one time there was no such efficient system for supporting the ware during the fire. Ceramists often piled the pieces one on top of another; sometimes touching, sometimes separated by wads of refractory clay. This method resulted in bare spots left on the surface of the ware. Other ceramists placed their work in saggers (refractory clay containers). The saggers were designed to be stacked one on top of another, which wasted a good deal of space in the kiln. Contemporary ceramists owe a great deal to those who developed the kiln furniture system. This is a wonderful system and it has become a standard part of the firing procedure.

This system is composed of flat shelves (called kiln shelves) and vertical modules to support the shelves (called kiln posts). Kiln shelves generally range in size from 9" to 30", kiln posts range in height from 1" to 12". Kiln posts must also be made from refractory materials such as a refractory fire clay.

For oxidation firing (including electric kiln firings) alumina shelves are generally used. They can be recognized by their light color (white or buff). They can withstand heat shock very well and are quite economical. For the reduction fire silicon carbide shelves are used. They can be recognized by their black color and crystalline grain pattern. While not as immune to heat shock as the alumina shelves, they are extremely durable.

Loading

When we begin to load a kiln, we construct a structure of posts and shelves inside the kiln chamber to support the ware. We begin with a base shelf, add three or four posts, load the ware, place the shelf on the posts, add more posts and ware, and continue the process until we have completed the loading process.

➤Check the height of the ware to be fired: from this you can determine what kiln posts you need. If you need just a bit more height, add kiln shelf fragments on top of the posts. Start with fairly low pieces and keep your tallest pieces for the top of the kiln. Don't waste space, don't put very low pieces with tall pieces - the height of the ware on each shelf should be fairly uniform.

➤Place the posts on the first shelf. Generally three posts are used, though large shelves for the electric kiln (more than 1,200 square cm or 200 square inches) require four posts.

➤Load the ware on the first shelf. Exercise care during the loading process: a great many pieces are broken at loading time.

➤Place the next shelf on the kiln posts. If you are using four kiln posts for each shelf, check for wobbling. If the shelf wobbles, place kiln wadding (a mortar-like substance made from grog and clay) under the low post.

➤Place posts on the newly set shelf.

➤Load this shelf with ware.

➤Continue until the loading is finished. If you are using cones to indicate conditions inside the kiln (a good idea even if you are firing with a kiln sitter or a computer firing controller), leave room for the cone on the shelf that is immediately below the spy hole. Check this by looking through the spy hole as you are loading the kiln.

Cone Numbering

020	018	016	014	012	010	08	06	04	02	01	1	2	3	4	5	6	7	8	9	10	11	12
▲	▲	▲	▲	▲	▲	▲	▲	▲	▲	▲	▲	▲	▲	▲	▲	▲	▲	▲	▲	▲	▲	▲

Low Temperature   High Temperature

Cone Chart

Cone number	60°C/108°F hr	150°C/270°F hr	300°C/540°F hr
022	579°C/1074°F	589°C/1092°F	625°C/1157°F
021	596°C/1105°F	611°C/1132°F	646°C/1195°F
020	620°C/1148°F	634°C/1173°F	664°C/1227°F
019	671°C/1240°F	685°C/1265°F	712°C/1314°F
018	708°C/1306°F	725°C/1337°F	755°C/1391°F
017	731°C/1348°F	752°C/1386°F	785°C/1445°F
016	764°C/1407°F	784°C/1443°F	825°C/1517°F
015	787°C/1449°F	807°C/1485°F	843°C/1549°F
014	807°C/1485°F	831°C/1528°F	880°C/1616°F
013	837°C/1539°F	859°C/1570°F	892°C/1638°F
012	855°C/1571°F	864°C/1587°F	900°C/1652°F
011	873°C/1603°F	884°C/1623°F	918°C/1684°F
010	887°C/1629°F	894°C/1641°F	919°C/1686°F
09	915°C/1679°F	923°C/1693°F	955°C/1751°F
08	945°C/1733°F	955°C/1751°F	983°C/1801°F
07	973°C/1783°F	984°C/1803°F	1008°C/1846°F
06	991°C/1816°F	999°C/1830°F	1023°C/1873°F
05½	1011°C	1023°C	1042°C
05	1031°C/1888°F	1046°C/1915°F	1062°C/1944°F
04	1050°C/1922°F	1060°C/1940°F	1098°C/2008°F
03	1086°C/1987°F	1101°C/2014°F	1131°C/2068°F
02	1101°C/2014°F	1120°C/2048°F	1148°C/2098°F
01	1117°C/2043°F	1137°C/2079°F	1178°C/2152°F
1	1136°C/2077°F	1154°C/2109°F	1179°C/2154°F
2	1142°C/2088°F	1162°C/2124°F	1179°C/2154°F
3	1152°C/2106°F	1168°C/2134°F	1196°C/2185°F
4	1168°C/2134°F	1186°C/2167°F	1209°C/2208°F
5	1177°C/2151°F	1196°C/2185°F	1221°C/2230°F
6	1201°C/2194°F	1222°C/2232°F	1255°C/2291°F
7	1215°C/2219°F	1240°C/2264°F	1264°C/2307°F
8	1236°C/2257°F	1263°C/2305°F	1300°C/2372°F
9	1260°C/2300°F	1280°C/2336°F	1317°C/2403°F
10	1285°C/2345°F	1305°C/2381°F	1330°C/2426°F
11	1294°C/2361°F	1315°C/2399°F	1336°C/2437°F
12	1306°C/2383°F	1326°C/2419°F	1355°C/2471°F
13	1321°C/2410°F	1346°C/2455°F	1349°C/2460°F
14	1388°C/2530°F	1366°C/2491°F	1398°C/2548°F
15	1425°C/2595°F	1431°C/2608°F	1430°C/2606°F

Cones

How can we know about conditions inside the kiln? Our kilns, with their closed firing chambers, offer many advantages but have one disadvantage - it is very difficult to know what is going on inside during the firing. The ceramist must have tools that enable the understanding of the conditions inside the kiln during firing. It is especially important to know about the heat conditions inside the kiln. This is influenced by two factors: time and temperature. These two factors work in concert to bring clay bodies to maturity and glazes to their melting point. This is called "heat work." Temperature can be indicated by a heat measuring device called a pyrometer but heat work can only be accurately measured by a device called a cone.

Cones are our most accurate indication of the conditions inside the kiln during firing. They are much more accurate than electrical or optical measuring devices. This is because cones contain the same materials as clays and glazes and have been carefully formulated to act in a consistent way during the firing. Their physical appearance is deceptively simple: they are merely elongated triangular pyramids. Cone are commonly available in two sizes. Use the larger of the two whenever possible. When the proper conditions occur inside the kiln (a combination of time and temperature) they soften and deform: it is this deformation that tells the ceramist that the firing is completed. Cones indicate the combination of time and temperature, not just temperature alone. For convenience we talk of the firing temperature of a cone but this is only a nominal figure used for comparison with other cones.

Cone Numbering

Beginners often find the cone numbering system to be quite confusing. High temperatures are numbered from 1 to 14, each step indicating a rise in temperature. The low temperature cones always have a zero as their first digit: they move from cone 020 to 01. As you ascend in temperature the numbers diminish. The beginner must learn the importance of the zero (it signals a low temperature cone) and must understand that the numbers fall in value as the temperature rises in the low temperature part of the firing spectrum and rise in value in the high temperature part of the spectrum.

Charting the Gap Between Commonly Used Firing Temperatures

This chart shows that the commonly used firing temperatures have been chosen with an eye to establishing a reasonable distance between one part of the firing spectrum and another.

Cone	Celsius 150°C/hr	Gap		Fahrenheit 270°F/hr
012	864			1587
010	894	30	54	1641
08	955	61	110	1751
06	999	61	79	1830
04	1060	60	110	1940
02	1120	60	74	2014
3	1168	48	120	2134
6	1222	46	98	2232
9	1280	58	104	2336
12	1326	46	83	2419

Sighting the Cone

If you are using a cone to guide the firing, you must make sure that you will be able to see it during the firing. During the latter stages of the firing, the atmosphere inside the kiln is brilliantly lit and the cone is visible. When loading, however, the kiln is dark and you must illuminate the interior of the kiln with a piece of burning newspaper or a flashlight. Close the door tightly and inspect the cone placement. You will probably have to move the cone a few times before it is perfectly placed. This is important because the cone must be fully visible if it is to be an accurate indicator of the conditions inside the kiln.

Placing the Cone in an Electric Kiln

In an electric kiln the cone may be placed nearly horizontally, supported by a piece of soft brick (the same kind of brick used to make the kiln) or may be pushed into a wad of clay, placed nearly vertically. The cone must be placed in the spot where it can be sighted from the spy hole in the door. It is advisable to use a guard cone (a cone rated for a lower temperature than your desired firing temperature). When the guard cone falls you know you are approaching maturation temperature.

Placing the Cone in a Fuel-Burning Kiln

In a fuel-burning kiln the cone must be placed at a slight angle from the vertical. The cone or cones are placed in kiln wadding (a mixture of clay and grog): this must be dry before the firing begins. It is wise to use guard cones to warn when you are approaching maturation temperature. It is also very important to place cones in various parts of the kiln because fuel-burning kilns can vary in temperature from one part of the kiln to another. This is especially true of reduction firings as reduction tends to cause localized temperature loss.

Kiln Sitters

Many ceramists who fire in the electric kiln use a kiln sitter, a device that holds a small cone. When the cone deforms a bar moves upward and activates a solenoid switch which switches off the current to the kiln. With care these devices are reliable and useful. They must, however, be kept clean and rust free and the cone must be placed very carefully. If care is not exercised the switch will not work and the kiln will overfire. Even if you are using a kiln sitter, it is a good idea to place a large cone near one of the spy holes as a backup.

One final note on this subject: the small cones used in these kilns were not originally intended for ceramic use, they are formulated differently from the larger cones and tend to bend a little earlier. You may find that the equivalent to a cone 3 in a small cone is cone 4 and that a cone 7 should be substituted for a cone 6. It is important to note that a triangular, bar-like device especially manufactured for use in kiln sitters may be substituted for the cone, with the promise of greater accuracy.

Pyrometers

Pyrometers are devices for measuring very high temperatures of the type that occur in a kiln. Their operating principal is that a voltage is created when two joined but dissimilar wires are subjected to high temperatures. This voltage can be used to drive a gauge which indicates the *approximate* temperature inside the kiln. The use of the word approximate here is emphasized because these instruments generally give only approximate readings. They are very useful in that they can tell you about the *rate* of heat rise inside the kiln but they are best used as supplements to pyrometric cones. Cones provide far more accurate and useful guidance as to when to terminate the main part of the fire and begin the soaking process.

Computer-Aided Firing

We are at the point where many ceramists use computers to aid in the firing. Most contemporary computer-aided firing schemes rely on pyrometers. As pointed out in the section on pyrometers, these instruments are not as accurate as cones. Even if you are using a computer controller it is a good idea to place a cone near one of the spy holes as a backup. Perhaps someone will design a kiln controller equipped with a sensor that can respond visually to the fall of the cone. In this way the ceramist could have the best of both worlds - the controlling power of the computer and the accuracy of cones.

15

Kiln Firing

The firing is the final step before the ceramic piece is complete and it may be the most dramatic. The final firing has a strong effect upon the look of the fired piece: in fact, in some cases, as in a wood or salt fire, it may be the most important influence on the character of the piece. It is here that the piece is likely to undergo its greatest stress and it is here that there is the greatest possibility for gratifying success or frustrating failure. We associate firing with drama; all firings end in a moment of truth when the kiln door is opened and the outcome of our work is revealed.

The Pace of Firing

The time when the kiln reaches maturation temperature depends on such factors as the efficiency of the kiln and the density of the kiln load. Perhaps the most important factor, however, is the rate at which the ceramist would like the temperature to rise. Some ceramists like the period before maturation to be marked by a very swift heat rise; others prefer a long, slow "stewing" kind of process. These preferences seem to depend mostly on the expectations of the ceramist and on the character of the imagery used on the work.

Cooling the Kiln

It is important to control heat rise and loss so that temperature changes inside the firing chamber are not abrupt. This is especially critical after the cone has fallen because crystals form in a glaze while it is cooling. These crystals strongly influence the look of the fired glaze, encouraging matness, depth, and richness: if the cooling is abrupt the crystals will not have a chance to form. Then, too, cracks may be caused by an overly rapid firing cycle (especially during the early stages of the fire) or by rapid cooling. To deal with cracks that occur during heating, the kiln should be heated slowly. To deal with cracks that occur during cooling, the cooling cycle should be extended. This is accomplished by firing the electric kiln for a time with

partial power or, if using a fuel-burning kiln, by closing up the kiln and letting it radiate heat into the firing chamber.

The Bisque Firing

Most contemporary ceramists fire their work twice, first at a comparatively low temperature (usually cone 08 to 06), which is referred to as a bisque fire. The ceramist then prepares the piece for the high firing (usually by applying glazes) and then fires to a higher temperature. By firing to bisque the ceramist prepares the piece to receive the glaze. This strategy is employed because most surface finishes are suspended in a water medium; the water can crack or break an unfired piece but has no effect on a bisque-fired piece. A piece that is bisque fired will not break down in water but its absorbent surface will readily accept glaze.

There are occasions when contemporary ceramists fire to higher temperatures in the bisque than in the final fire. Two come readily to mind: porcelain bisque firings and firings of very low-fire glazes. In high-temperature porcelain bisque firings the ceramist fires the unglazed piece to maturity in a container of silica sand to discourage warping. The piece is then glazed and fired normally, but to a temperature somewhat lower than the warping point of the clay body; the body is unaffected by the heat needed to fuse the glaze and does not warp. Glazes that are to be applied to mature clay bodies need to be thicker and stickier than normal glazes. This may be accomplished by using an oil rather than a water suspension material or by adding glue, a colloidal material, or bentonite (a very fine clay) to a water-based glaze.

Ceramists who work with very low-temperature glazes such as cone 06 or 08 will often fire to a cone 04 bisque; the body is still absorbent at this point but is more durable than if it were fired only to the maturation point of the glazes.

Bisque firing at the same temperature as the glaze is also possible. The advantage in this case is that bisque and glaze pieces may be fired in the same kiln. This method is appropriate when used with low-fire absorbent bodies or if the glazes have been formulated for application on a mature, nonabsorbent bisque. The great American ceramist Adelaide Alsop Robineau used this method to fire her porcelain.

A Day-Long Bisque Firing

Cone 08 (955°C/1751°F)

Bisque firings may be accomplished in one or two days (with an extra day for cooling). A one-day bisque firing is not quite as safe as the longer two-day firing but if care is taken to ensure that the work is completely dry and the heat rise is slow during the early part of the firing, this is an acceptable procedure.

- ➤ Day 1 - 9:00 a.m. The kiln is started on a setting that will produce a slow heat rise, with the door left ajar.
- ➤ Day 1 - 10:00 a.m. The kiln door is closed
- ➤ Day 1 - 6:00 p.m. The interior of the kiln is quite hot (around 1000°F). The kiln setting is changed to one that will produce a moderate heat rise.
- ➤ Day 1 - 7:00 p.m. The kiln setting is turned to one that will produce a strong rise in heat.
- ➤ Day 1 - 8:00 to 10:00 p.m. The kiln reaches maturation temperature and is turned off.
- ➤ Day 2 - 11:00 a.m. The kiln door is opened a bit.
- ➤ Day 2 - 3:00 p.m. The door is completely opened.
- ➤ Day 2 - 6:00 p.m. The kiln is unloaded.

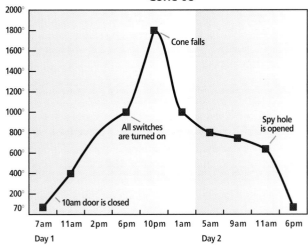

Firing Chart for a Day-Long Bisque Firing Cone 08

A Two-Day Bisque Firing

Electric kiln, cones 010 to 05

- ➤ Day 1 - 3:00 p.m. The kiln is started on a low setting with the door left ajar.
- ➤ Day 1 - 5:00 p.m. The kiln door is closed and the kiln is left to fire overnight.

- ➤ Day 2 - 9:00 a.m. The interior of the kiln is quite hot (around 1000° F). The kiln switches are turned up to medium or medium high.
- ➤ Day 2 - 9:30 a.m. The kiln switches are turned up to high.
- ➤ Day 2 - 1:00 to 2:00 p.m. The kiln reaches maturation temperature and is turned off.
- ➤ Day 3 - 9:00 a.m. The kiln door is opened a bit.
- ➤ Day 3 - 11:00 a.m. The kiln door is opened completely.
- ➤ Day 3 - 2:00 p.m. The kiln is unloaded.

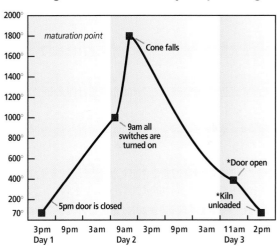

Firing Chart for a Two-Day Bisque Firing

(*67° is a typical kiln room ambient temperature)

The Final Fire

This is the final step before the ceramic piece is complete. It is here that the character of the finished piece is defined. The technology of the final fire is complex and demanding. It requires attention and discipline.

A Day-Long Final Firing

Electric kiln, cones 04 to 9

- ➤ Day 1 - 9:00 a.m. The kiln is started on a low setting
- ➤ Day 1 - 9:30 a.m. The kiln door is closed.
- ➤ Day 1 - 6:00 p.m. The interior of the kiln is quite hot (around 1000° F). The kiln switches are turned up to medium or medium high.
- ➤ Day 1 - 6:30 p.m. The kiln switches are turned up to high.
- ➤ Day 1 - 9:00 to 11:00 p.m. The kiln reaches maturation temperature. The heat setting is turned back to low and the kiln is soaked.
- ➤ Day 1 - 1 hour later. The kiln is turned off.
- ➤ Day 2 - 11:00 a.m. The kiln door is opened a bit.
- ➤ Day 2 - 2:00 p.m. The door is completely opened.
- ➤ Day 2 - 4:00 p.m. The kiln is unloaded.

A Two-Day Glaze Firing

Overnight preheat

- ➤ Day 1 - 3:00 p.m. The kiln is started on a low setting with the door left ajar.
- ➤ Day 1 - 5:00 p.m. The kiln door is closed and the kiln is left to fire on low heat overnight.
- ➤ Day 2 - 9:00 a.m. The interior of the kiln is quite hot (around 1000° F). The kiln switches are turned up to medium or medium high.
- ➤ Day 2 - 9:30 a.m. The kiln switches are turned up to high.
- ➤ Day 2 - 2:00 to 4:00 p.m. The kiln reaches maturation temperature. The heat setting is turned back to low and the kiln is soaked.
- ➤ Day 2 - 1 to 2 hours later. The kiln is turned off.
- ➤ Day 3 - 9:00 a.m. The kiln door is opened a bit.
- ➤ Day 3 - 11:00 a.m. The door is completely opened.
- ➤ Day 3 - 2:00 p.m. The kiln is unloaded.

Cooling an Electric Kiln

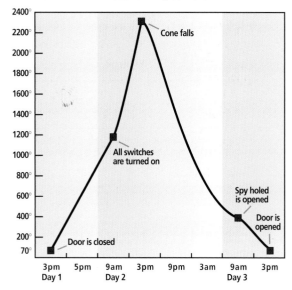

Firing Chart for a Typical Overnight Firing Electric kiln, cone 6

*(*67°F is a typical kiln room ambient temperature)*

It is especially important during the firing of an electric kiln that heat loss is controlled; most electric kilns can lose heat very quickly. Glazes are especially sensitive to abrupt changes during the cooling process. Crystals form in a glaze while it is cooling. These crystals strongly influence the look of the fired glaze, encouraging matness, depth, and richness; if the cooling is abrupt the crystals do not have a chance to form and they are sorely missed when they are not present.

To control the cooling process the ceramist turns the kiln off in stages, leaving it for an hour at medium heat, then an hour at a low setting before finally turning off all current.

Cooling an Electric Kiln With a Kiln Sitter

An electric kiln can be fired down or soaked even if it is equipped with a control mechanism. These mechanisms automatically shut off all current to the kiln; they are activated by a sensor which responds to temperature or to the deformation of a ceramic cone. Generally they allow for the manual restoration of current: now the coil switches should be turned to moderate settings and kept at these settings for an hour or so before the power is turned off.

Opening the Kiln

When the kiln temperature falls to 750°F open the spy hole. A few hours later open the kiln door slightly. When the temperature reaches 500°F open the door wider. When the ware is cool enough to hold, you may open the door fully and remove the ware from the kiln.

Fuel-Burning Kilns

Controlling the Atmosphere Inside a Fuel-Burning Kiln

A fuel-burning kiln demands a great deal of oxygen and it is very natural for the atmosphere inside to become depleted of oxygen during the firing. This phenomenon is called reduction. Reduction leaves its mark on both clay bodies and glazes. If you are firing a fuel-burning kiln, it is most likely that you wish to control and enhance the effects of reduction. This is a skill that must be learned - it is not a simple matter to maintain an effective reduction fire.

It is difficult to understand what is happening inside the kiln during the firing. Clues as to the character of the atmosphere inside the chamber are especially difficult to come by. The way the flame comes from the spy hole is the traditional indicator: a 2" flame indicates a heavy reduction while a ½" flame indicates a light reduction.

Many ceramists who fire a great deal in reduction come to feel that the body reduction is the most crucial part of the reduction process; they emphasize that body reduction should take place at a point below cone 08 (1750°F/955°C). Beyond this point many of the glaze fluxes may have begun to melt and body reduction will not be effective.

Many ceramists who fire in reduction keep careful records of their firing procedures. They feel that this helps them to create an effective firing strategy.

Flashing

Fuel-burning kilns allow the ceramist to subject the work to direct flame. This is called flashing and it often accompanies reduction. Work that has been flashed and reduced is valued for its rich and unpredictable character. Flashing causes changes in the character of sections of the piece which have been directly exposed to the flame. To accomplish this, the ceramist may modify the flame path inside the kiln. The ceramist may also create flashed effects by strongly reducing one or two burners in a multiple-burner kiln. In the flashed area color will be deepened and the transition from one color to the other may be marked by unpredictable visual effects.

A Typical Gas Kiln Cone 9 Reduction Final Firing

➤ Day 1 - 3:00 p.m. Start the kiln with the burners on very low. Open the damper quite wide. Allow the temperature to rise only 100° to 110°F an hour. Leave the kiln with the burners on low to fire overnight.

➤ Day 2 - 9:00 a.m. The interior of the kiln is quite hot (around 1600°F). As body reduction begins, close the damper slightly to restrict the amount of air allowed to enter the kiln. Raise the gas pressure as well. Keep the kiln in body reduction for 30 to 60 minutes.

➤ Day 2 - At this point reduction is moderated: keep the kiln in this state of moderate reduction for the rest of the firing. If you allow the kiln to reduce too much, the work will become muddy in color. If you allow it to reoxidize the effects of body reduction will be lost. Closely monitor the rate of rise in temperature, don't allow it to fall. It should rise in a consistent manner. If the temperature begins to fall, open the damper slightly. If the temperature climbs too rapidly at this point the kiln may have slipped into oxidation and you should partially close the damper.

➤ Day 2 - 2:00 to 11:00 p.m. The kiln reaches maturation temperature at some point in this time span. At this point many potters terminate the firing; others soak or fire down by turning down the gas to low, lowering the amount of air allowed to enter the firing chamber, and partially closing the damper.

➤ Day 2 - 30 to 60 minutes later. End the firing.

Controlling Cooling in a Gas-Fired Reducing Kiln

When the kiln is in reduction it may stall and there may be little or no heat rise. Since most ceramists put the kiln into reduction toward the end of the firing, heat loss is controlled in a natural manner. To end the firing, turn off the gas, close the damper, and the allow the kiln to cool. In some very open kilns the burner ports may also have to be stopped up with clay or spun kaolin. The cooling process will usually take one or two days.

When the kiln temperature falls to 750° F open the damper slightly. A few hours later open the damper wider. When the temperature reaches 500° F open the damper completely. The door can be opened at this time as well. If you have no way to

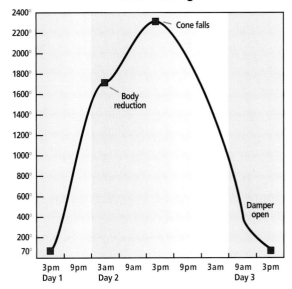

Firing Chart for a Typical Gas Kiln Cone 9 Firing

*(*70° is a typical kiln room ambient temperature)*

measure this, toss a bit of paper in the kiln; if it bursts into flame, the kiln is still too hot to open. When the ware is cool enough to hold, you may remove it from the kiln.

Multiple Firings

Multiple firing is the process of firing a piece to different temperatures during successive firings, starting with the highest temperature and then moving on down the scale. This process is generally used in color-oriented work: the guiding theory here is that each part of the firing spectrum is most effective for the production of some colors and that in multiple firing the whole range of the color spectrum will be covered.

The process requires great care, patience, and technical skill. The ceramist must be willing to spend a good deal of time and energy on each piece. Furthermore, multiple firing puts the ware in jeopardy: each successive firing increases the risk of cracking due to quartz inversion (see page 26). The best work of this sort, however, has an inventive character and a rich appearance.

The Kiln in the Imagination of the Ceramist

Kilns play a central role in the imagination of the ceramist. In fact, there have always been ceramists who take special interest in kilns and their complex ways. For a long time this interest was understood to be an expression of the technical side of ceramics. Yet when other ceramists talked of this concern, they said that these ceramists were "fascinated with the fire." This phrase betrays the underlying acknowledgment that this fascination was more connected with the drama of the fire than with its mechanics. In a recent development we have begun to hear from ceramists who see kiln building and firing as an

The U-shaped modules used to construct the kiln.

Shaping the kiln.

The half-formed kiln.

The firing.

"Sculpturkiln —
The House of Wales"

By Nina Hole

I built "The House of Wales" on the campus of the University in Aberystwyth, Wales, for The International Potters' Festival. For this special historical event I decided to make a sculpture that was a simple house form. I built it with the help of my assistant Debra English and students from Wales. It was built with paper between sections so it was possible to take it apart and later reassemble it at Battersea College in London.

What I wanted was to make a pure simple statement - a house form, enclosed in itself, containing the energy within the form. I wanted to build this shape with few openings apart from the small openings that the slab system of building gave.

As each sculpture kiln is different in form, the firebox that forms the base of the sculpture is different each time. It is a challenge to try to understand the mechanics of the firing and build the best firebox appropriate to each piece. In Aberystwyth the weather was very bad, pouring rain most of the time, so we had to build a little extra kiln to dry out the clay and the slabs as we built the piece.

The slab construction varies only a little from each sculpture I make but the condition of the clay determines the shape of the slab module. Here the module is a U-shaped slab about the size of a small firebrick. I made many of these and stacked them one on top of the other. This made a remarkably strong structure, strong enough to build a form four meters (13 feet) high, and strong enough so that I could fire it to 1000°C. I then covered the structure/kiln with a kaolin fiber blanket. At this point in the firing I removed the blanket and "unveiled" the kiln. It was a spectacular sight when the glowing structure stood there for all to see. I threw sawdust at the hot sculpture to reduce the surface and this also prolonged the glow of the fire.

The completed kiln after the firing.

Constructing an outdoor kiln.

A firing.

Louis Katz

The American ceramist Louis Katz has been making kilns as art and study objects since the 1980s. Their aesthetics, therefore, are very important, but they also are working kilns. Instead of firing these objects in a kiln with flame around their outside surfaces, Katz fires them as kilns with the fire inside the firing chamber. Therefore, their firing chambers are fired to maturity while their outer surfaces are only partially fired. This approach seems inside out, but it makes sense given the nature of these objects. Katz needs to make pots to fill these kilns and makes these in great numbers. The pots are consonant with the rugged character of the kiln. He has also become interested in bricks and has made many that he shows with his pots.

Katz has said of these kilns: "Many people don't realize that most kilns are made from clay. They tend not to understand that, like a tea bowl, a kiln is a functional object and can have the same kind of admirable qualities." He builds these kilns from discarded clay materials, wanting only that they be strong and heat shock resistant. Once the kiln structure dries, he covers it with a further layer of insulation made from wet clay and sawdust. He then loads the kiln with the ware. He fires the kiln with gas, mostly to cone 04. He often takes photographs to document the firings. When the firing and cooling are complete, he removes the sawdust and clay insulation layer "to reveal the colors of the fired kiln." He has exhibited these kilns, rolling them (presumably with a sense of ceremony) into the gallery.

avenue to aesthetic expression. They see the kiln as a living structure and the firing as a living process - as a type of happening. Two ceramists who have worked in this way are Nina Hole and Louis Katz.

The slide series on pages 194 and 195 documents the construction of a piece called "Sculpturkiln - The House of Wales" by the Danish ceramist Nina Hole at the Aberystwyth Art Center in Wales in western Great Britain. Hole is a ceramic sculptor who uses an experimental variant of raku firing as both process and spectacle. Her recent work has been on the theme of the house and she has constructed a number of large modular slab constructions which are both house and kiln. They create a spectacular effect during the firing and leave a sculpture at the end. She feels this gives her pieces a unique spirit in which technique and aesthetics are very closely intertwined and process is as important as product.

On pages 196 and 197 I show the kiln work of Louis Katz. In his work too the kiln takes on a central role.

16

An Overview of Ceramic History

As ceramists it is inevitable that we look at pieces from the past in a unique way. We tend to connect with this work very directly and to identify with certain examples almost as if we ourselves had made them. Which one of us has not looked at such a piece and tried to put ourselves next to its creator during the time of its creation? Looking at these works even has overtones of a detective novel: with a little study we are in a position to understand how they were created and why these methods were used.

Asia

There is a strong tradition of ceramic work in all of Southeast Asia. The ceramic traditions of China, Korea, and Japan are particularly strong. Furthermore, we can be grateful that in recent years these countries have developed vital contemporary ceramic movements.

China

Ceramics developed, in China, about 2200 B.C. Two types of work were developed almost simultaneously at this period - in western China a type called Yang Shao Redware, painted with highly burnished terra sigillatas, and in eastern China a monochromatic black ware known as Lung-Shan ware. Both are low fire. The Yang Shao ware is coil formed, it is very light and its construction and painted imagery are very skillful. The painted imagery is marked by a highly patterned and elegant geometry.

Lung-Shan ware is monochromatic. While not as striking as Yang Shao red ware, its carefully designed shapes seem to have been formed with the aid of a potter's wheel (probably a "slow" wheel). These cultures were succeeded by the Shang and Chou Dynasties. While many of us know the cast bronze vessels (molded from clay originals) made during these two dynasties, their artisans also produced highly carved ceramics of great refinement during this period.

The Han Dynasty (200 B.C. to 200 A.D.) was a time of

Vase, Yang Shao Red Ware, 3000 to 2000 B.C., 13½" x 11". The Everson Museum, Syracuse, New York. Museum Purchase. Photo by T.C. Eckersley.

great advances in ceramic technology. Both low-fire, lead-glazed and high-fire, ash-glazed work was made during this period. Most of the low-fire ware was mold formed. Its lead glazes, originally a transparent copper green, have usually changed over time to an opaque, metallic, silvery green.

The Han period also marks the development of the first large body of high-fire work. These pieces are examples of an early approach to stoneware. The work is thrown, often with great virtuosity and elegance. These pieces were fired in kilns fueled with wood. The glazes were derived from wood ash, a natural byproduct of the wood fire. The development of high-fire stoneware was brought about by advances in kiln

Platter, China, T'ang Dynasty, 618 to 906 A.D., 2¼" x 9¼". Everson Museum, Syracuse, New York. Photo by T.C. Eckersley.

design which resulted in the development of the hill-climbing kiln. These long narrow kilns were set on the upward slope of a hill (this encouraged a draft in the same way a tall chimney does and for the first time allowed high-temperature firings). This is also the period that saw the production of the clay armies of the Emperors of Ch'in. These unglazed sculptures are striking in their size and numbers.

The next great period of Chinese ceramics occurred during the T'ang Dynasty (618 to 906). A good deal of this work was thrown and these thrown pieces are marked by full, rich forms. Most T'ang ceramics were low fire, slip decorated, and lead glazed. Because lead bonds with the silica and alumina in clay, lead glazes can be used that have no clay in their makeup. The T'ang potters seem to have applied glazes composed entirely of lead over their clay bodies and colored slips. Because they had no alumina content of their own, these glazes ran and flowed in the fire: the Tang potters compensated for this strong glaze flow by leaving the lower part of the piece unglazed.

A small number of T'ang pieces were high fired, many of these in a stoneware body but a few pieces in porcelain. This work seems to be anticipating many of the explorations of the Sung Dynasty ceramists.

The Sung Dynasty (960 to 1279) was a time of great brilliance in Chinese ceramics and marks the widespread introduction of porcelain. From northern China came the porcelain called Ting ware. Ting ware can usually be identified by the metal banding on the lips of the pieces. The clay bodies often warped, so the potters fired these pieces resting on their lips in order to discourage this. The potters used metal bands to cover over the unglazed clay body at the lip. The body is marked by a light cream color and has a soft, fluid appearance. Ting ware pieces often were ornamented on the interior of the bowl forms. Many of these were carved; in others we see press-formed imagery created by using carved or stamped press molds. In southern China the porcelain is whiter, harder, and more restrained in shape. Most of this work was thrown, much of it over bisque clay press molds. It was fired in wood-burning, climbing kilns in a reduction atmosphere. The dense white clay bodies enhanced visual texture and glaze color.

At the same time, in northern China a highly decorated, popular ware was produced called T'zu Chou. It was made from a mid-fired stoneware clay body and fired in an oxidation atmosphere. This ware was generally thrown on the wheel and featured pictorial imagery. Most T'zu Chou pieces were finished in one of three ways: the piece was covered with a slip and the ceramist then partially carved away the slip to reveal the clay body; a dark slip based on a high impurity clay was applied over a lighter body and partially carved away to reveal the clay body; or a white slip was applied over the piece and a dark slip was used to paint pictorial imagery on this surface. In each of these strategies

Vase, Han Dynasty, 206 B.C. to 220 A.D. height 13¾", diameter 9¾", stoneware, glazed. Gift of Chao Ling and Fong Chow. The Schein-Joseph International Museum of Ceramic Art, New York State College of Ceramics at Alfred University. Photo by Brian Oglesbee.

Bowl, China, Sung Dynasty, 960 to 1279 A.D., diameter 7.3". Gift of Cloud Wampler, Everson Museum, Syracuse, New York. Photo by T.C. Eckersley

the ceramist finished the process by covering the piece with a light coating of a clear glaze.

After the Sung came the Yuan period (1280 to 1368) and the introduction of blue and white ware. In this kind of work the ceramist painted a cobalt decoration on a white porcelain body and covered the piece with a heavy coating of clear glaze. This work method remains a favorite of ceramists in China and it is still often used by them. After the Yuan came the Ming Dynasty, which lasted from 1368 to 1643. The Ming potters continued the tradition of blue and white ware but also explored the possibilities of layered glazes and multiple firings. This entailed the application of low-fire glazes to a glazed and fired porcelain piece. In this way the taut forms and durable glazes of porcelain could be combined with the brilliant color and graphic imagery of the low fire.

The potters of the Ch'ing Dynasty (1644 to 1912) carried on the Ming tradition of high-fire porcelain. The great achievements of Ch'ing pottery took place from 1662 to 1795 during the reigns of Kang Hsi, Wan Li, and Chien Lung. This work is noted for its complex polychrome decoration. The potters first fired to very high temperatures to harden the porcelain and establish the drawing. They then fired at progressively lower temperatures to create a broad spectrum of vivid color. The colors were created using the then innovative palette of brilliant low-fire overglaze colors that had their origin in France. Ch'ing Dynasty porcelains are aristocratic (many of the best pieces were created for the Imperial House), florid, fastidious, technically imposing, and highly inventive.

During the Ch'ing period another kind of work was developed that was quite different from the Imperial porcelains. Yixing red ware is hand carved or mold formed. The tradition has proved to be very vital and the work is still produced. The unglazed clay bodies vary in color from light tan to a brick red. Form and utility are the focal points of this work. These pieces convey a sense of care, reserve, and intellect.

The 19th and 20th centuries were difficult times for the Chinese, at first marked by great decay and then followed by great political turbulence. The production of porcelain and Yixing ware continued (and continues to this day) but none of it has attained the highest levels of technical skill and aesthetic conviction of the earlier work. We now see the beginning of a strong studio potter movement and ceramists creating work that is a blend of Chinese tradition and the international contemporary idiom.

Japan

The best known early Japanese work is from what has come to be called the Jomon culture. The name means "cord impressed" and is derived from the characteristic cord markings on the sides of the pots. Their pieces were coil formed and ornamented with sprigged clay relief. While some examples of very early Jomon have been found (I have seen a vessel piece credited to the 8th millennium B.C.), most of the great Jomon pots date from around 500 B.C. This work was built with coil-forming methods and fired to low temperatures in open fires. The Jomon potters knew nothing of glazes or colored slips, yet they were able to make the most of the surface creation strategies they knew. These large coil pieces are noted for their exuberant and inventive imagery.

The Jomon was an indigenous culture while the next Japanese cultures reflect the influence of newcomers from mainland Asia. The Yayoi culture (3rd century B.C. to 3rd century A.D.) was strongly influenced by new technology and form ideas from Korea and China. The Tomb culture (the Kofun period) followed (3rd to 6th century A.D.), marked by the creation of large burial mounds and ceramic

Vase, Japan, Kitoji Rosanjin (1883 to 1959), "Jar," circa 1954, stoneware with ash glaze, height 8½", diameter 7¼". Gift of the artist. The Schein-Joseph International Museum of Ceramic Art, New York State College of Ceramics at Alfred University. Photo by Brian Oglesbee.

Bottle, Japan, Shoji Hamada, (1892 to 1978), "Vase," height 7¾", width 4¾", diameter 2¾". Gift of David and Ann Shaner. The Schein-Joseph International Museum of Ceramic Art, New York State College of Ceramics at Alfred University. Photo by Brian Oglesbee.

sculptures called Haniwa that were placed on the mounds. These large, robust, simply modeled figural sculptures are evidence of a real understanding and love for the material.

The Nara period (672 to 780) is marked by a renewed interest in the creation of vessels and the learning of technical skills. At this time the potter's wheel and ceramic glazes were introduced from the Asian mainland. During the Kamakura period (1185 to 1338) the potters produced thrown pieces with rich, full forms. Simple geometric designs were often stamped on the surface of these pieces, which were then finished with wood ash glazes. The pottery of the succeeding Muromachi period (1338 to 1568) is similar but with a greater emphasis on loose thrown forms and highly textured glaze surfaces, often the result of long firings. Many of the great pieces from the pottery centers of Bizen and Shino were created during this period.

Noteworthy products of the Momoyama period (1568 to 1614) are large thrown jars with rich glazed surfaces and work intended for the tea ceremony. Particularly interesting is Oribe ware. It is named after Oribe Furita (died 1615), an aristocrat, tea master, and connoisseur of ceramics. These pieces seem to have been fired in mid- or high-fire kilns in an oxidation or neutral atmosphere. Many of the most important pieces were hand built, often over muslin-wrapped wooden press molds; others were thrown on the potter's wheel. The Oribe potters employed a complex system of imagery - a single piece might well be ornamented with two different colors of clay, a black glaze (used to create linear imagery), slips, and a translucent green glaze.

In the next period - the Edo period (1650 to 1857) - two approaches to clay coexisted, one very much oriented to the material nature of clay and the other oriented to the creation of rich imagery.

Bizen and Shigaraki ware is strongly clay oriented. This has always been a strong aspect of Japanese ceramics. The work is thrown, usually in a loose asymmetric manner. Glazes are usually splashed on the piece in such a way as to reveal a good deal of the rich color and texture of an earthy clay body. Pieces made in this tradition are spare and seemingly awkward yet they are carefully made and convey a sense of great sensitivity to detail.

The calligrapher Kenzan Ogata (1663 to 1743), on the other hand, followed an image-oriented approach. In this work Kenzan took cues from painting, fabric imagery, and the Oribe style. While his work was modest in size and the forms were quite simple, the painted imagery was complex and graphic. Kenzan or his brother Korin did the painting and Kenzan oversaw the glazing and the firing. This ware is low fire, painted first with a white slip, then with imagery (often created with a simple black slip), then covered with a clear glaze. A style very similar to Kenzan's work is Kyo-Yoki, (Old Kyoto Ware), a highly graphic style with a strong emphasis on color.

The 19th century was marked by a great interest in technical skill, a very precise imagery, and a good deal of work utilizing the multiple-fire techniques of Ch'ing Dynasty China. In the early decades of the 20th century the Japanese were ready for a revival of interest in the looser, more materials-oriented strategies of earlier periods. This revival was led by Soetsu Yanagi, its ideologist, and the potters Shoji Hamada and Bernard Leach (for more on Leach see the section on English pottery). Hamada and the calligrapher and potter Kitoji Rosanjin are seen as the premier ceramists in the period of Japan's reconstruction after World War II. At present the Japanese ceramists seem to be trying to integrate contemporary, international ceramic styles with their own traditions - often with much success.

Korea

The potters of the Silla Kingdom (about 57 B.C. to 935 A.D.) produced high quality ceremonial tomb ware, particularly covered jars with large pierced feet. This work was thrown on the potter's wheel, high fired in a reduction atmosphere, and left unglazed. Its gray color was derived from a heavy reduction firing with no reoxidation.

During the Koryo period (918 to 1392) the Korean potters came under the influence of the Chinese potters of the Sung Dynasty. They produced vessels with full and generous forms finished with celadon glazes. These pots were often decorated with inlaid clay designs that became the basis for the Mishima work of the Japanese. The Yi Dynasty followed (1392 to 1910) and was marked by work in a similar vein.

At the end of the 1500s Korea was twice invaded by Japan

Covered Jar, Korea, Silla Dynasty (57 B.C. to 935 A.D.), height 4", wheel formed, unglazed, reduction cooling to darken and gray the body.

and finally in 1637 it became a vassal state of China. Nothing of note seems to have been produced there over the next several centuries. Recently, however, in South Korea there has been a renaissance in ceramics by potters taking their lead from contemporary pottery (especially contemporary Japanese pottery) and from a revival of interest in ancient Korean pottery.

The Middle East

The potters of the ancient Middle East are responsible for many of the tools and techniques that are still a very important part of ceramics. These include the potter's wheel, terra sigillatas, and glazes. Pottery began here before 7000 B.C. By 4000 B.C. terra sigillata had been developed and was in common use. Much of this work was monochromatic but many of the most interesting pieces were ornamented with painted imagery. The painted ware of Susa, in Iran, is especially noteworthy for its graphic painted imagery.

The potter's wheel and true glazes were developed in Egypt as early as 3000 B.C. In Iran, during the Achaemenid period (1533 to 330 B.C.) ceramists created large, richly colored, glazed brick wall reliefs for use in royal architecture. The Sassanian period in Iran (3rd to 7th century A.D.) was marked by a decline in interest in ceramics - its rulers had become far more interested in the products of the metal arts.

It took the arrival of Islam in Iran, with its release of new energies, to revive interest in ceramics. Both vessels and tiles were formed using the press-mold process. The Iranian potters concentrated on the creation of ceramic imagery. Many image creation strategies were employed in this low-fire work, the most common being the application of a clear alkaline or lead glaze over painted slips. Ceramists employed many other materials and techniques as well, including the use of low-fire, fritted, white clay bodies made in imitation of porcelain, multicolored slip decoration and luster glazes. The work is elegant and colorful, with a single-minded concentration on rich surface imagery. Richly painted architectural tile work was especially important and large quarters of such Iranian cities as Isfahan became noted for their tile clad buildings.

Europe

We can begin our study of European ceramics with the islands Crete and Cyprus. Both are islands in the Mediterranean Sea closer to the Middle East than to Europe and potters in both places were influenced by the ceramic work of the ancient Middle East.

For the painted wares of Crete and Cyprus (2000 to 1000

B.C.) ceramists threw their vessels on the potter's wheel and employed terra sigillatas to decorate their surfaces with rich fabric-like patterns. The work was then fired to a low temperature.

Vessels from Crete and Cyprus served as precursors for the remarkable painted vases of Greece's golden age. Greek pottery was thrown on the potter's wheel and painted by skillful artists working in terra sigillata. It was then fired to a low temperature. Corinth and Athens were the two great centers of Greek pottery.

Corinth was a center of pottery from 700 to 550 B.C. Its pottery was low fired and thrown on the potter's wheel. Corinth had strong ties to Persia and its potters were strongly influenced by Persian ceramics. The work is noted for a style in which very little open space has been allowed. It is highly patterned and has an ornamental character. Animal images surrounded by florets are most often employed.

The preeminent period of Athenian pottery lasted from about 600 to 400 B.C. These pieces were thrown on the wheel: many are quite large and were thrown with great skill. The forms of Athenian pottery seem to be derived from stone and metal as much as clay. The act of forming was separated from that of painting; the painters were judged to be more important than the potters who threw the forms and indeed the sturdy Athenian pottery forms do seem to serve best as a background for the elegant, stylized painting defined by a sharp sgraffito line. This imagery is at once highly stylized and quite realistic, rich and well thought out. These images give us a vivid picture of Greek life and times. Since this was a time when many of the ideas we believe have shaped our culture were developed, these painted images have great significance for us. This body of work is at once the product of an iron-age technology and a very highly sophisticated imagery. This blend of primitive technology with highly sophisticated ideas is not unique in ceramics but it is carried out with an intensity in Greek ceramic work that is unrivaled.

Ceramics in the Roman Empire

The potters who worked in the Roman Empire created a body of work that has a mass-produced feel and both their ceramic forms and the imagery placed upon these forms are far less ambitious than that created by the Greek potters. True to their reputation for technical innovation, the Roman potters were pioneers in the art of slipcast forming. Much of the work we see from this period was finished with terra sigillatas. Their work did not feature the painted imagery of the Middle East and Greece. Their imagery usually took the form of low relief formed in the mold. A highly organized pottery industry was established by the Romans in many parts of their empire including northern Europe and England. The Romans inherited a flourishing pottery industry in the Near East and potters there continued their practice of using lead glazes.

Between the fall of the Roman Empire and the beginning of the Renaissance, European ceramic work was primarily utilitarian. Surfaces were either unglazed or finished with simple surfaces. Many pieces were finished with a dusting of lead powder (this forms a thin glassy coating on the surface of the piece) or a poured lead glaze. These pieces have a natural character and a lack of pretentiousness that has exercised a great appeal to ceramists of our time.

The Renaissance saw a revival of pottery in Italy under the influence of ceramics from the Islamic world. The Islamic tradition was first exported to Spain, which was under Islamic rule during this period. It was from Spain that the Italian potters learned many of the work strategies that they went on to make their own, including majolica. These Italian wares range widely in imagery from medallion-like patterns to highly painted scenes of myth and history common to the paintings of the time. Ceramic forms are modest and take a back seat to the painted imagery.

Bernard Palissy (1509 to 1590), a French ceramist, worked with the press-mold forming process. He finished his earthenware pieces by painting them with colored lead glazes. A writer as well as a potter, he described his research in the book *De l'art de la terre*. Palissy developed a rich imagery of mold-formed and realistically painted plant and animal life, and allegorical and mythological scenes. During the persecutions of French Protestants (Huguenots) he was imprisoned in Paris and died in prison.

The Development of Porcelain in Europe

During the latter part of the 1600s there was a strong penetration of Chinese export porcelain in Europe. While the methods used in making and firing porcelain were well known in Asia, European ceramists were unable to create a local equivalent. This was in part due to the access Chinese potters had to a white clay material that, as dug from the ground, had in its makeup both clay and feldspar components. It was a natural porcelain. European ceramists had no equivalent material. It only required a proper high firing to become a "true" porcelain. This gave the Chinese ceramists a huge advantage over their counterparts in Europe. The ware imported from China was rare, extremely expensive, and highly desired by members of the ruling classes of Europe. As a result, they strongly encouraged the development of their own version of porcelain.

Finally, in the early 1700s the effort to develop a European version of porcelain was successful. The effort was led by an unlikely pair, Johann Friedrich Böttger, a wandering alchemist, and Ehrenfried Walther von Tschirnhausen, a theoretician interested in creating artificial gems. Von Tschirnhausen had already worked with high temperatures in his experiments in which he tried to create gems, and this was a key to their success in developing porcelain. Sometime between 1705 and 1708 the two men were able to make a hard, dense, red porcelainous clay body, and by 1708 they began to experiment with white porcelain. By 1710 they were beginning to get promising results, and by 1720 they were successful.

Vase, Greco-Roman, Apulian Ware, height 21", attributed to the Arno painter, late 5th century B.C., earthenware, thrown and painted with terra sigillatas. Gift of Mrs. Morton C. Nichols, The Everson Museum, Syracuse, New York. Photo by T.C. Eckersley.

Pitcher, England, The Martin Brothers, height 6¼", wheel formed with engraved imagery, intaglio glazing, salt fired. The Everson Museum, Syracuse, New York. Photo by T.C. Eckersley.

Porcelain making was centered first in Meissen in southeast Germany. Though great effort was expended to keep the process secret, it soon spread to the rest of Europe. Though European porcelain looked similar to Chinese porcelain, it differed from it in its character and ingredients. It was really a very different material. The Chinese made their porcelain from a single white material that is partially clay and partially feldspathic, while the European version required three separate materials - kaolin, feldspar, and silica powder. Though the European product contained fewer impurities and was, therefore, whiter in color, it was much less workable. European porcelain work was highly refined, elegant, and aristocratic. While there is little sense of vitality in the later mass-produced European porcelain work, the

Coffee Pot, England, Thomas Whieldon. Gift of Cynthia B Benjamin, J. Lake Collection, The Everson Museum, Syracuse, New York. Photo by T.C. Eckersley.

early work at its best is marked by a sense of energy and an inventive quality that can be very persuasive.

In the late 19th century, experiments with imagery in Europe derived from the landscape painting of the time and led to a revolution in thinking about ceramics. This was called Barbotine ware. It flourished in France in the mid 1800s. It is a low-fire, slip-decorated ware finished with a clear lead glaze. Ceramics influenced by the Art Nouveau style came somewhat later. Its practitioners employed the same technology as Barbotine ware but its imagery was more highly stylized. The influence of these movements crossed the Atlantic and served as the genesis for the American Art Pottery movement.

In the early part of the 20th century much of the activity in European ceramics was associated with factories and the production of sophisticated luxury goods. In northern Europe ceramists employed simple, reserved forms and glaze treatments to create an elegant and intelligent work. After World War II this approach became very influential, particularly in the Scandinavian countries. In recent years the influence of the factories has ebbed and there has been a great interest in the creation of clay sculpture influenced by avant garde sculpture and painting.

England

Roman and Medieval Pottery in England

During the period of Roman rule a flourishing ceramic manufactory in England was established. Most of the work was in the vessel form and was finished with a red terra sigillata. The imagery took the form of low relief formed in the mold or was slip trailed over a thrown form. A highly organized pottery industry was established by the Romans. When the Romans left Britain in the early 5th century the ceramic infrastructure collapsed and succeeding work was inferior both in terms of technique and aesthetics. Early Medieval pieces were completely unglazed, but by the 13th or 14th century we again see pieces that were glazed. The ceramists created some of these glazed finishes by dusting the surface of the piece with a coating of lead powder (this formed a thin glassy coating on the surface of the piece). In other cases we see a thicker and more uniform glaze made by pouring a liquid glaze over the surface of the piece. Work continued along these lines (with some refinement of technique) for another 300 years.

Staffordshire Ware

Staffordshire is a county in central England. Both coal and clays were found there and it became a center for pottery in the 17th century. Particularly interesting are pieces decorated with slips under a clear lead glaze. The large, highly decorated slip-trailed and lead-glazed platters of Thomas Toft are particularly ambitious and noteworthy examples of the potter's art.

The next century brought a great flowering of technical and aesthetic invention. Staffordshire became a center of ceramic manufacture as the product became more sophisticated in both its technical and aesthetic aspects. Thomas Whieldon (1719 to 1786) was an important early figure during this period. He was born near Stoke-on-Trent in 1719. An innovator, he is well known for salt glazing, agate ware, cream ware, tortoiseshell slip-glazed ware, and for pieces resembling natural forms. Whieldon is also important for his influence on the course of English ceramics influencing the work of Josiah Wedgwood, Josiah Spode, and William Greatbatch.

Josiah Wedgwood (1730 to 1795) began his career from humble beginnings. He founded a firm that continues today. Under his guidance the firm developed a group of remarkable colored clay bodies known as Jasper clay bodies. These bodies were fired to maturity and became very dense. As a result, their surfaces were very rich and they required no glaze. These clay bodies are very unusual and work made with them has a very different look from other ceramic pieces.

In the late 19th century, experiments with imagery in England, derived from contemporaneous thinking about art, led to a whole group of new ceramic movements. These can be placed together in the category of "Arts and Crafts Ceramics."

In 1877 the Martin brothers started a ceramic studio in Southall (now a suburb of London) on the south bank of the Thames. The group was led by Robert Wallace Martin (1843 to 1923), the oldest brother and the most thoroughly trained. He modeled and threw the wares. Charles Douglas Martin (1846 to 1910) managed both the business and a shop where he sold their work in central London. Walter Fraser Martin (1857 to 1912) was the glaze and clay technician and Edwin Bruce Martin (1860 to 1915) was the decorator. The work was first ornamented with colored slips and then fired to a high temperature in a salt glaze kiln. We value the work of the Martin brothers mainly for its imagery marked by a rich sense of fantasy and humor. The Martin brothers have been called pioneers of studio pottery in Britain. Wallace Martin continued work until 1914.

In the 1930s Britain, ceramic work, though discouraged by the great depression, is marked by very interesting work in the Art Deco style. During World War II the use of fuel for creating nonessential objects was not allowed. As England recovered from the war in the 1950s, there was a renewed interest in pottery. This period was molded by the great influence of the work of the potter and writer Bernard Leach (1887 to 1979). In his work a renewed emphasis was placed on the character of the material. Leach, originally trained as a printmaker, learned the craft of ceramics in Japan and he was very influenced by the materials-centered approach of many Japanese ceramists. After a time he returned to England and began to make pottery strongly influenced by his experience in Japan. His influence, first on English ceramists and then on American ceramists, was profound. This influence was expressed in part through his work and in part through his ideas and his writing. Leach's writing is persuasive and always absorbing. He and his assistants threw much of his work on the potter's wheel. This was decorated simply and deftly. They also created tiles and hand-formed vessels. Most of this work was fired in fuel-burning, high-fire reduction kilns. Leach's mission was to bring to potters and those interested in pottery, a concept of simple, useful, and intelligently wrought forms - forms made with craftsmanship and a sense of the material and the process.

Contemporary potters in England tend to be vessel oriented and interested in explorations of ceramic materials and processes. There is a strong wish to blend tradition and contemporary attitudes and little interest in importing ideas from the popular arts, which is such a powerful theme in American ceramics.

Africa

The work of the village potters of Sub-Saharan Africa is an example of the survival of an ancient tradition. Most pieces are produced using a coil and paddle technique. In the hands of a skilled potter (always female) this is an effective method for quickly producing objects of beauty and usefulness. This surface is often ornamented with imagery in relief. It may be combed, stamped, drawn, or made from applied clay forms. It is fired at low temperatures and finished in a polished, monochromatic, carbon-darkened clay surface. The pieces are at once highly functional and elegant. It is reported that in recent years there has been a waning interest in this work as manufactured plastic and metal utensils (admittedly more durable and "convenient") have taken over the market. We

Vase, Nigeria, height 17". Collection of David MacDonald. Photo by Richard Zakin.

can hope that a new market, centering on its aesthetic character, will be established for this work.

Pre-Columbian America

America before Columbus was the site of a number of cultures that made remarkable pottery. Especially important is the pottery of what is now Peru, Panama, Nicaragua, Mexico, and the Southwest United States. This work was fired in bonfires at very low temperatures and finished with terra sigillatas.

Ancient Peru was the site of a number of cultures whose potters created important ceramic work. The Peruvian potters produced work that was intended for tombs and were therefore imbued with a strong sense of purpose. The ware was made in press molds and painted with terra sigillatas. The first important tomb ware from Peru was made by potters of the Chavin de Huantar culture (1800 to 500 B.C.). It is highly modeled and painted with a terra sigillata smoke fired to create a black surface. Applied decoration was mold formed separately and luted to the body of the piece. A little later than the Chavin culture and on Peru's southern coast, the potters of the Paracas culture

worked with mold-made forms that were finished with colorful, resin-based paint.

The Nazca culture (200 B.C. to 600 A.D.) followed the Chavin and the Paracas cultures and was strongly influenced by them. The Nazca potters, however, used a different surface treatment and employed a rich terra sigillata, polychromatic painted imagery. In fact, as many as 13 colored slips have been counted on a single piece.

The Moche culture was based on the northern coast of Peru. It flourished from 200 B.C. to 700 A.D. and thus was nearly contemporary with the Nazca culture but the work was quite different. Its potters produced tomb ware strongly influenced by Chavin pottery. Moche potters specialized in compound press mold forms of great complexity and sculptural character. Perhaps because of the emphasis on sculptural form, color was subdued and was limited (most often to tan and cream colors).

Successor to the Nazca was the Chimu kingdom. Most Chimu pottery is sculptural and form oriented. It is painted with a monochrome black terra sigillata. Chimu work is very uneven in quality. Some of it seems to have been stamped out very quickly and without great care. Other pieces are of very high quality. Because the ware has a very wide

Covered Jar, Nigeria, height 7¾". Gift of Warren Jacqueline Ziegler, The Everson Museum, Syracuse, New York. Photo by T.C. Eckersley.

Jar with stirrup spout, Peru, Chimu Kingdom, A.D. 1100 to the late 1400s, 7¾". Gift of Mr. and Mrs. W. H. G. Murray, The Everson Museum, Syracuse, New York. Photo by T.C. Eckersley.

Footed Vessel, Mexico, Olmec culture, Funerary Urn, 800 to 600 B.C., 11⅜", earthenware, hand or press-mold formed. Gift of Janos Szekere, The Everson Museum, Syracuse, New York. Photo by T.C. Eckersley.

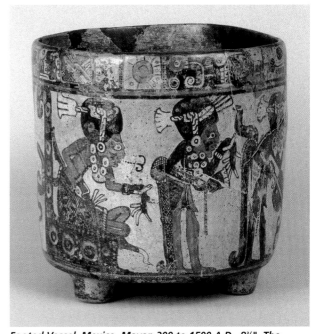

Footed Vessel, Mexico, Mayan 300 to 1500 A.D., 8¾". The Everson Museum, Syracuse, New York. Photo by T.C. Eckersley.

distribution, it has been surmised that many of these pieces were intended as trade items. These would not have received the same attention as pieces for their own funerary use.

In Central America, the first great work came from the Olmec culture in Mexico, which flourished from 1500 B.C. to 200 A.D. The Olmec potters specialized in a highly stylized, figural imagery. Particularly interesting is a group of large scale figurines with unusual baby-like features.

From about 300 to 1500 A.D., in what is now Guatemala, Honduras, and Mexico, Mayan potters created a low-fire pottery with simple and strong forms, finished with terra sigillatas. The essentially linear imagery drawn over the surface of the piece tells us a great deal about the beliefs of these people. The imagery is drawn with vigor and

Vase, Anasazi, 700 to 1200 A.D., height 13½", diameter 13", earthenware. Gift of Mr. and Mrs. Johnathan Holstein, The Everson Museum, Syracuse, New York. Photo by T.C. Eckersley.

intelligence and a flair for characterization.

During the period before the arrival of the Spanish conquerors, ceramists from many Mexican cultures produced noteworthy ceramics. The ceramics of Oaxaca and Vera Cruz in eastern Mexico and Colima in Western Mexico are particularly interesting.

The Nicoya potters from Nicaragua, and Coclé potters from Panama created vigorous, folk-like imagery that appears to be influenced by Mayan pottery.

The American Southwest

The Indians of the American Southwest, both before and after the arrival of the Europeans, created a low-fire painted utilitarian ware that was influenced by pre-Columbian ware from Mexico. The work is highly developed in both form and imagery. Form was developed using carefully executed coil techniques. Early work was often left without applied

surface imagery, later the imagery was created with terra sigillatas.

Anasazi Pottery

Anasazi (from a Navajo Indian word meaning "the ancient ones") is the term archaeologists use to designate the cultures of the prehistoric Basket Makers and the Pueblo Indians of North America who dwelled in the Four Corners region, where Arizona, Colorado, New Mexico, and Utah meet in what is now the southwestern United States. At the time of its greatest extent, the Anasazi culture was spread over most of New Mexico, northern Arizona, southwestern Colorado, and much of Utah. The Anasazi built many of the numerous pueblos (many now in ruins) found in these areas. The climax of Pueblo development was reached during the Pueblo III period (1100 to 1300) and the finest

Bowl, Madeline Naranjo, Santa Clara Pueblo, height 3". Photo by T.C. Eckersley.

examples of corrugated Anasazi pottery come from this period.

Anasazi pottery was of two general types: culinary wares in which the coils were pinched to produce a corrugated effect, and decorated wares with black designs in elaborate patterns on a white background.

The ceramic work of the contemporary Hopi potters has moved far from its utilitarian roots. The ware is both inferior in usability to contemporary cookware and far too expensive to encourage this sort of use. Instead, this work is valued for its elegance, decorative character, and its Indian identity. Such a change of intent may rob objects of their authenticity and strength but this has not happened to this work. Its practitioners zealously guard the tradition and the work remains vigorous even today. As a result contemporary American Indian pottery is very highly regarded and featured in both private and museum collections.

North America Since Columbus

The settlers who came to North America from England and Europe had a very different ceramic tradition from the Native Americans. While it too had a strong utilitarian cast, it was different in character and technology. Some of it was low-fired slip ware and some was high-fired, salt-glazed stoneware; all of it was based on European and English models.

As society in North America evolved toward a goal of cultural democracy, new needs developed. A new, more sophisticated type of ceramics known as American Art Pottery came to serve as an indicator of the social status and aspirations of its owners. American Art Pottery began in 1878 with the creation of the Cincinnati Faience style. This work was highly influenced by the Barbotine style from France. It was fired in low-temperature oxidation kilns and its imagery was derived from low-fire slip painting covered with a clear lead glaze. The Rookwood studio in Cincinnati, Ohio, was the foremost studio producing work in this style.

By the turn of the century other methods of creating

Vase, U.S., Rookwood, 1910, height 8", painted Rookwood, painted by Ed Diers. Photo by T.C. Eckersley.

surface imagery were employed. Noteworthy here were the remarkable pieces of George Ohr and the tiles and vases from the Grueby studio finished with its highly influential "Dead Mat" glazes.

While some art potters worked alone or with a staff of one or two, the typical American Art Pottery establishments were organized on the factory plan. Many jobs were specialized and mass-production methods were used where possible. Many establishments such as Roseville and Fulper, very early in their development, organized themselves along factory lines. After many years of emphasis on handmade work, the highly regarded Rookwood studio turned in the 1920s to a highly industrial model. Pots were no longer hand thrown but rather mold formed and glazes were applied with a sprayer.

Vase, The Fulper Pottery, 1909 to 1930, height 6". Photo by T.C. Eckersley.

Vase, U.S., The Grueby Pottery, circa 1900, 12½", wheel formed with hand-formed coil additions to create the ornament. Earthenware clay body with low-fire "Dead Mat" lead glaze. Gift of the Dorothy and Robert Reister Ceramic Fund, The Everson Museum, Syracuse, New York. Photo by T.C. Eckersley.

Plant Bowl, The Rookwood Pottery, 1921, height 3". Photo by T.C. Eckersley.

Adelaide Alsop Robineau (1865 to 1929) was one of the most famous individual artists working in the Art Pottery movement. She began to work in porcelain in 1904. She threw her work on the wheel and then ornamented it with excised and carved imagery. She then glazed it with the beautiful but difficult to use crystal and flowing mat glazes. Her work is especially noteworthy for its rich and inventive surfaces requiring skill and patience. Robineau's work

conveys a spirit of great intensity and coherence.

In the 1930s ceramic work was discouraged by the great depression. During World War II the fuel necessary for firing was directed instead to the war effort, further discouraging ceramic production. After the war a few of the factories (most notably Roseville) tried to recover their position but soon faded away. Instead there was a renewed interest in pottery made by artisans working on an individual basis. This approach to clay, strongly advocated by Bernard Leach, soon became the model for American ceramists. This led to the widespread use of warm-colored, reduction-fired clay bodies and glazes marked by strong visual textures. This utilitarian pottery tended to be emphatically thrown: its mood emphasized its ties to nature and the earth. Its prevailing mood was serious and reverential. For a time this movement swept all other approaches aside.

Perhaps in reaction, a movement called Funk or Pop Pottery evolved on the west coast of the United States in the late 1960s. The movement's practitioners claimed to have little interest in the material basis of ceramics, they wanted to create strong imagery. They borrowed freely from popular culture and attitudes of irreverence and irony. Its technology was also borrowed: the Funk potters used the prepared clays and glazes that had been developed to meet the needs of ceramic hobbyists, a group long held in low esteem by those who thought of themselves as ceramic artists. This work was fired in the electric kiln (also at the time held in low esteem).

Contemporary Ceramics in the U.S. and Canada

By the early 1980s references to popular culture and to tongue-in-cheek humor were set aside in favor of thoughtful explorations of color and form. In the 1990s up to the

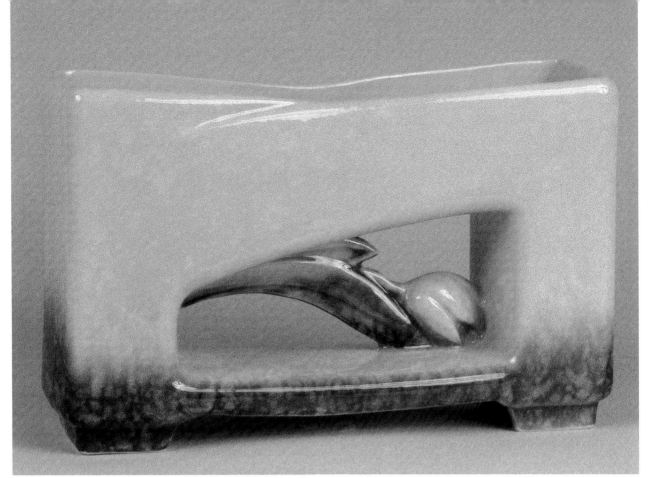

Vase, Roseville Pottery, "Wincraft," 1948, height 6½". Photo by T.C. Eckersley.

Sculpture, U.S., William Parry, ca. 1960, height 15". Photo by T.C. Eckersley.

Ruth McKinley, Teapot, Canada, ca. 1965, height 5". Photo by T.C. Eckersley.

Adelaide Alsop Robineau, "The Crab Vase," 1908, height 7⅜". Photo by T.C. Eckersley.

present ceramists have continued working along these lines, placing great emphasis on sculptural form in vessels and on figural sculpture in which there is a strong desire to blur the lines between craft and art. Due to increased opportunities for travel and the influence of international publications, there has been movement to a heightened internationalism in the field and a greater interest and knowledge in work from many parts of the world. The situation of Canadian ceramists is particularly interesting. They have had a high level of support from government and government-sponsored education and an influence on ceramics in North America disproportionate to their numbers. They have tended to blend the influence of their contemporaries in the United States with that of England and Europe.

Footed Vase, Daniel Rhodes, ca. 1950 to 1960, height 12". Photo by T.C. Eckersley.

Appendix A
Analysis in Ceramics

Many ceramists use analysis methods in their work. Analysis is defined as the separation of a whole into its component parts. Analysis can be concerned with the material aspects of ceramics or it can be concerned with an intangible, such as a process. We ceramists have a number of very important roles for analysis in our work. These roles include:

➤The analysis of ceramic recipes based on their oxide makeup.
➤The analysis of ceramic recipes based on their material makeup.
➤The analysis of surface creation strategies.

Analyzing the Oxides in Ceramic Recipes

Oxides are compounds of an element and oxygen. The most common type of analysis in ceramics is the analysis of the oxides in a clay body, slip, or glaze recipe. To do this we use an analysis procedure in which we calculate the amount of each of the oxides in all of the materials in the recipe. This can be an invaluable tool to help us understand why a recipe acts as it does. It can also help us develop new recipes. This kind of analysis is important because we make our ceramic recipes, clay bodies, slips, engobes, and glazes from complex compounds. Ceramists have used most of these compounds for millennia. There is a great body of knowledge of the way they behave in a wide variety of recipe types and firing temperatures. Like all compounds they are made up of two or more elements, some are very complex and contain as many as eight or nine elements. In our recipes we typically combine five to eight of these complex compounds. Many recipes, therefore, contain a whole group of elements derived from many sources. This complexity creates rich glazes but makes analysis a complex proposition. It is not possible to track the total element makeup of any recipe

without the aid of analysis tools and it is difficult to learn how to use such tools. Typically, glaze analysis is learned only by the most advanced students of ceramics.

Contemporary ceramists use computers and computer programs to carry out these analyses. Before access to computers became widespread we were required to employ complex, tedious procedures to carry out an analysis of the oxides in recipes. These procedures demanded a great deal of patience, they were liable to error, took a long time to learn, and were difficult to use. Now we have access to computer programs that automate the process and the analysis procedure is nearly instantaneous.

The Analysis Format

The most common analysis method is called molecular analysis. To summarize the molecular analysis process, we first find the type and amounts of the oxides contributed by each material in the recipe. We then add up the total of each oxide and place it in a standardized format.

In the molecular analysis process the weight of the compound in a recipe is converted to a figure which represents the relative number of the molecules of each of the oxides in that compound. In this way the molecular analysis method takes into account the differing densities of materials. Because it is based on the relative number of molecules of each oxide in the recipe, it can give us a special view of the role of each element in the recipe.

The molecular analysis is presented in a format in which the oxides are listed by molecular type. The ceramist places the oxides in a chart format divided into three parts. The first are fluxes, which have one (or more) atom of the fluxing element and one oxygen atom (RO). The fluxes encourage silica to melt. Various fluxes encourage melting at different parts of the temperature range. In the second group are stabilizers, which have two atoms of the element plus three of oxygen (R_2O_3). They stabilize the glaze and control glaze

Glaze Oxides Categorized by Oxide Structure

Alkaline - RO/R$_2$O	Neutral - R$_2$O$_3$	Acid - RO$_2$
Barium (BaO)	alumina (Al$_2$O$_3$)	silica (SiO$_2$)
Calcium (CaO)	boron (B$_2$O$_3$)	tin (SnO$_2$)
Lead (PbO)	iron (Fe$_2$O$_3$)	titanium (TiO$_2$)
Lithium (Li$_2$O)		zirconium (ZrO$_2$)
Magnesium (MgO)		
Potassium (K$_2$O)		
Sodium (Na$_2$O)		
Strontium (Sr$_2$O)		
Zinc (ZnO)		

melt and crystallization, thereby controlling glaze flow. The third type is the glass-forming oxides. These have one atom of the element in question plus two of oxygen (RO$_2$). The theory here is that oxides of the same type will act in a similar manner. This is especially useful in pointing out the role of the fluxes and stabilizing oxides in influencing the melt and the role of silica (the prime glass former) in giving the glaze its glassy nature.

Glaze Oxides Categorized by Oxide Structure

The analysis is now normalized (brought into unity). The total of the flux column is used as a "factor." All columns (including the first) are divided by this factor number. In this way the second and third columns are written in ratio to the oxides in the first. For example:

Sample Glaze Recipe
65 nepheline syenite
19 whiting
02 zinc oxide
12 kaolin

Sample Glaze Molecular Analysis

alkalies	neutral	acid
(zinc, calcium	(alumina)	(silica)
sodium & potassium)		

Na$_2$O .296	Al$_2$O$_3$ .567	SiO$_2$ 2.09
K$_2$O .098		
CaO .536		
ZnO .067		

Because all the oxides are factored by the sum of the alkaline column, the strength of this format lies in its clear expression of the relationship of the oxides to each other. To the ceramist who uses this system a great deal, this reveals a great deal about the glaze. The first column tells the ceramist what the major fluxes are and the number of molecules of any flux in the glaze. Next the ceramist will look at the ratio of silica to alumina by dividing the silica amount by the amount of alumina to reveal the silica to alumina ratio. In this recipe the ratio is 3.71 to 1. This tells the ceramist that this recipe is going to be a mat glaze. Now, looking at the fluxes it is easy to see that there is more calcium in the list than any other oxide and it will be the most significant flux. This will be a calcium mat glaze.

Percent by Weight Analysis

Another system has been developed in which the ceramist tracks the oxides in the ceramic recipe using a percent by weight format. This method does not enable the ceramist to deal with the density of the different materials but it is easier to grasp than the molecular method. There are ceramists who prefer the percentage analysis method because it is easy to grasp its results - they value it for its simplicity and clarity. In the percent by weight method you simply multiply the amount of the material in the recipe by a listing (of the percent of the whole) of the element oxides in that material. You then normalize the oxide total to 100%.

Most computer analysis programs offer the percentage method as an alternative to the molecular format. The percentage format always lists the results in percentages of 100%. This makes it easy to compare one percentage analysis with another and with many others. It emphasizes relations between recipes while the Unity Formula format emphasizes the relationships of the various oxides within a single glaze. For example:

Sample Recipe
65 nepheline syenite
19 whiting
02 zinc
12 kaolin

Percentage Analysis

SiO$_2$: 51.1	Al$_2$O$_3$: 22.3	
K$_2$O: 4.0	Na$_2$O: 7.8	CaO: 12.3
ZnO: 2.3	Fe$_2$O$_3$: 0.1	

Analyzing a recipe.

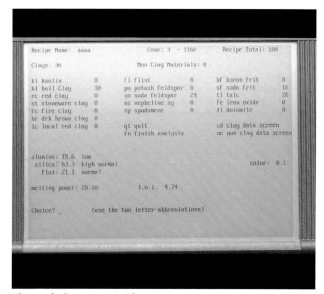

The analysis as seen on the computer screen.

For someone who uses it a great deal, this system too reveals a great deal about the makeup of the glaze. The ceramist sees the oxides listed by percentage and from this listing can quickly come to an understanding of the major oxides and their percentages in the glaze. The listing we see here reveals a fairly high percentage of alumina and a moderate percentage of silica. This points to a mat glaze. Now, looking at the fluxes it is easy to see that there is more calcium in the list than any other oxide and it will be the most significant flux. So here too in this analysis we see that this will be a calcium mat glaze.

New Developments

Ten years ago it was predicted that computers would revolutionize the process of recipe analysis. This revolution has now taken place. In computer-aided analysis you open the analysis program and enter the recipe. All the information needed to perform the analysis has been written into the program. The program performs the computation and the answer is given in a matter of seconds. The computer program automatically puts the analysis into the appropriate format. These computer programs are powerful analysis tools. They make it possible to quickly and easily analyze recipes. They are reasonably priced and available for most computers including those running Apple and Windows operating systems.

Analysis formats are tools for representing information we need. We have inherited analyses formats appropriate for use by chemists but perhaps not as useful to most ceramists. This includes the way we list numbers of molecules (the unity system), the placement of the data on the page, and the whole idea that numbers are the best way to show the results. We now look forward to a time when ceramists will use new formats to analyze our recipes.

The most promising format for ceramists may be graphic representation. Instead of representing the analysis in numeric terms, it is a simple matter to write a computer program that will represent the element components of a glaze graphically in the form of a diagram or chart. Since ceramists are visual people there are great advantages to this approach. A number of observers predict that in the future all analysis systems intended for use by studio ceramists will feature this format for presenting oxide analyses.

Interpreting and Using Molecular Analysis Figures

Once a molecular analysis is completed, you must learn how to interpret and use the results. These tasks may be accomplished in two ways: by comparing the analysis with analyses of other similar recipes and by comparing the analysis to a group of limit formulas (these list minimum and maximum values for oxides in particular recipe types). Both methods can help you predict a great deal about the way a new recipe will work.

To use limit formulas you compare the recipe to the limit formulas to see if any oxides appear in amounts that are too low or too high. These can be a sign of an improperly written recipe. The limit formulas allow a lot of latitude in guiding you to the proper use of an element in a recipe. Limit formulas are not a perfect solution. They can keep you from making really foolish mistakes but they may prejudice you against really interesting recipes that stray from the usual glaze types.

The limits listed below are based on the idea that the silica, alumina, and flux ratio should remain consistent from one firing temperature to another. If this strategy is employed, the ceramist varies the recipe from one temperature to another not by changing the amount of silica, alumina, or flux in the recipe, but by varying the melting range of the fluxes.

Glaze Building Recommendations

For Molecular Analysis Systems

For the low fire:

Na_2O/K_2O .04-1.0   CaO/MgO 0-1.0
ZnO 0-.28 B_2O_3 .08-1.4
Al_2O_3 .01-1.0 SiO_2 .90-6.0
Li_2O 0-.2

For the mid fire:

Na_2O/K_2O .04-1.0   CaO/MgO 0-1.0
ZnO 0-.28 B_2O_3 .03-1.3
Al_2O_3 .2-1.0 SiO_2 2-6.0

For the high fire:

Na_2O/K_2O .1-1.0   CaO/MgO 0.0-1.0
ZnO 0.0-.28 B_2O_3 0.0-.5
Al_2O_3 .2-1.0 SiO_2 2-6.0

Limit Formulas for Percentage Systems

For the low fire:

K_2O/Na_2O 4-11 B_2O_3 5-18
ZnO 0-3 TiO_2 to 0-3
CaO/MgO 0-11 Li_2O 0-3
Al_2O_3 10-15 SiO_2 45-70

For the mid fire:

K_2O/Na_2O 4-11 B_2O_3 3-16,
ZnO 0-3 TiO_2 0-3
CaO/MgO 0-11 Li_2O 0-3
Al_2O_3 10-20 SiO_2 45-70

For the high fire:

K_2O/Na_2O 4-11   CaO/MgO 8-28
B_2O_3 0-10   ZnO 0-3
TiO_2 0-3 Li_2O 0-2
Al_2O_3 10-20 SiO_2 45-70

Appendix B
Materials-Based Creation and
Evaluation of Ceramic Recipes

Not all ceramists use calculated analysis procedures to evaluate and create glaze recipes; in fact, the majority do not. The noted potter and author Robin Hopper has written the following about glaze analysis: "From my experience over 30 years of teaching and making pots, I can honestly say that I have almost never seen a calculated glaze that was better than those produced by a solid, sensitive, empirical understanding of the materials we use." (*Ceramics Monthly*, Sept. 1988). Hopper is advocating here an approach that is based on the ceramist's understanding of the character of the materials as opposed to the approach that requires the ceramist to break ceramic materials down to create a representation of their constituent elements.

As Hopper points out, this method is based on an understanding of a recipe as a group of materials rather than of its constituent elements. Most experienced ceramists can and do evaluate glazes in this way. Some see it as a quick way to assess a recipe before carrying out an analysis of its oxides, others find that this procedure is the only one they need. They can do a good job of "reading" the recipe and are able to develop an intuitive understanding of its overall character. In this method the ceramist first tries to get a feel for the materials in a recipe and the elements that they are contributing. It is these factors which most influence the character of the glaze at any given firing temperature. This acts as a kind of quick snapshot of the glaze - it is somewhat imprecise and is certainly not state of the art, but it is simply carried out and very useful.

While this method has generally been carried out in a wholly intuitive manner, it can be organized in such a way as to combine the advantages of the intuitive approach with the organization we associate with a numerical-based analysis. It then becomes a much more effective and widely useful method for appraising ceramic recipes.

In the first part of this section you will see guidelines for

glaze recipes: both general guidelines for all glazes and specific guidelines for glazes at various firing temperatures. The second part is a demonstration of the way this method can be used to solve common problems such as interpreting, adapting, or developing a glaze recipe.

General Guidelines for Glazes of Any Firing Temperature

In this system the ceramist divides the glaze materials into clays (mostly silica and alumina), feldspars and frits (silica, alumina, flux), silica powder (100% talc and wollastonite - silica and flux), and finally other materials, that contain no silica or alumina but whose ingredients exercise an influence on the character of the glaze.

Clays Useful in Glazes

➤Kaolin
➤Stoneware clay
➤Ball clay
➤Red clay

Clays enhance the viscosity or stiffness of the glaze; they keep it from running off the piece during the firing. The darker glaze clays can also modify glaze color - stoneware clays and red clays have significant impurities and will darken the glaze.

A 2% to 7% clay content in a glaze encourages shiny surfaces, 8% to 14% satin or mat surfaces, any amount above 15% will in most circumstances encourage mat or dry surfaces. A glaze is likely to be successful if its total clay content is 2% to 20%.

Feldspars

The feldspars contain silica, alumina and soda, and potassium. Feldspars encourage melting, durability, and stability in glazes. At cone 6 and above they can usefully serve as the central material in the glaze. Those feldspars with the most sodium are called soda feldspars, those with the most potassium are called potash feldspars. A few contain lithium (spodumene and lepidolite). It is suggested that lithium feldspars not be used in amounts more than 20% as in higher amounts they can encourage a poor glaze fit.

Frits

Frits contain silica, alumina, and fluxes. There are many frits - those that contain the fluxes boron, sodium, and calcium are the most common. Like feldspars, they encourage melting, durability, and stability in glazes. Almost always they encourage earlier melts than the feldspars and so are especially useful in low-fire glazes. Frits, as is the case with feldspars, can usefully serve as the central material in the glaze. Frits and feldspars can also be combined to create a useful glaze recipe for the low- or mid -fire range.

A glaze is likely to be successful if its total feldspar and frit content is 50% to 85%.

Talc and Wollastonite

These contain calcium or magnesium combined with silica. They are very useful in clay bodies and to a lesser extent in glaze recipes.

Ground Silica or Flint

This is 100% silica. By itself silica is refractory (requires very high temperatures to melt). However, it is readily melted by those materials that act as fluxes. Ground silica is especially useful in glazes that need to be very glassy such as transparent glazes.

Materials That Contain No Silica or Alumina
- Dolomite
- Whiting
- Magnesium carbonate
- Strontium
- Titanium (at 1% to 3%)
- Zinc (at 1% to 3%)

These cannot form a glaze but can influence the character of the glaze. The two materials at the end of the list, titanium and zinc, can be very useful if you understand their behavior. Small amounts (up to 3%) of zinc and titanium encourage strong melting, stable and durable surfaces, and are useful in recipes for most firing temperatures. They encourage very different dry, mat surfaces when used in large amounts, 8% to 20%.

Tin and zirconium opacifiers can be added to the glaze to encourage opacity. Tin encourages rich, satiny surfaces and rich color. It is expensive, however. Zirconium is much less expensive than tin and generally does a fine job. It can discourage melting, especially in the low fire but the ceramist can compensate for this by adding materials (such as frits) that contain significant amounts of a low-temperature flux, especially boron.

Guidelines for Specific Firing Temperatures

Cone 04

Requires the most powerful melting materials.

- Sodium or boron frits - 45% to 85%
- Soda feldspar - up to 40%
- Spodumene - up to 20%
- 04 glazes are likely to be successful if total frit and feldspar content is 65% to 90%
- Powdered silica - up to 10%
- Calcium or magnesium silicate such as talc or wollastonite - up to 15%
- Magnesium carbonate, dolomite, or whiting may be useful in amounts up to 5%
- Titanium or zinc for strong melts - up to 3%
- Opacifiers - tin oxide is suggested in amounts up to 3%

Note: Though they are wonderful fluxes at cone 04, I do not discuss the use of lead containing compounds due to their toxicity.

Cone 02

Much less demanding, simple to create, lead-free, durable, formulations.

- Sodium or boron frits - 45% to 85%
- Nepheline syenite or soda or potash feldspar - up to 30%
- Spodumene - up to 20%
- 02 glazes are likely to be successful if total frit and feldspar content is 60% to 85%
- Powdered silica - up to 10%
- Calcium or magnesium silicate such as talc or wollastonite - up to 15%
- Magnesium carbonate, dolomite, or whiting may be useful in amounts up to 10%
- Titanium or zinc for strong melts - up to 3%
- Opacifiers: tin oxide - up to 3%, zirconium compounds - up to 10%

Cone 3

Still requires fluxes that melt strongly at low temperatures. Sodium and boron frits, feldspars, and spodumene are very useful in these glazes. Both tin oxide and zirconium compounds are useful as opacifiers.

- ➤ Sodium or boron frits - 10% to 60%
- ➤ Nepheline syenite, potash or soda spar - up to 70%
- ➤ Spodumene - up to 20%
- ➤ Cone 3 glazes are likely to be successful if total frit and feldspar content is 50% to 85%
- ➤ Powdered silica - up to 20%
- ➤ Calcium or magnesium silicate such as talc or wollastonite - up to 30%
- ➤ Magnesium carbonate, dolomite, or whiting may be useful in amounts up to 15%
- ➤ Titanium or zinc - for strong melts - up to 3%. For mat surfaces - up to 12%
- ➤ Opacifiers: tin oxide - up to 3%, zirconium compounds - up to 10%

Cone 6

Has much of the character of the high fire; can have less emphasis on low-temperature fluxes.

- ➤ Sodium or boron frits - up to 40%
- ➤ Feldspars nepheline syenite, potash, or soda spar - up to 50%
- ➤ Spodumene - up to 20%
- ➤ Cone 6 glazes are likely to be successful if total frit and feldspar content is 50% to 85%
- ➤ Powdered silica, calcium, or magnesium silicate such as talc or wollastonite - up to 20%
- ➤ Magnesium carbonate, dolomite, or whiting - up to 20%
- ➤ Titanium or zinc for strong melts - up to 3%, for mat surfaces - up to 12%
- ➤ Opacifiers: tin oxide - up to 3%, zirconium compounds - up to 12%

Cone 9

The big difference between cone 9 and cone 6 is the action of calcium/magnesium containing materials. They become powerful fluxes by cone 8. Potash feldspars are particularly well suited to this temperature and most cone 9 recipes contain them. Spodumene is also a useful cone 9 feldspar, not for its strong melting power but because it encourages exciting colors and visual textures. Boron/calcium frits of moderate melting power are useful in amounts under 40% but more powerful frits may cause overmelting.

- ➤ Boron/calcium frits of moderate melting power - up to 40%
- ➤ Sodium/boron frits - up to 10%

- ➤ Nepheline syenite and soda feldspar - up to 40%, potash feldspar - up to 80%
- ➤ Spodumene - up to 20%
- ➤ Cone 9 glazes are likely to be successful if total frit and feldspar content is 50% to 85%
- ➤ Powdered silica - up to 20%
- ➤ Calcium or magnesium silicate, such as talc or wollastonite - up to 40%
- ➤ Magnesium carbonate, dolomite, or whiting - up to 40%
- ➤ Titanium or zinc for strong melts - up to 3%, for mat surfaces - up to 12%
- ➤ Opacifiers: tin oxide - up to 3%, zirconium compounds - up to 12%

How the System is Used

Interpreting a Glaze Recipe

You may need to be able to look at a glaze recipe in a magazine or book and see if it is worth trying. This can be done with these charts. Use the following recipe intended for cone 6 as an example:

Whiting	54
Titanium dioxide	02
Potash feldspar	30
Ball clay	10

Using the guidelines for feldspars and frits, we see that this recipe has a total of only 30% feldspar. Dolomite, whiting, and titanium dioxide total 60%. Therefore it is much lower in silica sources than is suggested in the general guidelines. This would not be a stable glaze.

The following glaze recipe, with the same materials in very different proportions would work well: it is within the limits for clay, feldspar, and fluxes that contain no silica or alumina.

Whiting	24
Titanium dioxide	02
Soda spar	64
Ball clay	10

In another example we look at a cone 02 recipe:

Boron frit	56
Ball clay	14
Whiting	28
Zinc	02

While this glaze conforms to the general guidelines it does not conform to the guidelines for cone 02 - its whiting content is too high for a cone 02 recipe and the resulting glaze will most likely be underfired.

Adapting a Glaze - Materials Substitutions

These charts can be used as a basis for making materials substitutions. Frits and feldspars are similar in their basic structure and tend to vary mostly in their flux content. Simply substitute any frit or feldspar for the frit or feldspar in the recipe. Clays too are fairly uniform in their basic structure, though the amount and type of their impurities may vary. It is useful to substitute one clay for another in the recipe since these substitutions will significantly alter the look of the fired glaze while retaining much of its basic character.

Similarly, one flux can be substituted for another. This method can also be used to adapt a glaze recipe for use with new materials or a new firing temperature. For example:

Ball clay	05
Potash feldspar	45
Silica powder (flint)	20
Whiting	26
Titanium	04

You can substitute a red clay for the ball clay and in this way darken the glaze. The recipe has now been adapted from a light color to one which is dark. The substitution of frit for feldspar allows you to increase the melting range, thereby making it useful at a lower firing temperature.

Red clay	05
Boron frit	45
Flint	20
Whiting	26
Titanium	04

Developing a New Glaze Recipe

You can use this method to develop a new glaze recipe. Start with an appropriate figure for the clay, move on to the feldspars and frits, then to the materials that modify the melt. For example, to build a cone 3 glaze I did the following:

New Glaze #1

Potash feldspar	47
Boron frit	16
Ball clay	18
Dolomite	16
Tin oxide	03

The guidelines allow for 2% to 20% clay. In this example I chose to use 18% clay to encourage a satin mat glaze surface. From 50% to 80% total feldspar and frit is suggested; from these figures I chose to use 47% potash feldspar and 16% boron frit (I anticipated that this would encourage a satin shiny or shiny surface). I finished the glaze by adding dolomite, a moderately powerful flux at cone 3, in the amount of 16%. I also added 2% tin oxide (and brought the recipe to 100%). This percentage of tin encourages opacity and satin glaze surfaces.

I never tested this recipe because I wanted to create a glaze with a good deal of visual texture. I assume that it would have been an acceptable glaze with a simple, smooth surface. I wanted, however, to make this glaze more interesting. I did the following:

New Glaze #2 (Estacada Green)

Potash feldspar	27
Spodumene	20
Boron frit	16
Red clay	18
Dolomite	16
Tin oxide	03

Copper carbonate 2%

I first changed the feldspar by subtracting 20% from the potash spar and putting spodumene in its place. Spodumene is a fine feldspar in cone 3 glazes because it encourages strong melting and rich visual textures. I also changed the clay from ball clay to red clay to encourage a rich earthy color. I added copper carbonate to make a green glaze. This recipe looked much more promising on paper and upon firing we found that it was green in color where it was thick and earth orange where it was thin, resulting in a rich color contrast. It went on to become a favorite in the studio.

Combining Materials-Based and Molecular Analysis Approaches

I feel that there are advantages to both the materials-based analysis approach and those analysis types that allow you to break the recipe down into its molecular and element parts. Therefore, I like to employ some sort of blending of the two. I most often begin the development of a glaze or group of glazes by taking the materials-oriented approach. I then analyze the resulting recipes to see if they seem promising. At this point the recipes exist only on paper. If both the recipes and the analyses seem promising, I make up a small sample of each of the glazes to test them in the fire. I do this work with the knowledge that the only results that really count are the ones that come from the kiln.

Other Analysis Strategies

While contemporary ceramists most commonly use element analysis, other analysis strategies are also useful. Two of these are database analysis and image creation analysis.

Using Database Tools to Analyze the Impact of Materials and Oxides in Recipes

A database is a computer program that allows you to store and analyze data. It can also be built into another program such as an analysis program to increase its usefulness. Most ceramists begin their work with a database program in order to store their glaze recipes. Because the program can help you find your recipes very quickly, it is a far more flexible storage medium than a paper-based notebook or card file.

A few of the best computer analysis programs include well-integrated databases. Two of these are *HyperGlaze* and *Insight*. These help you store data and examine the data from various points of view. There are great advantages to having both calculation and database resources linked into one package. These integrated databases let you carry out a number of important tasks. To begin, you enter the recipe title, the recipe, and the analysis. This will enable you to go beyond using the database to help you find a particular recipe by its name, for this is only a small part of its power. For example, you will also be able to use the database to help you find all recipes that contain titanium or all that have a high feldspar content. To harness this power you may learn to use the sorting and filtering tools built into the database.

Sorting Recipe Data

The sorting procedure allows you to place the recipes in any order; most ceramists start out by sorting by cone range and within each cone range, by name. Many stop at this point. Of course you can do these things with a box full of index cards. The next task, however, cannot be easily or quickly performed with the index cards - you can perform a sort with a special purpose in mind.

Example #1
Sorting each recipe by its silica content. This will tell you a great deal about the effect of silica in your recipes.

Example #2
Sorting each recipe by both its silica and alumina content. This will tell you how these two in tandem influence your recipes.

Example #3
Sorting each recipe by its talc content. This will help you understand the impact of various amounts of talc on your clay body recipes.

Filtering

Filtering is a selection process. It too lets you select for any field criteria you like; this will allow you to select all recipes that contain a particular material or combination of materials. You can filter your recipe list so that, temporarily, only those recipes appear which have an ingredient or characteristic you are interested in finding. You can also select recipes that contain a material in a particular range of values.

Example #1
Filtering to eliminate all recipes that contain 60% or more soda feldspar.

Example #2
Filtering to eliminate all recipes that do *not* contain 2% to 6 % titanium dioxide.

Example #3
Filtering to eliminate all cone 3 glazes in the database that are not mat. In this way you will be able to find the common aspects of cone 3 mat glazes. To begin you need to establish a field that allows you to characterize the degree of matness or shininess of the glazes in the database. Now you can use a filtering tool to temporarily filter out all recipes that are not mat. You then can look for the causes of matness, for example, looking at materials such as clay and magnesium as causes of matness in your recipes. You may also wish to track the effects of an element such as boron on matness. Many databases allow you to sort by three or four fields in descending order. This allows you to use these procedures to track the interaction of two or even three materials.

The result here is more than a way to track an individual glaze recipe and its ingredients. It is far more powerful than that. The power of the computer to allow us to organize information has turned this into an analysis system based on a pragmatic approach. This is a way to study new recipes by comparing them with others that we are familiar with. As you may have realized, this does not have to be a substitute for traditional analysis systems, it can enhance their usefulness.

Image Creation Analysis

You may find that your application procedures have a greater impact on the look of your work than glaze recipes. If you are in this group, you may find that a system that helps you track application procedures can be extremely helpful. The question is: are recipes the most important influence on the look of the work or is what we do with our recipes as important? The next question is: if application is important, can we track it and does such an analysis tell us anything important?

I personally have started to develop this system because I am one of those who finds that my application strategies strongly influence the look of my work. I have found it to be a useful analysis strategy. It is my hope that others will take up this system and find it as helpful as I have.

A tile piece made from low-clay content clay bodies.

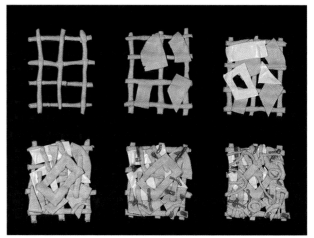

A group of sequential tiles used to map the way a complex tile imagery was constructed.

Visual Material: The Image Creation Diagram

This is a two-part analysis instrument. The first part is a diagram of the image creation process. This will show us a diagram created by combining a photograph with drawings.

Text-Based Material

The second part of this procedure is text based. This part of the analysis procedure supplements and gives detail to the diagrammatic material. In the text-based part of this program track the following:

➤ Background material - name, place of origin, date.
➤ Image tracking - text-based step-by-step descriptions of the image creation process.
➤ Firing - temperature, type, and atmosphere and kiln type.

Creating an Image Creation Diagram
➤ Take a photograph of the piece using good quality color print film.
➤ Cut the background away, leaving a photograph of the profile of the piece.
➤ Mount the photograph on a piece of paper.
➤ Next to the photograph draw the various layers of clay, slip, and glaze.

➤ Indicate a sprayed glaze that trails off with a slanted edge and a dipped or poured glaze with a straight edge.
➤ Fill in the layers with color. In this illustration colored pencils have been used to draw in the color.

This procedure, as you see it here, blends photographic and hand-drawn imagery to produce the image creation diagram. It is used with computer-generated text.

It has now become possible to create and store the images as well as the text electronically using computer writing and a drawing programs, imaging devices, and data storage media. This seems to be the direction that this kind of analysis will take. It allows for the easy and inexpensive storage and distribution of the image creation diagrams.

Metric and the U.S. Customary Systems of Measurement

For a long time we in the English-speaking world used a system of weights and measures of very ancient origin called *The English System of Weights and Measures.* Then the English abandoned this system and adopted the metric system. The metric system is the official system in the United States as well, but we stubbornly cling to the older system in everyday practice. For want of a better term the older system is now called the *U.S. Customary System.* Ceramists, however, have specific needs that are often best met with the metric system. Contemporary ceramists in North America favor the metric system of weight and size measurements for many of their measurement tasks because they are much more precise than their equivalents in the U.S. Customary system. To further complicate the situation we tend to favor the U.S. Customary system of temperature listing because it is convenient and familiar. Therefore, almost all of us weigh our recipes in grams and kilograms but many of us still use the Customary

A Roseville pot.

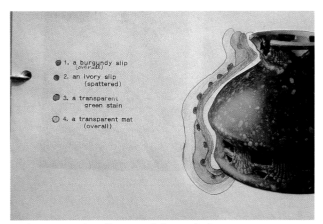

1. a burgundy slip (overall)
2. an ivory slip (spattered)
3. a transparent green stain
4. a transparent mat (overall)

An image creation diagram of the analysis.

scale to specify the temperature inside our kilns. This mixing of systems makes sense in terms of convenience if not of logic. The situation in Canada is somewhat different because the Canadian government has made a concerted effort to persuade its citizens to convert to the metric system.

Conversion Charts

You may encounter directions or descriptions in which the ceramist has used a system of measurement that you do not often use. The following charts have been written to help you convert these citations into ones you can use.

Size

U.S.	Metric
1" = 2.5 cm	1 cm = .39"
10" = 25.4 cm	10 cm = 3.9"
100" = 254 cm	100 cm = 39.3"

Weight

U.S.	Metric
1 oz. = 28.3 gr.	1 gr. = .03 oz.
1 lb. = 453.6 gr.	10 gr. = .35 oz.
10 lbs. = 4536 gr.	100 gr. = 3.52 oz.
(4.5 kilograms)	

1000 gr. (1 kilogram) = 35.2 oz (2.2 lbs.)
5000 gr. (5 kilograms) = 11 lbs.

Temperature

U.S.	Metric
32°F = 0°C	0°C = 32°F
70°F = 21°C	21°C = 70°F
212°F = 212°C	100°C = 212°F
500°F = 260°C	200°C = 392°F
1000°F = 537°C	500°C = 932°F
1400°F = 760°C	800°C = 1472°F
1600°F = 871°C	900°C = 1652°F
1800°F = 982°C	1000°C = 1832°F
2000°F = 1093°C	1100°C = 2012°F
2100°F = 1149°C	1150°C = 2102°F
2200°F = 1204°C	1200°C = 2192°F
2300°F = 1260°C	1250°C = 2282°F
2400°F = 1315°C	1300°C = 2372°F
2500°F = 1371°C	1400°C = 2552°F

Appendix C
In the Studio

A ceramic studio is a complex workplace. In these sometimes chaotic spaces we spend a great deal of our lives; we owe it to ourselves and our work to make them as easy to work in and as safe as possible.

The Work Space

Ceramic work spaces may be in a garage, a basement, a side room, or a building dedicated to clay work. The floor should be washable, either bare cement or covered with linoleum and should be fitted with a drain in the floor. There should be provision for the ventilation of dust and fumes. Adequate overhead lighting is essential. A sink is very useful.

The worktable, work stand, and potter's wheel should be designed for safety and should be comfortable. Unfortunately, worktables that are too high or too low, or potter's wheels that encourage back strain are common. As you design your studio space keep comfort and efficiency in mind. The way you arrange your work space can make a big difference in the way you work and your level of fatigue at the end of the day.

Plan your studio by mapping your work space. Do this by hand on a large sheet of graph paper or use room planning computer software. It is a good idea to make a three-dimensional scale model of your wheel, worktables, storage areas, glazing areas, and kiln. You can shift and arrange these shapes with an eye to safety, convenience, and efficiency. This kind of modeling is fun and will help you design a studio that will be a good place to work.

Studio Equipment

Basic Tools and Furnishings

➤ Worktables
➤ Potter's wheel (a necessity for some, optional for others)
➤ Forming tools
➤ Shelves for work
➤ Shelves for materials
➤ Stool or chair
➤ Damp storage
➤ Sink
➤ Sprayer
➤ Spray booth (if you apply glazes with a sprayer)
➤ Gram scale (.05 to 500 grams)
➤ Gram scale (1 to 10,000 grams)
➤ Electric kiln (at least 7 cubic feet) or a fuel-burning kiln (at least 12 cubic feet capacity)
➤ Electric kiln for test firing (300 to 400 cubic inches - optional)

Economy Class - An Inexpensive Studio

It is possible to set up a small ceramic work space for building and firing hand-built pieces - one that takes up little space and costs very little money. These kinds of restraints require a very small, electric fired kiln, useful for firing small pieces. Such work spaces require only a worktable and some shelving to be complete. They are appropriate as a starting studio for the beginner or as a temporary studio for the experienced ceramist.

Small Tools for General Use

➤ Plastic bucket, to hold water
➤ Needle tool, for cutting and scoring clay
➤ Wooden knives, for cutting and shaping
➤ Kitchen sponge
➤ Small, fine-grained sponge such as a cosmetic sponge

➤ Rib or ribs - wood, plastic, or metal, for smoothing and shaping clay
➤ Thin sheets of plastic, for wrapping wet pieces

Useful Small Tools for the Hand Builder

➤ Roller, for rolling uniform sheets or slabs of clay. This may be a length of 2" thick dowel from a lumber yard or a roller from a cooking supply store.
➤ Knives with disposable blades, for cutting and carving the clay. These range in size and durability from large-bladed utility knives to the fine, thin blades of scalpels. You will find such knives in craft supply houses and catalogs, hardware stores, pharmaceutical supply and art supply stores.
➤ Scissors, for cutting templates (widely available with specialized types from hardware stores and art supply stores)
➤ Thin zinc/aluminum sheet (zinc lithography plate), for durable templates. These are available from printers, newspapers, and offset lithographers.

Tools for Throwing

➤ Loop tool, for trimming the clay
➤ Sponge mounted on a long dowel, for cleaning the interior of the thrown piece
➤ Chamois cloth (or equivalent), for smoothing the lip of the piece
➤ Calipers, for measuring lids

Tools for Glaze Formulation and Application

➤ High quality dust mask
➤ Gram scales, 0.1 gram to 500 grams and 5 grams to 20,000 grams
➤ Sieves, for clays and glazes
  • Large - 10-mesh. Kitchen sieves are excellent. Try to find a rust-free model. Kitchen supply stores sell stainless steel versions of the standard kitchen sieve and these are quite useful.
  • Large 30-mesh sieve
  • Large 60-mesh sieve
  • Large 100-mesh sieves (from ceramic supply houses)
➤ Glaze pencil, for labeling glaze and clay body tests
➤ 3 brushes:
  ½" stiff bristle brush (artist's bristle brush)
  ½" soft brush (Japanese "Hake" brush is excellent)
  2" sponge brush (inexpensive and useful)
➤ 30-power magnifying scope, for examining the surface of glazes

Tools for Testing Ceramic Formulations

➤ High quality dust mask
➤ Gram scales, 0.1 gram to 200 or 500 grams
➤ Sieves, for test lots of clay bodies and glazes. A small sieve is very useful in preparing test lots of glaze. An enameling sifter (60-mesh) is an excellent tool for these tasks. They are readily available from craft supply houses and do a fine job.
➤ Glaze pencil, for labeling glaze and clay body tests
➤ Stiff brush, for forcing materials through sieve
➤ Soft brush, for applying test slips and glazes
➤ 30-power magnifying scope, for examining the surface of glazes

The Potter's Wheel

The potter's wheel is one of our most important pottery forming tools. Potters have been throwing on the wheel for millennia and during that time they have developed a great many wheel designs. The design task is a difficult one and no one design is perfect. The potter's wheel must be powerful, easily controlled, and must be capable of a wide range of speeds (with no loss of power), varying from a very few revolutions per minute to speeds of 200 revolutions per minute or more. These are very demanding specifications.

We distinguish between kick wheels and electric wheels. Kick wheels derive their power (at least part of the time) from the kicking action of the potter's foot. To increase the wheelhead speed the potter merely kicks faster, to slow it the potter kicks more slowly or uses a dragging foot to brake the flywheel's speed. Many kick wheel designs also allow for motor drive. The motor's power is transmitted through a friction wheel to the flywheel. Kick wheels are reliable and durable and are excellent for throwing small and medium sized forms. Unfortunately, the motor drive is inefficient and is not as useful for throwing really large pieces. Furthermore, they are fairly expensive and prone to vibration. Look for a kick wheel that is well built and does not vibrate excessively. The emphasis should be on structure rather than economy.

The electric wheel's sole source of power is an electric motor. The power in an electric wheel is usually transmitted from the motor to the wheelhead by belts or gears. It is difficult to develop smooth and steady speed controllers for wheels of this type but they can be compact and very powerful. Electric wheels can be quite efficient and are excellent for throwing very large forms. Speed control (especially at low speeds, where control is needed most) is often insensitive and may require frequent adjustments. Look for an electric wheel that is quiet, compact, has responsive controls and good speed control even at the lowest speeds.

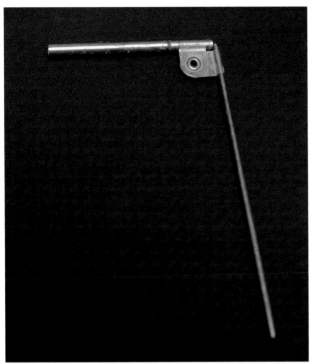

The atomizer sprayer.

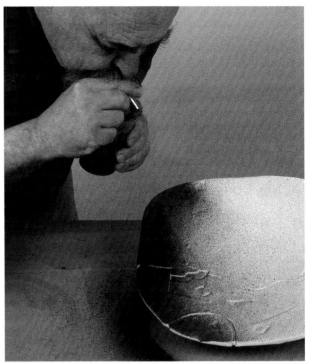

Applying glaze with an atomizer.

Slab Rollers

Slab rollers are the near equivalent of the potter's wheel for hand builders. Slab rollers can speed up the hand builder's work considerably. These tools are expensive, take up a good deal of room, need periodic adjustment and repair, but make uniform, very strong slabs.

Ceramic Scales

An accurate gram scale is a necessity for weighing ingredients for body or glaze recipes. Spring-loaded scales are the least expensive but also the least accurate. Most ceramists continue to use triple beam scales; the design of these scales is characterized by parallel beams that serve as tracks for sliding weights. As the ceramist slides the weights along their calibrated tracks, the beam is brought to a horizontal resting position. The ceramist uses the calibrations to read the weight of the material.

Ceramic ingredients must be placed in a container. Accurate scales are designed with mechanisms to compensate for the weight of this container. In a mechanical scale care must be taken to perform this task accurately.

Electronic scales are quick and responsive and do not require the ceramist to move weights along a track. Their digital readout allows quick and effortlessly accurate readings. Furthermore, their compensation for the weight of the weighing container is almost automatic. Accurate electronic scales are much less expensive than they were a few years ago and they are very well suited for ceramic work.

You may also want to invest in a large capacity gram scale (100 to 5,000 or 20,000 grams) in your work. Mechanical versions can be expensive. Large capacity electronic gram scales have become popular in recent years. Sources of these scales are ceramic suppliers and scientific supply houses. Large capacity electronic scales are also available from kitchen supply stores. Though a bit less accurate than those sold in scientific supply houses they are often reasonably priced.

Sprayers

A sprayer is a device consisting of a container from which stain, slip, or glaze is sprayed through a nozzle by air pressure. Most contemporary sprayers derive their air pressure from an air compressor. Lung power or bellows mechanisms may also be used as sources of air under pressure.

There are many types of sprayers. They can be categorized by capacity and the size of the spray pattern. Large sprayers with a broad spray pattern are known as a spray guns, smaller sprayers for detail work are known as airbrushes. They may be categorized by the way air is mixed with the liquid to be sprayed. The internal mix sprayer is constructed with a chamber inside the gun. In an external mix mechanism there is no chamber, and, as the name implies, air and liquid are mixed externally.

Safety Note: The fine dusts associated with glaze spraying can be harmful. Always wear a good dust mask (see page 234) and use a spray booth when using a sprayer.

External Mix Sprayers

External mix sprayers are simple, robust devices. In this type of sprayer the air from the compressor and the liquid glaze do not mix inside the sprayer but rather at a point midway between the air and glaze nozzles. By this simple strategy, the weaknesses of most spray mechanisms are avoided and very few blockages occur. If there is a blockage, it is in the feed tube connected to the glaze container; since this tube is open and straight, it can be cleaned easily. Typically, only air pressure can be controlled in external mix sprayers. Their ease of use and immunity to clogging are important advantages, however. Ceramic materials are comparatively coarse and may clog the spray mechanism so this is an important advantage. External mix sprayers require very little air (25 p.s.i. will do) and are less expensive than other spraying units. Furthermore, they may be fitted with a wide nozzle at the top of the feed tube to accommodate rough, unscreened mixtures.

Internal Mix Sprayers

These are more complex than external mix sprayers. They allow much more control than the external mix mechanisms. Because they are subject to clogging, you should ball mill the mixture.

Compressors

There are two very different types of compressors. The first is used only with an airbrush; it is small, quiet, and very carefully made, but it is not a multipurpose tool. Compressors of this type are available mainly from art supply stores. The second type is stronger, larger, and noisier; it is not as carefully built, but it has many uses. This type is available from hardware outlets. Both compressors work very well and can be recommended safely.

Atomizer Sprayers

Spraying may also be accomplished with atomizers. Atomizer sprayers have two pipes that together form an L. The bottom pipe (the long end) is placed in the liquid to be sprayed; the top pipe (the short end) is placed in the mouth. The user blows through the short pipe, causing a weak vacuum to form at the top of the long pipe. The liquid at the bottom of the long pipe is drawn up and then sprayed out. This simple machine is a useful leftover from another era. It is quiet, reliable, inexpensive, and very small and portable. Because its spray is not broken up into fine particles, these sprayers are safer than high pressure sprayers. Atomizers are not as appropriate when spraying large areas as are compressor driven sprayers but they are very useful for spraying localized areas. Furthermore, they can serve as an excellent introduction to the spraying process.

Appendix D
Safe Practice for the Ceramist

Toxicity

In recent years we have become far more keenly aware of the danger ceramic materials pose to both ourselves and those who eat or drink from our pieces. Some of our materials are toxic, others, though nontoxic, are potentially dangerous irritants. These problems can be surmounted; they should not keep us from working in clay or from making pieces that people will want to use. We can make sure that our work is not dangerous to those who use it. While there is no way to completely eliminate danger to ourselves as ceramists we can minimize the danger. We can eliminate the most hazardous materials and practices in our work. Unfortunately, we may have to modify some of our work methods and materials and avoid others entirely to do so.

The following materials are *toxic* and their use should be avoided:

➤Barium carbonate
➤All cadmium compounds
➤All chrome and chromate compounds
➤All lead compounds
➤Lithium carbonate
➤Manganese dioxide (powdered)
➤All nickel compounds
➤Vanadium pentoxide

Some of the materials ceramists use contain these toxic elements but they are combined with other materials to create compounds (frits and stains) that are fairly safe to use. Note, however, that some highly acidic or alkaline foods may release these toxic elements, so you should never use these compounds in pieces that might hold food. In addition, they may produce toxic gases during firing. Fire them only in a well-ventilated kiln room. These compounds include:

➤Lead frits
➤Lithium feldspars
➤Vanadium stains

Substitutes for Toxic Materials

Titanium dioxide, tin oxide, or zirconium opacifiers, will (in amounts more than 7%) partially serve as substitutes for barium carbonate. These materials encourage soft, satin mat surfaces somewhat reminiscent of barium's mat effects.

Chrome and chromate compounds: copper oxide or carbonate will serve as a partial substitute for greens derived from chrome; there are no real substitutes for pinks and crimsons derived from chrome or for the brilliant fire engine red and brilliant orange colors derived from chrome/lead combinations.

Boron and sodium are strong melters and can serve as useful substitutes for lead compounds and lead frits.

The lithium feldspar spodumene is much less toxic than lithium carbonate and can serve as a useful substitute for this material.

Black iron oxide is a fairly close substitute for powdered manganese dioxide.

Nickel carbonate has no substitutes.

Titanium yellow stain is a safe and effective (and inexpensive) substitute for vanadium pentoxide or vanadium stains.

Silica-Containing Materials

➤All clays
➤All feldspars
➤Ground silica (flint)
➤Talc (calcium, magnesium silicate)
➤Wollastonite (calcium silicate)

Until it is fired, any material that contains silica is dangerous to the ceramist. These include clays and feldspars. These are the core materials of ceramics: we must use them every day. They are especially dangerous in their dry form. The problem is made more complex because it is difficult to predict how people will react to materials that contain silica. There is no doubt that they can cause health problems but the problems vary greatly from person to person. Constant exposure to silica over a period of years can cause respiratory damage. While all ceramists must learn to control the amount of ceramic dust which reaches their lungs, some ceramists are particularly at risk. Those who should be most careful either have a disposition to respiratory problems or are heavy smokers. The elimination of smoking among ceramists is the most important step in eliminating work-related health problems.

Other respiratory irritants include:

➤ Bone ash
➤ Cobalt colorants
➤ All copper compounds
➤ Gerstley borate (calcium, sodium borate)
➤ Wood ash
➤ Zinc oxide
➤ All zirconium compounds

Cleaning Strategies

The rule here is that it is always best to deal with wet rather than dry dust. It is better to mop up dust than to sweep or vacuum it. Wet dust is muddy but will not end up in your lungs. Ceramic machinery is best sponged down as well.

Safety Equipment

Respirators

When working with dry materials the ceramist should wear a NIOSH (U.S.A.) or Factory Inspectorate (G.B.) approved dust respirator.

A respirator filters the air just before it enters the body. If used carefully a respirator can effectively protect us from the hazards of our work. Some respirators purify the air of dusts, others purify the air of both dusts and fumes. In an ideal world we would not create dangerous dusts and fumes. In a slightly less ideal world we would be able to completely filter all impurities out of the air and no one would be threatened by toxic dusts or fumes. Since the world is not ideal, we must sometimes filter impure air as it is about to enter our lungs. While such protection is a bit inconvenient it is highly efficient because of its localized nature.

Respirators fit over the nose and mouth and contain filters that let air pass through while filtering dusts or fumes. Some respirators are meant to be used once or twice and then discarded. Though they are light and easy to wear, disposable masks cannot protect you from fine ceramic dusts.

Most contemporary respirators are made from a modular design with a reusable face piece and disposable filter cartridges. The sophisticated multi-layer filters can be designed to filter extremely fine dusts including ceramic dusts. The body of the mask (the face piece) is made from a rubber-like material that seals out dust and fumes. Disposable filtering cartridges are attached to this face piece. Most manufacturers offer a whole line of cartridges, each designed for a specific job. Ceramists need cartridges that filter very fine dusts. Occasionally, we may also need the extra protection of filters that protect us from fumes, especially during the kiln firing.

The mask will lose its effectiveness if you neglect to change the filter. Change the filter immediately if you sense irritation or experience an unpleasant smell or taste. Place a mark on the filters for every hour the mask is worn and change to a new filter after ten hours. When you change the filter also wash the face piece.

A new and promising design is a two-part device with a fan installed behind a plastic mask. The mask effectively evacuates all dust. This is a complex and relatively expensive device but very effective in high dust situations.

Disposable Safety Garments

If you work in a highly dust-laden environment, it may be a good idea to wear special protective clothing (including headgear); paper safety suits are useful for this purpose.

Disposable safety garments, made from a paper-like material, are inexpensive and durable and offer good protection.

Procedures for Safely Preparing Ceramic Recipes

Clay body and glaze making can be dangerous. The dry powders needed to make clay bodies and glazes are very dusty and can settle in the lungs. Add water to dry materials as soon as possible and avoid sieving dry mixtures. Sieving a wet mixture is far safer than dry sifting (and quicker as well). Once the recipe is wet, it is safe to use unless it contains toxic materials.

Preparing and Forming Clay Bodies

The ceramist needs to develop good work habits when forming clay bodies. A great deal of clay dust can be created during these procedures. Without care our work areas can easily become as dusty as the mixing area. The dust should be cleaned with a mop because wet dust is far less dangerous to us than dry dust. Clay bodies can be irritating to the skin and cause contact dermatitis. Those ceramists with a predisposition to skin irritations must be especially wary. Clays by themselves do not seem to be particularly irritating to the skin. It is additions to the clay body that make them so. Clay bodies that contain highly alkaline materials such as strongly alkaline fluxes and feldspars are particularly at fault here. Also potentially irritating are clays in which mold growth has been encouraged. Molds enhance workability but they can irritate the skin and trigger allergic reactions. It may help to apply a barrier skin cream.

Colored clay bodies can be quite dangerous if made with hazardous materials. Particularly dangerous are bodies colored with powdered manganese (granular manganese is benign) or chromium colorants. Create colored clay bodies from naturally occurring clays or from commercially produced stains.

Preparing and Applying Glazes

If working with highly alkaline slips and glazes, it may be a good idea to wear special protective clothing (including headgear); paper safety suits are useful for this purpose. Wear a good dust mask. Add water to dry materials as soon as possible. Never sieve dry mixtures for this can be extremely dusty - sieving a wet mixture is far quicker and safer. Once the recipe is wet, it is safe to use unless it contains toxic materials.

Most methods of glaze application are not particularly dangerous procedures. Spraying, however, can be quite hazardous. Always wear a mask while spraying and spray into a well-vented spray booth.

Bench Grinders

Contemporary bench grinders are made from an electric motor fitted with carborundum grindstone that turns rapidly. Bench grinders are especially useful for grinding glaze off the bottom of a piece. They can, however, produce flying ceramic chips that can cut the skin and damage the eyes. The rapidly turning grinding wheel can catch articles of clothing or hair in a sudden motion and pull you toward the machine. When using the grinder always wear a protective face shield, tie back long hair, and don't wear clothing that can become entangled in the grinding wheel.

Procedures for Safe Kiln Firing

Kilns can be the source of fires or explosions. Electric kilns carry heavy current loads and gas kilns need large volumes of gases. The connections to electrical sources or gas lines should be professionally installed. The same is true for safety mechanisms that interrupt electric current and gas during an emergency.

The ventilation of dangerous gases produced during firing is also a problem and one that is especially serious because it may be hard to associate these gases with their bad effects. Kilns should be placed in a separate room or building. Fuel-burning kilns may be placed outdoors. Kilns located indoors should be fitted with an efficient exhaust system vented to the outside. Electric kilns may be fitted with an under-kiln or overhead hood. Fuel-burning kilns installed indoors should have an overhead exhaust canopy.

Viewing the Kiln Interior During Firing

When you fire with cones, you will need to look into the incandescent firing chamber to check the position of the cone. This can cause eye damage. You should purchase and use "tuned" safety glasses to look into the kiln chamber during the latter part of the firing. Tuned glasses are readily obtained from a safety supply house; the supplier merely needs to know the maximum firing temperature that you use and will supply glasses of the appropriate shade. Dr. Michael McCann in his book *Artist Beware* (Watson-Guptill, 1979) recommends welder's glasses with the designation 2 to 2.5. These glasses are inexpensive and aside from protecting the eyes make it easier to see the cone.

Procedures for Insuring That Fired Pieces Are Safe to Use

As well as attending to our own health you should also be attentive to the welfare of those who will use your work. There is no need to use glazes that contain toxic materials on work that may be used to contain food. In theory, toxic materials can be "locked" in the glassy matrix of a glaze. However, they can also be "unlocked" during the firing. We have many alternative nontoxic materials that melt strongly and encourage rich glaze surfaces. The important message here is that with a little bit of rethinking we can produce work that is safe for our customers, and we can work in a way that does not threaten our own well-being.

Appendix E
Ceramic Recipes

In ceramics, more than in many other arts, technological matters strongly influence the look of the finished piece. One place where this is strongly in evidence is in the phenomenon of the ceramic recipe. Ceramic recipes are composed of materials which are sources of silica, alumina, and various other elements that influence the character of the melt. Ceramic recipes are written in a format that allows them to be compared to one another and to be used easily by contemporary ceramists. For example, they are generally formulated for a total of 100% in order to allow easy comparison with other recipes. Colorants are often written as percentages over and above the 100%. This is because other colorants can be used in their place with few substantive changes in the character of the fired product other than color. Ceramic recipes draw from a limited palette of materials - those that have been proven in use and are readily available from ceramic suppliers. While we have a limited choice of materials, their proportions vary a great deal. These different proportions are what give each recipe its unique flavor.

Cone 04 Recipes

Clay Bodies

Standard Talc Body
50 ball clay
50 talc

This is the standard 50/50 low-fire clay body. I was surprised by the fact that upon computed analysis we see that a standard 50/50 low-fire talc body is very low in alumina and very high in flux.

Clay Body #1
20 ball clay
10 talc
50 red clay
20 soda feldspar

This body is fairly workable and durable. After a few weeks it becomes highly thixotropic and more difficult to form.

Engobe 04-1
33 ball clay
11 talc
12 Gerstley borate
42 soda spar
02 titanium

This engobe is dry surfaced and very durable.

Engobe 04-1 K2
20 soda feldspar
33 boron frit 3124
12 talc
33 ball clay
02 titanium
clay 33, silicates 65, fluxing materials 4

In this suggested version of the recipe I use frit 3124 instead of Gerstley borate.

Glazes

Opaque 04 Glaze
10 ball clay
10 boron frit 3124
44 talc
24 Gerstley borate
12 zirconium opacifier

The most significant secondary flux in this glaze is Gerstley borate. It accepts both stain and standard colorants very readily. It has little visual texture. This glaze is very durable and reliable.

Opaque 04 K2
34 boron frit
40 talc
14 ball clay
12 zirconium opacifier
clay: 14 silicates: 74 fluxing materials: 12

In this suggested version of the recipe I use frit 3124 instead of Gerstley borate.

Clear Glaze 04
08 ball clay
08 flint
18 talc
26 Gerstley borate
02 zinc
38 boron frit 3134

The most significant materials in this glaze are the two frits, one a sodium frit and the other a boron frit. Its transparency is encouraged by its high glassmakers and moderate clay content. Unfortunately, this glaze crazes. It is very difficult to create a cone 04 clear glaze which contains no toxic materials and does not craze.

Clear 04 K2
54 boron frit
32 talc
12 ball clay
02 zinc oxide
clay 12, silicates 86, fluxing materials 2

In this suggested version of the recipe I use frit 3124 instead of Gerstley borate.

Robin's 1b Clear Glaze
10 ball clay
30 boron frit
20 talc
24 Gerstley borate
14 spodumene
02 zinc

The most significant fluxes in this glaze are sodium, calcium, boron, and lithium, derived respectively from a soda frit a boron frit, Gerstley borate (both frits are also sources of calcium), and spodumene. This glaze crazes a bit less than the previous one but due to its clay content (which I think is high for a clear glaze) is slightly milky.

Robin's 1b Clear K2
18 spodumene
46 boron frit 3124
24 talc
10 ball clay
02 zinc oxide
clay 10, silicates 88, fluxing materials 2

In this suggested version of the recipe I use frit 3124 instead of Gerstley borate.

Mohawk Green F
30 Gerstley borate
16 kaolin
02 lithium carbonate
38 soda spar
12 talc
02 zinc
03 copper carbonate

The most significant secondary fluxes in this glaze are sodium, calcium, boron, and lithium derived respectively from soda spar, Gerstley borate, and lithium carbonate. Its color is a rich saturated green. It has a fairly strong visual texture.

Mohawk Green F K2
20 soda feldspar
12 spodumene
50 boron frit 3124
16 kaolin
02 zinc oxide

In this suggested version of the recipe I use frit 3124 instead of Gerstley borate.

Cone 02 Recipes

Clay Bodies

Red Body
25 ball clay
50 red clay
25 talc

A light brick red color, low absorption, good workability.

Ivory Colored Body
20 ball clay
40 goldart
10 soda spar
30 talc

A light buff (ivory) color, good workability.

Glazes

Chemung Base
10 ball clay
54 soda frit 3110
24 Gerstley borate
12 zirconium opacifier
03 copper carbonate

A shiny, translucent glaze. It takes stain color very well. Its most significant flux is sodium derived from soda frit and boron derived from Gerstley borate. Its turquoise color is derived from the reaction of copper to sodium.

Chemung Base 2K
76 boron frit 3124
06 talc
06 ball clay
12 zirconium opacifier
clay 6, silicates 82, fluxing materials 12

In this suggested version of the recipe I use frit 3124 instead of Gerstley borate.

Spencer Base
10 ball clay
54 boron frit 3124
24 wollastinite
12 zirconium opacifier
1.5 cobalt carbonate

The most significant flux in this glaze is calcium derived from the wollastonite. It has no visual texture, its surface is smooth and waxy. Its color is a soft blue.

Baldwin Base
10 ball clay
46 boron frit
12 red clay
20 spodumene
12 zirconium opacifier
06 iron oxide

The most significant fluxes in this glaze are the boron frit and spodumene (a lithium containing feldspar). Its color is a soft ochre cream. It has some visual texture.

Wellsburg Shiny Brown Glaze
30 barnard clay
48 Gerstley borate
20 spodumene
02 titanium

The most significant fluxes in this glaze are boron, iron, and lithium. Boron is derived from Gerstley borate. Barnard is a source of iron and spodumene is a source of lithium. Its color is brown and its surface is quite shiny with some visual texture.

Wellsburg Brown 2K
20 spodumene
48 boron frit 3124
30 barnard
02 titanium
clay 30, silicates 68, fluxing materials 4

In this suggested version of the recipe I use frit 3124 instead of Gerstley borate.

Barton Spodumene Base
10 dolomite
32 boron frit
22 red clay
20 spodumene
12 zirconium opacifier
6% iron oxide

The most significant flux in this glaze is lithium derived from spodumene (a lithium containing feldspar). Its surface is satin or satin shiny, its color a warm ivory.

Tioga Clear Glaze
04 ball clay
24 flint
48 boron frit 3124
22 spodumene
02 zinc

This kind of recipe is desirable for transparent glazes. Its most significant fluxes are lithium (derived from spodumene) and zinc, both of which aid melting. It is craze-free on both the buff and red bodies. It has a tendency to a slight opacity.

Rosstown Dry Surfaced Glaze
03 ball clay
50 flint
26 Gerstley borate
16 spodumene
03 titanium
02 zinc

The most significant fluxes in this glaze are lithium derived from spodumene and boron derived from Gerstley borate. Its surface is extremely dry and it is not appropriate for use on functional pieces. It is not shiny (although high in glassmakers) because it is too low in melters to form a glassy melt. An unstable surface was desired for this recipe.

Rosstown Dry 2K

36 silica
16 spodumene
40 boron frit 3124
03 ball clay
02 zinc oxide
03 titanium

In this suggested version of the recipe I use frit 3124 instead of Gerstley borate.

Mohawk Green

30 Gerstley borate
16 kaolin
02 lithium carbonate
38 soda feldspar
12 whiting
02 zinc
03 copper carbonate

Originally written for cone 04, it also works well at cone 02. The most significant secondary fluxes in this glaze are sodium, calcium, boron, and lithium derived respectively from soda spar, Gerstley borate, and lithium carbonate. Its color is a rich saturated green. It has a fairly strong visual texture.

Cone 3

Clay Bodies

Buff Body

20 ball clay
55 goldart stoneware clay
25 talc

A durable, workable body. Its color is a light ochre yellow.

1988 Buff Body

60 ball clay
05 goldart stoneware clay
25 talc

This body is durable and quite workable. Its color is a buff yellow and it works well with glazes.

Red Body

10 ball clay
10 fire clay
55 goldart stoneware clay
25 red clay

This body is ochre orange in color. While it darkens many glazes it is quite compatible with most of them.

Glazes

Granby Base

12 ball clay
08 soda frit
10 Gerstley borate
10 zirconium opacifier
58 soda spar
02 tin oxide

The most significant flux in this glaze is sodium derived from both the soda feldspar and the soda frit. This is a smooth satin shiny glaze. It is very durable; it is quite opaque due to its zirconium and tin content. It is an excellent base glaze and works very well with most colorants and stains.

Granby Base 2K

58 soda feldspar
20 boron frit 3124
12 ball clay
08 zirconium opacifier
02 tin oxide

In this suggested version of the recipe I use frit 3124 instead of Gerstley borate.

Fairdale Cream

12 ball clay
10 dolomite
10 soda frit 3110
10 Gerstley borate
12 zirconium opacifier
24 soda spar
20 spodumene
02 rutile

The most significant fluxes in this glaze are lithium derived from spodumene and sodium derived from soda frit and soda feldspar. Its color is a soft ivory cream and its surface is mat.

Fairdale Cream 2K

24 soda feldspar
20 spodumene
20 boron frit 3124
12 ball clay
02 rutile
10 dolomite
12 zirconium opacifier

In this suggested version of the recipe I use frit 3124 instead of Gerstley borate.

Dewitt Dark Tan

08 ball clay
16 dolomite
24 boron frit 3124
12 zirconium opacifier
10 soda spar
20 spodumene
10 rutile

The most significant fluxes in this glaze are iron derived from Barnard clay and lithium derived from spodumene. Its color is a dark, earth colored tan. Its surface is strong and durable. It is marked with a tight pattern of visual texture.

Fulton Glaze

10 ball clay
10 soda frit
18 Gerstley borate
10 zirconium opacifier
50 soda spar
02 rutile
01.5 cobalt carbonate

The most significant flux in this glaze is sodium derived from soda frit and soda feldspar. It is bright blue in color. Its surface is shiny and unmarked by visual texture.

Fulton Base 2K

40 soda feldspar
38 boron frit 3124
10 ball clay
02 rutile
10 zirconium opacifier

In this suggested version of the recipe I use frit 3124 instead of Gerstley borate.

Class Base

08 boron frit 3124
16 Gerstley borate
34 red clay
36 soda spar
06 rutile

The most significant fluxes in this glaze are iron derived from red clay and boron derived from boron frit and Gerstley borate. This is a dark base glaze which can be used with a number of colorants. It is a durable, reliable glaze base.

Class Base 2K

26 potash feldspar
34 boron frit 3124
34 red clay
06 rutile

In this suggested version of the recipe I use only frit 3124 and no Gerstley borate.

Class Black

Add 2% copper carbonate to the Class Base to get a rich black.

Class Brown

Add 8% black iron oxide to the Class Base for a very rich brown color.

Cone 6

Clay Bodies

Buff Body

10 fire clay
14 flint
62 goldart stoneware clay
14 potash feldspar

A light cream colored clay body. Its workability is good.

Red Body

12 ball clay
10 flint
33 kaolin
45 red clay

A brick red body. Its workability is good. The most significant flux in this body is iron derived from its red clay.

Glazes

Emerald Transparent

08 kaolin
22 Gerstley borate
51 nephaline syenite
08 titanium
08 dolomite
03 zinc
03 copper carbonate.

The most significant fluxes in this glaze are calcium derived from dolomite and sodium derived from nepthaline syenite. It is a fairly durable glaze. Its surface is mat with a lot of visual texture. Its cool green color is derived from copper influenced by sodium (derived from its nepthaline syenite content).

Emerald Transparent 2K

26 potash feldspar
34 boron frit 3124
17 kaolin
12 dolomite
03 zinc oxide
08 titanium

In this suggested version of the recipe I use frit 3124 instead of Gerstley borate.

New Soft Waxy Transparent Glaze

08 ball clay
10 flint
20 Gerstley borate
47 nephaline syenite
02 titanium
10 wollastonite
03 zinc

The most significant secondary fluxes in this glaze are sodium derived from nepheline syenite and calcium derived from wollastonite. It is shiny and fairly durable. Due to its balanced recipe and its titanium and zinc content it resists crazing.

New Soft Waxy Transparent 2K

36 potash feldspar
38 boron frit 3124
12 ball clay
10 whiting
02 zinc oxide
02 titanium

In this suggested version of the recipe I use frit 3124 instead of Gerstley borate.

Catlin Base

08 ball clay
15 Gerstley borate
42 soda spar
12 spodumene
03 rutile
10 wollastinite
10 zirconium opacifier

The most significant fluxes in this glaze are lithium derived from spodumene and calcium derived from wollastonite. The surface is satin shiny and has some visual texture. Its viscosity is fairly low and it fills interstices well. Its color is a white softened by the presence of titanium.

Catlin Base 2K

26 potash feldspar
12 spodumene
31 boron frit 3124
08 ball clay
03 rutile
10 whiting
10 zirconium opacifier

In this suggested version of the recipe I use frit 3124 instead of Gerstley borate.

Gumrak 3

18 dolomite
12 boron frit 3124
12 red clay
34 soda feldspar
14 spodumene
10 zirconium opacifier
12 rutile

The most significant fluxes in this glaze are calcium/magnesium derived from dolomite and lithium derived from spodumene and titanium. Where thin its color is a dark tobacco brown, it is mustard where thick. Its color is derived from iron (from the red clay and rutile) and influenced by lithium and titanium. The version without colorant is a soft cream breaking to a light amber.

Zakin Base 2

06 ball clay
12 dolomite
12 Gerstley borate
52 soda feldspar
08 titanium
10 zirconium opacifier
03 copper carbonate

This recipe can also be used without colorant. The most significant fluxes in this glaze are titanium and calcium/magnesium derived from dolomite. Due to its titanium content this glaze is more durable than its low glassmaker content would indicate. Titanium also encourages its strong visual texture and satin mat surface. Its green color is derived from copper softened by calcium/magnesium (from dolomite) and titanium.

Zakin Base 2 2K

32 potash feldspar
24 boron frit 3124
10 ball clay
16 dolomite
08 titanium
10 zirconium opacifier

In this suggested version of the recipe I use frit 3124 instead of Gerstley borate.

Zakin Base 3

06 ball clay
12 Gerstley borate
28 soda spar
36 spodumene
08 titanium
10 zirconium opacifier

Used by itself and with 3% copper carbonate. This glaze is much like Zakin Base 2. The most significant fluxes are lithium derived from spodumene and titanium. A mat glaze with only a hint of shine. Its color is a muted light amber. Its visual texture is very rich. Durability is enhanced by the titanium, color and visual texture are influenced by the spodumene and titanium. With 3% copper, a soft green.

Zakin Base 3 2K

28 potash feldspar
26 spodumene
20 boron frit
08 ball clay
08 titanium
10 zirconium opacifier

In this suggested version of the recipe I use frit 3124 instead of Gerstley borate.

Zakin 4

10 dolomite
12 Gerstley borate
10 red clay
28 soda feldspar
22 spodumene
08 rutile
10 zirconium opacifier
12 iron oxide.

The most significant fluxes in this glaze are lithium derived from spodumene, iron derived from red clay and titanium. This glaze has no visual texture. Its smooth velvety surface reminds one of a barium mat glaze. Its color is iron red derived from a red clay and red iron oxide.

Zakin 4 K2

20 soda feldspar
22 spodumene
20 boron frit 3124
10 red clay
08 rutile
10 dolomite
10 zirconium opacifier
12 iron oxide

In this suggested version of the recipe I use frit 3124 instead of Gerstley borate.

Cone 9

Clay Bodies

Buff Body

08 dolomite
12 fire clay
58 goldart
22 kaolin

A buff colored body. Its workability is excellent.

Buff Talc Body

12 fire clay
60 goldart
22 kaolin
06 talc

A buff colored body with excellent workability.

Porcelain Body (Classic)

25 flint
50 kaolin
25 potash spar

This is the classic porcelain recipe which has been used by ceramists in the western world since its development in Germany. It is a pure white body of highly limited workability.

Woodbourne 2 Vitreous Engobe

10 stoneware clay
18 red clay
28 dolomite
24 potash feldspar
20 talc

The most significant fluxes in this vitreous engobe are iron from the red clay, calcium/magnesium derived from dolomite, and talc. With no colorant it is a very rich burnt orange to cream in color. It has a soft waxy mat surface.

Woodbourne 3 Vitreous Engobe

08 ball clay
34 red clay
24 potash feldspar
14 dolomite
20 spodumene

The most significant fluxes in this vitreous engobe are calcium/magnesium derived from talc and whiting. Its color is a mottled iron green and its surface is a soft waxy mat.

Woodbourne 3 Vitreous Engobe With Iron

24 red clay
12 stoneware clay
30 potash feldspar
14 talc
20 whiting
12 iron oxide

The most significant fluxes in this vitreous engobe are calcium/magnesium derived from talc and whiting and iron derived from red clay, and iron oxide. A highly mottled, runny, waxy mat. Rich caramel brown color.

Glazes

Northfield Transparent 3

08 kaolin
16 dolomite
58 potash feldspar
02 titanium
14 wollastinite
02 zinc
03 copper carbonate

The most significant fluxes in this glaze are potassium derived from potash feldspar and calcium derived from wollastonite. Its transparency is encouraged by its high glassmakers content.

Allen Creek 4

10 stoneware clay
32 dolomite
34 potash feldspar
14 talc
10 zirconium opacifier

The most significant fluxes in this glaze are calcium/magnesium derived from talc and dolomite. It is buff white to burnt orange in color. Its surface is soft looking. Add 3% copper carbonate for a green.

Webster 2

12 stoneware clay
28 potash feldspar
10 spodumene
35 talc
15 whiting
3 copper carbonate.

The most significant fluxes in this glaze are calcium/magnesium, derived from talc and whiting and titanium. Its color moves from burnt orange to gray-green.

Webster 3

12 ball clay
36 potash spar
10 spodumene
34 talc
08 titanium

The most significant fluxes in this glaze are calcium/magnesium derived from talc and whiting, titanium and lithium derived from spodumene. It has lots of rich glaze flow, orange-tan to white to dark green-gray.

Webster 4

15 stoneware clay
12 spodumene
46 talc
12 rutile
15 whiting

The most significant fluxes in this glaze are calcium/magnesium derived from talc and whiting. lithium derived from spodumene and titanium. For a soft green add 3% copper carbonate.

Appendix F
Glossary

Absorption: The ability of a material (such as a fired clay body) to take in moisture.

Alumina: One of the basic building blocks of clays and glazes. Clays, feldspars and frits contain alumina. Alumina promotes plasticity and strength in clay bodies, it promotes durability and viscosity in glazes. Alumina is refractory (it discourages melting). Glazes with a moderate alumina content tend to be mat, opaque, nonrunning and very durable; glazes with a high alumina content may be dry surfaced.

Analysis: The separation of a whole into its component parts.

Atmosphere: (kiln atmosphere): This term refers to the amount of oxygen in the firing chamber of the kiln during firing. In an oxidation atmosphere the kiln is amply supplied with oxygen from the air intake. In a reduction atmosphere the air intakes are shut for a time during the firing, temporarily depriving the firing chamber of oxygen. This strongly influences the character of the ware.

Atomizer: A simple sprayer device composed of two thin metal tubes set at a 90° angle to each other. One of the tubes is inserted in a liquid. As the ceramist blows through the other tube a mild vacuum is created and the liquid is sprayed over a small area. Atomizers are excellent tools for spraying small areas of ceramic pieces. They are simple, inexpensive, and useful.

Ball clay: A fine particle, plastic clay. These clays are used in clay bodies to improve workability and plasticity. They encourage shrinkage and cracking so their use must be carefully controlled and they generally are not used in amounts over 15% of the body.

Bentonite: A very fine particle clay-like material. It finds common use in ceramics as a plasticizing agent for clay bodies.

Bisque firing: A preliminary firing of unglazed ware. While bisque firing temperatures may vary widely, it is most common to bisque fire to cones 08 to 04. This kind of fire prepares the work for glazing - the ware may be immersed in the watery glaze without cracking or breaking down.

Boron: This is a glass former, finding great use in low and mid fire glaze recipes because it encourages strong melts. It is usually used in the form of a boron frit.

Breakup: Visual texture marking the surface of the glaze. The textures vary a great deal. They may be composed of small dark spots, of small patterns created by a change of color, of color variations triggered by changes in the thickness of the glaze, or of places where the glaze runs away from a sharp edge, causing a color change. Ceramists often value breakup and try to encourage it.

Calcine: The process of heating a material to drive off organic impurities, water, or carbon (these are driven off as gases). Calcined materials are used to make recipes more stable and more useful. For example, in high clay glazes the plasticity of the clay may cause difficulties during firing; calcining is used to diminish the plasticity.

Calcium: In the low and mid fire this oxide does not encourage melting. At cone 8 and above it strongly encourages melting. It is found in a number of ceramic materials including whiting, (calcium carbonate), dolomite (calcium, magnesium carbonate), and talc (calcium, magnesium silicate). It is used in slips, engobes, and glazes, and occasionally in clay bodies.

Clay body: A compound of clay and nonclay materials chosen for their individual characteristics that, when combined, meet the specific requirements of the ceramist.

Cobalt: In its carbonate or oxide form, this is a colorant. It encourages strong blue colors. It is stable over the whole range of the firing spectrum.

Colloids: Materials with a very fine particle size. Colloidal particles are useful to the ceramist because they encourage workability in clay bodies and good suspension in engobes and glazes.

Colorant: A mineral or compound of minerals used to color ceramic materials. The most common colorants are iron oxide, cobalt oxide or carbonate, copper carbonate, rutile (a compound of titanium and iron), and manganese dioxide.

Compounds: These are substances formed by two or more elements or molecules in defined proportions.

Cones: Elongated pyramids made from clay and glaze materials. They are designed to deform when specific time and temperature conditions pertain inside the kiln. They are very useful indicators and many ceramists rely on them for information on the firing, how it is progressing and when it should be ended.

Copper: In its carbonate or oxide form, this is a colorant. In the oxidation atmosphere it encourages green and greenish blue colors, while in reduction it encourages red and oxblood colors. It is stable over the whole range of the firing spectrum.

Crawling: A glaze defect in which the glaze forms in separate droplets during firing rather than in a smooth surface. When this phenomenon occurs on a dust- or dirt-free bisque fired piece, it generally indicates that the glaze formula is too viscous, due to an overly high alumina content. In this case, the clay content of the glaze must be lowered.

Crazing: A network of thin glaze cracks. It occurs when the glaze shrinks more than the clay body during the firing.

Crystals: A three-dimensional structure composed of atoms or molecules arranged in an orderly, repeating pattern. The outer form of the substance they make up mirrors this internal structure. Crystals play an important part in the makeup of the materials and products of the ceramist.

Deflocculant: An alkaline material which encourages clay particles to repel each other.

Deflocculated: Lowered or entirely negated clay plasticity. Clay bodies which have been somewhat deflocculated (generally by alkaline melters in the formula) lose much of their plasticity. Clay which has been highly deflocculated becomes a completely nonplastic material, used in slipcasting to make clay bodies liquid.

Density: In ceramics, a clay body is said to be dense when it is fired to a point at which its particles are closely packed together and it cannot absorb moisture.

Dolomite: Calcium, magnesium carbonate. A compound of calcium and magnesium. In the low and mid fire this oxide does not encourage melting. At cone 8 and above it strongly encourages melting.

Earthenware: A low fire body made in some significant part from clays with a high content of iron and other "impurities."

Efflorescence: A powdery deposit over a surface. In ceramics, a white powdery deposit of calcium whose source is calcium in the clay.

Electric kiln: A closed box made of lightweight refractory brick for firing ceramic ware. Its interior walls are lined with tightly wound metal coils. When current is sent to the wires they become hot. The heat is retained inside the firing chamber and the ware is fired.

Element (as the term is used in the chemistry of clay and glazes): A substance composed of identical atoms. Ceramists need to know the element makeup of a ceramic recipe because the elements in the recipe are the prime influence on the character of that recipe.

Engobe: Originally, this term was related to the concept of an envelope - that is, an overall coating of slip. Slips used as engobes were almost always porcelain slips intended to disguise modest clay bodies so that they might be confused with porcelains. The term has come to mean a porcelain or semiporcelain slip applied in any fashion. Engobes have a clay content of 25% to 50% and a nonclay content of 50% to 75%.

Eutectic: A mixture of two compounds (often in specific proportions) that creates a melt at a temperature lower than the melting point of either of the two individual compounds.

Extruder: A device that allows the ceramist to shape clay by forcing it through a form or die. It is composed of a reservoir that holds clay and a mechanism to force the clay from the reservoir into a die. The die is pierced with an opening or openings that cause the clay to take on a shape desired by the ceramist. At present most extruders are limited to forms that are 4" in width or less. Dies can be designed to create either solid or hollow forms.

Feldspar: A blend of silica, alumina, and the fluxes sodium, potassium, calcium, and lithium. The product of decomposed igneous (formerly molten) rocks. There are many varieties of feldspar, all meeting different needs.

Filler: A neutral material. Clay body fillers are nonplastic additions generally used to increase strength and lower shrinkage. Their particle size varies from very coarse to very fine. Fillers for slips, engobes, and glazes are finely ground, nonmelting, nonclay materials, employed to strengthen and stabilize the formula.

Fire clay: A coarse, large-particle clay which contributes strength and workability. In itself it is only moderately plastic but it may significantly enhance plasticity by encouraging particle size differentiation. Fire clays tend to be buff, tan, or ocher in color due to a moderate iron content (1% to 3%) and titanium (1% to 3%).

Flashing: An alteration in the color of an area of the glaze surface. It is the result of the play of the flame over the surface of the ware and is found only in fuel-burning firings.

Flocculent: An acidic material which encourages the aggregation of clay particles (for its opposite, see deflocculant listed above).

Flocculate: To cause clay particle aggregation (which can encourage plasticity) by the addition of acidic materials.

Flocculated: A state in which clay particles tend to aggregate or clump together; the clay mass acts as a coherent, workable material that can be shaped and formed.

Flux: An oxide that encourages silica oxide to melt. Fluxes include the oxides of barium, calcium, boron, sodium, and potassium. Related to this is the term anti-flux - a material that discourages melting.

Frit: Manufactured compounds containing silica, alumina, and melters. While more expensive than many materials which find use in ceramics, they are highly valued and used widely for their stabilizing and strong melting powers. Sodium, calcium, and boron are the most common melting ingredients in frits. There are many varieties of frits, all meeting different needs.

Glaze: A glassy coating especially formulated to fit over a clay form. Glazes contain silica, alumina, and melter.

Greenware: Finished ware which requires drying before it can be fired.

Grog: A coarse-particle filler for clay bodies. The presence of grog ensures that the clay body will contain a wide variety of particle sizes. Grog also discourages warping and encourages durability.

Ground silica: (also called flint): A finely ground silica powder, free of impurities. This is an important source of silica in ceramic recipes (clay bodies, slips, engobes, and glazes).

Impurity: A material that, when present, creates a mixture (often an undesirable mixture). In ceramics, iron and titanium are considered impurities in white clays and clay bodies.

Inlay: A process in which clay elements of more than one color are worked together to create a multicolored clay piece.

Installation: An artist-constructed environment whose purpose is to create a large scale art object. It is usually made with a variety of materials and often includes objects from everyday life.

Intaglio: A design carved into the surface of the clay.

Intaglio glazing: Here the ceramist carves a design, fires the piece to bisque, applies a slip or glaze to the surface of the piece, and wipes it off so that it remains only in the intaglio carving.

Kaolin: Clay distinguished by its great purity and whiteness. Kaolins tend to be less easily worked than other clays but this difficulty is compensated for by their beauty and refined character.

Kiln: A chamber made from refractory (heat resistant) materials. The kiln is designed with mechanisms that generate heat and the chamber is designed to hold that heat. Ceramic ware is placed inside the chamber, where it is fired.

Kiln furniture: A system of refractory ceramic modules. It is composed of flat shelves supported by vertical posts. Ceramists use these to construct a temporary structure inside the kiln to support ceramic ware.

Majolica: A brilliantly colored glaze painting technique employing an opaque white glaze which serves as a base for the application of glaze color. This technique was extensively used in European ceramics in the 15th and 16th centuries.

Majolica glaze: A low-fire glaze type, the main ingredients of which are lead oxide (a strong melter) and tin oxide (an opacifier). These opaque white glazes are formulated to work well with applied color.

Maturity, maturation: When applied to clay bodies, an optimum point at which warping and brittleness are kept to a minimum and the absorption rate is reasonably low. When applied to glazes, the point at which the glaze produces a desired effect. Generally, glazes are called mature when they are fully melted in the fire and are glassy in surface.

Melter: A compound that causes melting, facilitating glaze formation. Melters include silicates, feldspars, and fluxes.

Mixed media: The use of two or more materials to create a piece. For example, clay and metal, clay and rope, or clay and wood.

Modular: A repeated structural component. The term has use in ceramics as descriptive of a construction strategy in which the ceramist uses repeated small elements to construct a large form.

Mold: A matrix designed for shaping materials. Ceramists make extensive use of molds. They may press clay against the mold, slump clay in the mold or over the mold, or pour slip into the mold.

Opacifier: A material which blocks the passage of light through the glaze, thereby rendering the glaze opaque. Opacifiers encourage the formation of small bubbles or of crystals which change the structure of the glaze and block the passage of light.

Oxidation: The combination of a material with oxygen.

Oxidation firing: Allowing ready access of oxygen to the firing chamber at all times. Generally, electric kilns are constructed in such a way as to fire in oxidation.

Oxide: Any element combined with oxygen. During the firing, oxygen combines with the elements to create oxides and therefore all our ceramic materials are oxides once they are fired.

Plasticity: The way a clay or clay body reacts when it is shaped and formed.

Plasticizing agent: An ingredient added to a clay body recipe to improve workability. Two types of plasticizer are available, organic based and extremely fine particle materials. Organic materials, such as yogurt, encourage bacterial action which makes the clay more elastic and slippery. Fine particle materials, such as bentonite and colloids, increase the variety of particle sizes in the body and lessen the impact of coarse particles. The two can be used in combination.

Platelet: A small, flat sheet-like particle. Clay particles come in the form of hexagonal, flat crystals.

Porcelain: A pure white clay body which is translucent where thin. To be defined as porcelain, bodies contain no more than half white clay, with the other half being composed of ground silica (flint) and feldspar. Because of their low clay content and the nonplastic character of their clays, porcelains are difficult to work with: however, they can be very beautiful and they are used in spite of their limited workability.

Porcelainous: Similar to porcelain but different in some respect. Usually the difference lies in the amount of clay or the type of melter in the recipe. Most porcelainous bodies contain more clay than porcelain bodies (this encourages workability) and/or melters (such as talc) that encourage maturity at comparatively low temperatures.

Pug mill: A machine for the thorough kneading of clay bodies. De-airing pug mills have, as part of the mechanism, a vacuum mechanism to remove excess air from the clay body.

Pyrometric cones: Narrow, three-sided pyramids. Mimicking clay bodies and glazes, pyrometric cones react to the combination of time and temperature (often called heat work). As time passes and the temperature increases, the cones soften and bend. The ceramist uses the deformation of the cone as an indication that the clay bodies are mature and the glazes are melted and glassified and that the firing is complete.

Raku: A low fire method of finishing ceramic work. The ware is glazed and put into an already heated kiln. When the glazes are seen to have melted the ceramist removes the pieces with tongs. At this point the ceramist may smoke reduce the surface of the piece using flammable materials such as wet leaves. The spontaneous character of the results is highly regarded.

Ram press: A device harnessing a great deal of pressure to press-form clay between molds or dies.

Reduction firing: Firing with a minimum amount of oxygen. In reduction firing, the potter interrupts the flow of adequate oxygen to the firing chamber of the kiln at certain crucial periods during the firing. This is most naturally accomplished in the fuel-burning kiln. Reduction firing strongly influences the character of clay bodies and glazes.

Refractory: Resistant to heat.

Respirator: A device consisting of a flexible, tight fitting mask with filters attached that clean the air entering the lungs. Some filters are designed to deal only with dusts while others can deal with both dusts and fumes.

Rutile: A colorant compound of iron and titanium.

Shrinkage: In ceramics refers to loss of size when the clay loses moisture and chemically combined water (the H_2O that is chemically bound to clay and is lost only in firing).

Shivering: Glaze patches forced away from the ware, leaving sections of unglazed body visible; most easily observed at the corners and edges of the piece. Shivering occurs when the glaze shrinks less than the body upon which it rests. It can be eliminated by increasing the shrinkage of the glaze or by decreasing the shrinkage of the clay body.

Silica: A crystalline material that, along with alumina, is one of the building blocks of all clays and glazes. Sources of silica are powdered silica, feldspars, clays, and silicates (talc and wollastonite). Silica promotes plasticity and durability in clay bodies, and glaze flow, durability, and a glassy melt in glaze formulas.

Slip: A mixture of clay and water. Slips are used as: 1. Bonding materials. 2. Decorative surfaces. 3. A highly liquid clay used in slipcasting.

Slip trailing: A strategy in which the ceramist creates a raised line of wet slip on the surface of the piece. Also called "tube lining" to acknowledge the collapsible applicator used by many ceramists to create the trail line.

Slip ware: Work created in plaster molds using a liquid clay slip. The process is illustrated in a photo essay on page 92, "Creating a Mold-Formed Vessel."

Slurry: A mixture of a finely divided material and a liquid (usually water). In ceramics, the term generally refers to a soupy mixture of clay and water.

Soda ash: Sodium carbonate. This is an important source of sodium in frits and is also used as a substitute for salt in soda firings.

Soft paste porcelain: Traditionally, porcelain is fired to very high temperatures, 1260°C or higher (cones 9 to 12). Porcelain fired to lower temperatures must contain very strong melters (due to the refractory character of the clay content of porcelain); these strong melters unfortunately deprive porcelain of some of the dense and durable qualities for which it is so admired. On the other hand, the material is still quite durable and beautiful and worthy of use. These slightly softer, less dense, highly fluxed clay bodies are termed soft paste porcelain to distinguish them from the material fired to the higher temperature.

Spodumene: A lithium feldspar. It encourages strong melts and rich glaze textures.

Sprigging: Clay imagery applied to the surface of the form. It is usually made in the form of small slabs or coils.

Stains: Calcined compounds of kaolin and naturally occurring ceramic colorants which have been modified by additions of oxides that affect their color. They have created a whole new color palette for the ceramist. These colors are brilliant, safe to use, and very reliable. Stains are added to the glaze in varying amounts, usually 3% to 8% of the total recipe. While relatively expensive, they have certain advantages over naturally occurring colorants: they are predictable and reliable and their color is WYSIWYG (what you see is what you get). They may be affected adversely by an ingredient in the recipe and must be tested in a recipe before normal use.

Stoneware clay: A term used in the United States and Canada to designate a raw clay that matures at cones 8 to 9, is buff or tan color in oxidation, and is plastic and workable. Their color is due to a moderate iron content (1% to 3%) and titanium (1% to 3%). They are valued for their blend of workability and strength.

Stoneware clay body: A body that contains a high percentage of clay and a low percentage of nonclay materials (some stoneware bodies contain no nonclay materials whatsoever). In color, stoneware bodies are buff, tan, orange, or brown. They have good particle size variation and tend to be very workable and durable. They mature at cones 6 to 11.

Talc: Calcium, magnesium silicate. It is a strong melter and is especially useful as a flux in low and mid fire clay bodies.

Talc body: A clay body which contains a significant amount of talc (usually 25% to 50%).

Terra cotta red clay: A high iron clay. Due to their impurities, especially iron, these clays are valued for their rich, hearty color. Iron content is generally over 6%. Iron serves not only as a coloring agent but as a powerful melting flux as well. These clays, therefore, are often used as an ingredient to encourage clay body maturity. Terra cottas mature at a low temperature; they are usually fired in oxidation to take advantage of their rich earth-red fired color.

Terra sigillata: A highly refined slip. The ceramist begins by partially deflocculating a slip. This breaks the bonds that hold the large particles in suspension, allowing the ceramist to decant the mixture and clean the slip of large particles.

Toxic: Poisonous or health threatening. Many ceramic materials are toxic. Some are dangerous only before firing (thereby endangering only the health of the ceramist). Others are potentially dangerous to the user as well, especially if used in food containing vessels.

Translucent: A material that partially transmits light.

Transparent: A material that transmits light.

Visual texture: *see breakup.*

Vitreous: A glass or glass-like material. Nonvitreous: not a glass or glass-like, usually dry in surface.

Warp: To bend or twist. In ceramics, clay bodies warp during the drying and firing procedures.

Wash: A thin watery coating.

White body: A clay body containing only white and colorless clay and nonclay materials. Porcelain bodies are a type of white body; they are high fire and translucent, but other white bodies may be opaque or intended for the lower fire.

White stoneware: An opaque white clay body. These bodies, like porcelain, must contain only white or colorless materials such as kaolins, ball clays, and noniron bearing melters. Unlike porcelain, they may have a fairly high clay to nonclay ratio, and tend to be much more workable than porcelain.

Whiting (calcium carbonate): In the low and mid fire this oxide does not strongly encourage melting. At cone 8 and above it strongly encourages melting. It is used in slips, engobes, and glazes, and occasionally in clay bodies. In both clays and glazes it promotes durability; in glazes it also may promote rich glaze surfaces.

Wood ash: The burnt ashes of a wood fire. This material encourages rich and varied visual textures when added to glazes.

WYSIWYG: What you see is what you get. In ceramic parlance this means: if it goes into the kiln with a particular look it will come from the fire with a similar look. Originally imported from the computer world it has a very useful place in our lexicon.

Zirconium opacifiers: A group of similar compounds, all containing the element zirconium, which interferes with the passage of light in glazes. Not all zirconium opacifiers are of equal purity or do they all encourage the same level of opacity. However, all tend to produce similar results, and substitutions between various zirconium opacifiers are often successful. Generally, additions of 10% to 12% are sufficient to ensure opacity.

Annotated Bibliography

Berensohn, Paulus. *Finding One's Way With Clay*, Simon and Schuster, New York, 1972. This book is mostly about feelings and ideas, by an artist who has thought deeply about the creative process in clay.

Branfman, Steven. *Raku - A Practical Approach, 2nd Edition*, Krause Publications, Iola, WI. A useful guide for the ceramist who wants to work with raku.

Conrad, John W. *Ceramic Formulas: The Complete Compendium*, Macmillan, New York, 1973. Many of the recipes here are very nicely done and very useful.

Constant, Christine, and Ogden, Steve. *The Potters Palette*, Krause Publications, Iola, WI, 1996. A fascinating exploration of the reactions between colorants and glaze materials.

Doat, Taxile. *Grand Feu Ceramics*, Keramic Studio Publishing Co., Syracuse, NY, 1905. This book has been out of print for many years and is very rare. Only a few of the largest libraries have a copy. It is a wonderful source of knowledge about stoneware and porcelain practice at the turn of the century.

Darling, Sharon (with a contribution by Richard Zakin) *Teco: Art Pottery of the Prairie School*. The Erie Art Museum, Erie, PA, 1989. A thorough discussion of this important American Art Pottery studio.

Evans, Paul. *Art Pottery of the United States - An Encyclopedia of Producers and Their Marks*. Feingold Lewis, New York, 1987. A complete guide to the American Art Pottery movement.

Frith, Donald E. *Mold Making for Ceramics*, Krause Publications, Iola, WI, 1985. A useful guide for the ceramist who wants to work with molds.

Hamer, Frank. *The Potter's Dictionary of Materials and Techniques*, Watson-Guptil, New York, 1975. This is a useful guide to ceramic materials, techniques, ideas, and technical history in dictionary form.

Hopper, Robin. *The Ceramic Spectrum, 2nd Edition*, Krause Publications, Iola, WI, 2001. In this book Hopper deals with color and glaze character in a thorough and personal way.

Hopper, Robin. *Functional Pottery - Form and Aesthetic in Pots of Purpose, 2nd Edition.* Krause Publications, Iola, WI, 2000. In this book Hopper writes with conviction about a subject which he believes in passionately.

Lane, Peter. *Studio Porcelain*, Krause Publications, Iola, WI, 1980. A very thorough treatment of this special medium.

Lawrence, W.G., and West, R.R. *Ceramic Science for the Potter,* Krause Publications, Iola, WI, 1982. A dense, technically oriented text; it is authoritative and useful. While it takes concentration, it is accurately aimed at the needs of the studio ceramist.

Leach, Bernard. *A Potter's Book*, Trans-Atlantic Arts, Hollywood-by-the-Sea, FL, 1962. This book is a kind of epistle in praise of clay from a man who took the potter's mission most seriously.

Parmelee, Cullen W., and Harman, C.G. *Ceramic Glazes*, Cahners Books, Boston, MA, 1973. Though this book requires a good deal of concentration, it is thorough and useful.

Perry, Barbara, *American Ceramics - The Collection of Everson Museum of Art*, Rizzoli International Publications Inc., New York, 1989. This book is based on the collections of American ceramics at the Everson Museum in Syracuse, New York. The museum is a treasure house of American ceramics. Barbara Perry, former curator of ceramics there, has written a brilliant survey of the collection.

Poor, Henry Varnum. *Ceramics - From Mud to Immortality,* Prentice Hall Inc., Englewood Cliffs, NJ, 1958. In this book Poor talks of pottery as "a way of life." Not many know of this book but many who do value it very highly.

Rhodes, Daniel, revised and expanded by Robin Hopper. *Clay and Glazes for the Potter, 3rd Edition*, Krause Publications, Iola, WI, 2000. This handbook is an intelligent and sensible overview of the field.

Schreiber, Toby. *Athenian Vase Construction: A Potter's Analysis*, The J. Paul Getty Museum, Malibu, CA, 1999. This book reflects the studies of Athenian pottery by a very knowledgeable ceramic researcher. Her work on forming and the pot forms is especially thorough.

Troy, Jack. *Wood Fired Stoneware and Porcelain*, Krause Publications, Iola, WI. Troy is a wonderful writer and is deeply committed to ceramics and to the wood fire.

Weiss, Peg, editor. *Adelaide Alsop Robineau: Glory in Porcelain*, Syracuse University Press, 1981. Although this is a highly specialized book, it will tell you a great deal about the history of ceramics in our country and about an important figure in that history.

Wood, Nigel. *Chinese Glazes, Their Origins, Chemistry and Recreation*, A&C Black, London/University of Pennsylvania Press, PA, 1999. This book is an excellent guide to the way in which the Chinese potters created their glazes. It is extremely complete, trustworthy, and very well written. Wood's first book, *Oriental Glazes,* was very good, in this new book he has built upon that foundation. It is a great achievement.

Zakin, Richard. *Electric Kiln Ceramics*, Krause Publications, Iola, WI, 1993. A guide for the ceramist who wants to use the electric kiln.

- *Hand Formed Ceramics*, Krause Publications, Iola, WI, 1995. A guide for the ceramist who uses hand forming methods to create ceramic pieces.

- *Ceramics: Ways of Creation,* Krause Publications, Iola, WI, 1999. Biographies and essays on the thoughts and work of 36 artists working in varied aspects of ceramics.

Magazines
Available at most public and university libraries.

American Craft, 401 Park Ave. South, New York, NY 10016. This well designed magazine covers all aspects of the crafts, including ceramics.

Ceramics Monthly, Box 12448, Columbus, OH 43212. This very well illustrated magazine covers every aspect of the ceramic world, with special emphasis on the ceramics of North America.

Clay Times, PO Box 365, Waterford, VA 20197-0365. This magazine takes an informal and conversational stance.

Studio Pottery, Box 70, Goffstown, NH 03045. Written by and for people who spend their lives in the clay field. Each issue has a focus and takes on the character of a book about that theme.

Ceramics: Art and Perception, 35 William St., Paddington, Sydney, NSW 2021 Australia. Here we see a very wide variety of work from Australia, Japan, the U.S., and England.

Kerameiki Techni - International Ceramic Art Review, PO Box 80653, 18510 Piraeus, Greece. Published three times a year. There is an English language version. This magazine shows us work that ceramists in North America might not see. It has a European cast, it is sophisticated and shows us another side of clay.

Index

Artist Index

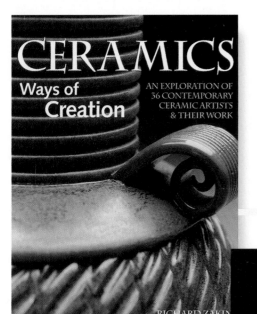

Richard Zakin:

"The Object Is To Turn the Undiscovered Into What's Obvious."

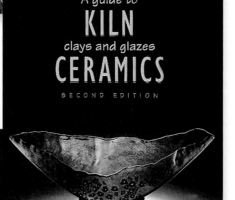

Ceramics - Ways of Creation
by Richard Zakin
How do ceramic artists create their work? Where do their ideas spring from and what is the source of their work methods? If you've ever wanted to explore the artistic process, this fascinating study of **36 ceramic artists** and the "ways of creation" they employ to produce their unique works of art will delight and inspire you.
Softcover • 8¼ x 10⅞ • 288 pages
250 color photos
Item# TCC • $39.95

Electric Kiln Ceramics
A Guide to Clays and Glazes, 2nd Edition
by Richard Zakin
This inclusive guide will assist you in using the electric kiln to produce clear, brilliant colors and richly textured surfaces. Provides you with completely revised glaze recipes, information on commercial glaze for low fire and updated health and safety information.
Hardcover • 7¼ x 10⅛ • 304 pages
16-page color section
Item# EKC2 • $39.95

Hand-Formed Ceramics
Creating Form and Surface
by Richard Zakin
Follow author Richard Zakin on a global survey of techniques for creating sculpture, vessels, and wall pieces. You'll find complete instructions and learn the advantages and disadvantages of forming methods. Plus, you'll get tips aplenty on the art of combining forming methods.
Hardcover • 8¼ x 10⅞ • 244 pages
16-page color section
Item# HFC • $39.95

krause publications

Credit Card Customers Call Toll-free
800-258-0929
Mention Offer: CRB1

Krause Publications, Book Offer CRB1, PO Box 5009, Iola WI 54945-5009